The
Spirit
of
Adventure

The true story of a summer-long discovery of Europe
while flying an open-cockpit biplane.
The adventure of a lifetime…

Michael McCafferty

All profits from the sale of this book are donated to
Rutgers University's Keck Center for Collaborative Neuroscience - Spinal Cord Injury Project
to find a cure for paralysis caused by spinal cord injury.

Michael McCafferty
PO Box 2270
Del Mar, California
USA

e-mail: FastMikie@Gmail.com

website: AirMikie.com

Table of Contents

Preface

I consider myself to be one of the luckiest guys on the planet. How else can you explain being able to fly my own open-cockpit biplane around Europe for the summer? Oh, sure, I worked for many years to be able to make this happen, but there are plenty of people who work hard all their lives and never get to do something like this. So there must be a big element of luck involved in Life.

Many times over the years since this great adventure, friends suggested I write a book about it. My reply was always that I would work on the book someday "when I got old". Thirteen years have passed since my epic tour of Europe. I still don't consider myself *old* but the recent death of a classmate from high school inspired me with a sense of urgency. Barry Dunleavy was a good friend for 54 years. His passing got me thinking that maybe I might not have much time left and that some of the things I've been putting off might not get done at all unless I "Begin it now."

So here it is, the story as it was experienced, and written, day-by-day, during that magical summer of 1997. The story is told primarily in the 96 daily e-mails I sent to a list of friends back home. The book starts with two additional chapters to set the stage leading up to this adventure, and finishes with an added Epilogue that tells the bizarre story of how, several years later, my flying adventures ended.

All profits from the sale of this book are donated to Rutgers University's Keck Center for Collaborative Neuroscience - Spinal Cord Injury Project to find a cure for paralysis caused by spinal cord injury. Your purchase of this book, for yourself and for gifts, supports a good cause to help others. The story of why I have chosen to support this organization is told in the chapter Day 11 – Who is this Guy?

If you are unfamiliar with the Waco YMF-5 biplane, you should take a quick look at Appendix B before starting in on the story.

There are more stories and full color photos available at AirMikie.com that will make your reading of this book even more enjoyable. Thank you for sharing this with your friends.

The Fantasies

The Spirit of Adventure I

I accepted delivery of this incredibly beautiful biplane fresh from <u>the factory</u> on July 19, 1993. It was the 50th one they built, and they were very proud of it.

I informed them I couldn't fly it and they were okay with that, that is, until after I paid for it and went for my "orientation" flight with the factory chief pilot. After one hour of spectacularly bad landings, the pilot and I had this brief conversation:

Chief Pilot Carl Dye: "Tell me again how long you've been a pilot?"

Me: "I'm not a pilot."

Carl: "We just build 'em here, we don't teach people how to fly 'em."

Me: "No problem. Help me get it back to San Diego, and I'll take it from there."

Carl: "Well, okay..."

And so the adventure began.

I knew virtually nothing about flying at the time, but I was committed to mastering the art and science of it. I had two different instructors checked out by Carl: Vince Moore and <u>Lowell Williams</u>. Vince was young, detailed, rational and patient. Lowell had been a P-51 Mustang fighter pilot in WWII, and a finer man/pilot could not be found. With their help, I eventually earned my ticket to fly solo.

A solo license, or even a private pilot license, is just one of many steps in the long path of learning when it comes to flying. Over the next several years, I achieved advanced ratings for instrument flying, multi-engine aircraft, gliders, seaplanes, etc.

About a year into my flying education, instructor Vince Moore was doing a solo test flight to check things out after some routine maintenance. Due to an undocumented feature of the parking brake, and his use of the brake during a ground run-up of the engine, the brake stayed partially engaged during the subsequent flight. When he touched down, the parking brake engaged fully and instantly flipped the plane over, resulting in a total loss of the plane. Vince was unhurt, thankfully. I traded the parts and the insurance payoff for a new biplane, same as the first one, and gave it the following registration number in remembrance of the first one: N250YM.

During the months between Vince's accident and the delivery of the new biplane, I had some time to continue my flying education, in different airplanes. It was during this time I flew the legendary WWII fighter, the P-51 Mustang, and the B-17 bomber. However, the next couple of years with the new biplane were some of the best times of my life. Flying consumed me completely.

Each new adventure fueled the next. At first I flew just around Southern California, then the southwest (Monument Valley, etc.), and up the coastline to Big Sur, Half Moon Bay and the coastline of Oregon. Bolder adventures took me through Nevada, Utah, Wyoming and Montana. In 1995, flying buddy Art Annecharico and his Waco joined me on a trip along the coastline from San Diego to Canada. In 1996, Art and I flew our biplanes across the USA, from Southern California to Maine, down the east coast to Kitty Hawk, then back home again. I wrote daily e-mails from that six-week trip, and the story is online at this link: http://michaelmccafferty.com/adventures/usa/.

After the coast-to-coast adventure, I got the itch to do a round-the-world flight. When I looked further into the idea, I was amazed to learn that an open-cockpit biplane had flown around the world only once, in 1924, and required the resources of the US military. It wasn't a solo flight as I had imagined but rather involved two pilots. And so, a worthy challenge presented itself to me at that moment: to become the only man to fly solo around the world in an open-cockpit biplane.

Initial research indicated it would take at least a year in the planning, and six months in the execution, and a whole lot of money. It was big goal for a pilot who had never flown outside of the USA. So a prudent step in the planning was for me to get international experience, and the best place to do that was Europe, because of the many countries in close proximity. It would give me a lot of international flying experience in a tidy logistical package.

A low-level tour of Europe was looking like it could be a lot of fun. I thought of all the cool stuff I could do, like finding a way to fly a Spitfire while in England, flying to my ancestral home in Ireland, flying the Alps (wow!), the English Channel, the Irish Sea, the

Mediterranean and over the South of France. Yes, this could be a great adventure, but I had no idea how I was going to do it.

The first challenge was getting my biplane over there. The Waco YMF-5, the type of biplane I owned, was designed for the "sportsman pilot" according to the original factory literature in 1935. It was not designed for long distance flights. To fly the Atlantic, my Waco would need major modifications that would take a lot of time to design and build, so I had to find another way. Plan B was to disassemble the biplane, pack it into a shipping container, put it on a boat to Europe, then reassemble it to go flying. When the summer was over, I'd reverse the procedure.

Of course, this would be an enormous logistical challenge as well as a paperwork blizzard, and I hate paperwork, so I looked for someone else willing to handle all of those details for me. Luckily, I worked out a deal with the Waco factory. They wanted to display a Waco at the Paris Air Show, which worked perfectly into my plans of flying my biplane in Europe. I agreed to let them display my biplane in the show if they handled all the details and logistics involved in getting it there and back, including disassembly and re-assembly. My sole responsibility was to cover the cost of shipping. It was a win-win situation. We both wanted a biplane in Europe in the summer of '97, and I was the lucky one who was going to be flying it. The Paris Air Show was in June, and I was looking to stay in Europe all summer, until it got too cold to fly. This was shaping up to be huge!

To get my biplane to Paris in June, I would have to fly my open-cockpit biplane to Lansing, Michigan in the closing days of winter! As I now type these words, it seems like madness, but at the time I was very enthusiastic about this first leg of my European adventure. That flight took 10 days and I was the coldest I have ever been in my life. The worst of it occurred in La Mesa, Texas when I was forced to land in 30 mph winds due to rapidly deteriorating conditions. Safe on the ground, I was fascinated to witness my first multiple tornadoes, up close!

Once the biplane was in the capable hands of the factory craftsmen, there was nothing more I could do for the next two months except wait until it arrived in France. This was a difficult time for me, because I had to endure several weeks of perfect spring flying weather in Southern California without my biplane.

Waiting for the Slow Boat to Paris

<u>Borrego Springs, CA</u>

I've been waiting now for 50 days for the Waco factory to call me with news that my biplane is in France. When the phone rings, this great adventure will begin.

These are perfect days in the desert. The air temperature is warm, 95 to 100 degrees in the afternoons, and completely lacking in humidity. The best time of day is evening, when the glare of the sun fades over the mountains to the west, creating a rose coloring to the mountain ranges surrounding the valley. The wind goes calm and there is absolute silence. I push the button to roll back the pool cover, and slip into water that is un-noticeably warm. I can feel no difference between the air temperature and the water temperature. It couldn't be better if it were Tahiti. This is the best time for me to relax, meditate, and exercise, all at once.

Sometimes, underwater in the pool, I'll simulate flying my biplane, doing loops and rolls, and other aerobatic maneuvers, just for fun. Sometimes, I'll hover in one place, swimming forward with my legs and backward with my arms, going nowhere, but exercising mightily. Sometimes, I'll simply float on my back and watch for the first stars to appear in the darkening sky. After the sky goes black, it's easy to see the reflected light of satellites streaking by.

At night, I climb to the roof deck and lay out in the hammock, becoming one with the universe of stars all around me. There is very little light pollution here in the desert, and the stars are startling in their clarity and sheer number, visible all the way down to the horizon. The air temperature at night is very comfortable, hovering in the mid-70s. It's a great place to sleep with all the advantages of camping out, but none of the challenges of living in the wild (i.e. ants, spiders, scorpions, rattlesnakes, etc.). It's a very civilized way to commune with nature, while enjoying all the comforts of home.

These days at the Fun House are calm and comfortable, and without stress. I take time for creative writing, correspondence, planning, browsing the Internet, and sometimes, a nap, or a drive into town about 10 miles away. There's plenty to occupy my time. Of course, there are the many `toys,' including the pool table, bikes, audio/video, books, cars, and so much more. Sometimes, I even try to see if I can actually play with all the toys in one day. I haven't succeeded yet. Usually, I fail when I come across one of the hammocks and give it a try. From that point, I lose all ambition, and fall into a deep contented sleep.

How different these days are from the days of being a hard-charging entrepreneur, chasing the carrot while keeping only a half step ahead of the stick. Those days were filled with fear and stress, yet sometimes enormously rewarding when I would get a kind letter or call from a customer who used the software I had invented. It was their gratitude that kept me going, in spite of the pain in my side that grew worse each year until I finally sold the company and the new owners took the pain and replaced it with freedom and cash.

These days of comfort at the Fun House are the payoff for the preceding 30-plus years of exhausting work. Sometimes, there were setbacks that many people would call failure, but which in the end only taught me the lessons I used to build future success. Each day I now live contains some element of reward for those years of persistence. And yet, I know deep in my gut that I have been lucky to get to this point. I know that it could have turned out much differently. I could have died at any time along the way, with no earthly reward whatsoever for my efforts. Competition could have overwhelmed my fledgling company — or simple mistakes on my part, poor timing or bad luck. Somehow, it all turned out okay.

When the phone finally rings, my easy life at the Fun House will come to an end. For most of the next three months I'll be dealing with the forces of nature, the winds and weather, mountains, and seas. I will fly over the countrysides and coastlines of Europe in a single engine, open-cockpit biplane designed over 60 years ago with fragile wings of wood and fabric. I will take off and land in places unknown to me now, and meet all sorts of strange people, whose languages I don't understand, and whose food I won't be able to eat. I'll be sleeping in a great variety of places from the very worst to the best. I'll be at the whim of the winds, the weather and the fortunes of Lady Luck.

Seldom will I know when I wake up where I'll sleep that night. Sometimes, my plans will change in an instant in the air as cloudbanks loom ahead blocking my path and forcing me to land in different places. It may happen that I'll get stuck for days on the ground, held down by bad weather. No matter what happens, each day will be an adventure. It will be a summer of living by my wits, of play and of hard work, of discovery and of sharing with you, dear reader, some of the insights that occur to me in the process.

It's this sharing part that adds an extra dimension to this adventure. It is my intention to publish a daily account of the adventure with photos via the Internet, leveraging an e-mail account and website set up for this very purpose. It is my intention to leave an account of my day's activities each evening before falling asleep.

This means that if I screw up, I'll do it in front of all my friends, as well as an Internet audience of complete strangers. Why would I want to put this extra pressure on myself?

The primary reason is that I am a writer. I must write in the same way I must fly. Secondly, I'm a computer geek of sorts and I see the Internet as an extraordinary new tool that can enable great, new things. In this case, it will enable a photojournalistic account of a continuing adventure, accessible on a global scale, reported in real-time. The World Wide Web is only two years old. There will be great things to come from the Internet, and I need to learn more about it by doing.

And so, in the fullness of time, the phone rings…

Day 1: Silent fears

Mikie's Fun House, <u>Borrego Springs, CA</u>

When I wake in the morning, a great new adventure will begin. Over the past months I have been preparing for this moment. The anticipation is overwhelming! This is the culmination of four years of learning and experience, and it is the bliss of fantasies come true. And yet, this moment, right now, before I go to sleep, this is the moment of my greatest fears.

Fear of humiliation: Many people know of my plans. To fail would be a dent in my carefully crafted armor of invincibility and achievement. What if I did something completely stupid and broke the biplane, or violated some international law that got me imprisoned, or... the scenarios are infinite when fears are given free reign. Fear of disaster, tragedy, and death: Gravity is the aviator's constant killer companion.

And of course, there is the matter of my own insecurity: who am I to attempt such an outrageous thing? I have only four years of flying experience, all in the USA. I am a simple wannabe flying in a sky of legends. Will I be found out, or will I unwittingly demonstrate my ignorance and lack of skill for the entire world to see?

These fears are real and reasonable, and each must be examined, learned from, dealt with and discarded. Action is the antidote to fear. I am resolved to move forward in the morning. But now I need sleep. In a few minutes, I'll be dreaming of landing my beautiful open-cockpit biplane on sweet grass somewhere by the sea, somewhere in Europe.

Day 2: A Day of Challenges

Paris, France

The fully loaded Boeing 747 made the smoothest landing I have ever experienced in a commercial airliner. I was hoping it was a good omen for my adventure. It wasn't.

Upon arrival at Orly, a major airport in the south of Paris, the first challenge was to purchase a ticket to Bordeaux. Apparently, my travel agent back home had forgotten to include that ticket with my travel packet, so I was now on my own for this leg of the journey. I had no idea where to find Air Liberte', and simply kept walking straight until it magically appeared before me. Thankfully the clerk spoke English and the transaction was easy. As she was helping me, this same clerk was also speaking French to her co-worker. I told her that I couldn't understand a word she was saying, but that her language was quite beautiful. She smiled and blushed very nicely!

The next challenge was to make a phone call to my contact in Bordeaux to make sure everything was okay with the plane. To make a phone call, I needed some French money and handled that easily enough with the help of a cashier at the airport. The clerk gave me all bank notes, and when I asked for some change for the phone, she informed me that French payphones do not take coins! They require credit cards or prepaid phone cards. So all I had to do was figure out how to use the machine that dispensed the prepaid phone cards, using my credit card as payment.

After several attempts at decoding the international symbols on the dispenser, and feeling quite stupid for doing all the wrong things, I finally succeeded at purchasing my prepaid phone card and proceeded to attack the payphone itself. This again proved to be a humbling experience, and I could feel the eyes of every Frenchman in the airport laughing at my stupid attempts to master this basic machine. (Hey, I'm a software guy, not a hardware guy!) Of course, eventually, I got it all sorted out and made my first French payphone call. Suddenly I felt very much the world traveler.

The call itself wasn't a very pleasant experience, actually. I got some very bad news that my biplane, shipped overseas and delivered on time to the seaport of Le Havre, had progressed no further. It had not been forwarded to Bordeaux as required, and was in fact not going to be sent anywhere without the payment of a deposit of 15 percent of the value of the airplane (15% of 250k = $37,500). Ouch! My contact Bernard Chabbert was continuing to haggle with the Customs people, and brilliantly convinced them to truck the plane to Le Bourget airport, the site of the Paris Air Show where the plane was to be displayed by the Waco factory, without paying the deposit. So now all of our plans for re-assembly had to be shifted 400 miles north to Le Bourget, from Bordeaux. Bernard handled it all superbly.

Since I wasn't going on to Bordeaux, I returned to the blushing Air Liberte' clerk and returned my ticket, then found a taxi to take me to a hotel at Le Bourget airport. The driver spoke no English; so needless to say, it was a very quiet ride.

The room at the hotel offered more challenges: I was prepared for the differences in electrical and phone outlets, having purchased adapters in the US. No problem. They worked and I felt smug about my foresight. But I wasn't ready for the challenge in the next room. None of the rooms in the hotel have showers, only bathtubs! This would be my first bath since I got out of short pants, some 50 years ago. What a completely uncivilized experience, wallowing in one's own gravy while attempting to get clean, all the while refraining from the normal shower activities which are distinctly unsavory in a bathtub.

I am really starting to feel the effects of sleep deprivation and the time zone differences. But there is much work to be done yet. I had to figure out how to access an Internet connection and send e-mail to 227 friends and family from my TeleMagic database. I also made some minor changes to my web site and tweaked other technical details to allow for global communications. The challenges were easily overcome.

By this time, I was totally wasted, but still wanted to check out the local television programming. Most channels were USA reruns with French-dubbed voices or subtitles. There was one German-speaking channel that alternated between Japanese martial arts violence on the one hand and German porn on the other. And then there was CNN — in English! How sweet it is to hear the sound of one's own language in a sea of babble.

Sleep came easily, in spite of the bed, which was simply a mattress on a wood frame with no box spring. It was definitely uncomfortable, but by that time I could have slept on a bed of nails.

My sleep was soon filled with dreams of flying low over the coastlines of Europe. Tomorrow, I would get to see my beloved biplane for the first time in 50 days.

Day 3: A Lesson in French Hospitality

Great news! Sometime around mid-morning, Bernard Chabbert called to announce that the Waco would be trucked into Le Bourget by late afternoon. I had given up hope that the plane would be delivered on Friday, assuming that the truck driver would probably want to avoid Friday afternoon rush hour traffic, and make up some excuse to postpone until Monday. Fortunately, I was wrong.

At mid-day, the world's greatest Waco biplane pilot called and said he had just checked into the hotel and would be right up. Carl Dye, the chief pilot for the Waco factory, and certainly the man with the most knowledge about this awesome airplane than any man alive, was here in Paris to oversee the re-assembly of my plane and to test fly it when it was all put together.

We spent a couple of hours going over some aeronautical charts of England and Ireland that I had brought from the US. We were looking for the differences in chart notations between the US and Europe maps. (There were plenty!)

I then received a call from Francois Bricheteau, the Directeur General of Euralair Industries. He called to inform me that my biplane had arrived at their hangar at Le Bourget (only a half mile from my hotel) and would I please come to his office to deal with unloading it. Carl and I set out immediately.

Within an hour we had half a dozen Frenchmen and two Americans standing around this 40-foot container on a truck, all trying to figure out how we could get the biplane out of it and onto the ground. We all had our own ideas, and it was more than a little difficult to communicate to each other with our limited understanding of each other's language. We finally settled on a method that involved a mobile loading platform and a winch, and within four hours we had the biplane out of the truck and safely on the ground.

Carl Dye, world's greatest biplane pilot, with a box full of Waco

To celebrate our achievement, Francois Bricheteau appeared with several bottles of superior French champagne and lots of glasses to share it with everyone involved in our endeavor. What a wonderful surprise! What a very hospitable host we had taking care of us. We stopped mid-task (for we still had to unload the wings from the back of the container), and poured bubbly, toasting cheers among us, especially to my successful three-month tour of Europe.

Another of Euralair Industries' chieftains, Jean-Yves Bonnetain, the quality assurance manager, was clearly smitten by the Waco. He seemed to be a vintage airplane buff, taking the time from his busy schedule to show me a French magazine brimming with stories of several vintage airplane shows coming up later in the summer.

Euralair Industries was a major player in the aircraft industry, and they were surely going out of their way when it came to this little insignificant Waco. It was not because of business that they did this. After all, they rolled a Boeing 737 out of their main hangar just to accommodate us! It was not because of their pure love of biplanes either, I found out later. Francois Bricheteau mentioned to me that my friend, Bernard Chabbert, had contacted the very highest level at Euralair requesting help in getting us airborne for the Paris Air Show. Bernard, an aviation writer in France, was well known, so when he called, people were apt to listen up. His simple request was enough to activate huge resources (even late on a Friday afternoon) to get us going!

Unfortunately, the schedule did not include mechanics to work through the weekend, so even though we got the biplane off the truck, we would have to wait until

Monday to put the wings on and test fly it. This meant I had the weekend to explore Paris.

All I can say is that it was a great pleasure to see my beautiful biplane again after almost two months. It was shipped by rail, truck, ship and winch, and arrived without a scratch after travelling more than 4,000 miles to its final destination. It survived numerous opportunities for disaster and yet came through with flying colors. What a great airplane!

After the work was done, we returned to the hotel for some refreshments, and spent the evening quaffing pints of Guinness with some Brits who were in town for the air show. I met a fellow Irishman named Brian Duffy whose uncle runs the airport at Knock, in the west of Ireland, and made a note to look him up when we arrive there.

The rest of the evening was devoted to figuring out how to get a photograph out of my new digital camera and onto my web site. The pints didn't make it any easier!

Day 4: An Excursion into the Streets of Paris

<u>Paris, France</u>

I awoke just before noon, catching up on the sleep I missed last night. The morning began with lightning, thunder and rain showers, and it seemed as if the day would be ideally suited to visiting museums. I checked The Weather Channel's website to find the Paris forecast to be sunny all day. Sure enough, the isolated thunderstorm passed through quickly, and the sky became scattered puffballs in a sea of blue. I really wanted to fly.

I wasn't ready to rent a car yet. I wanted to tour the city by taxi and get my bearings, and learn more of the ways of the streets before risking my life behind the wheel. Carl and I arranged for an English-speaking taxi driver, a native of Ghana, to drive us into Paris (only 15 kilometers) and give us a tour.

First stop was a brief photo opportunity at the Eiffel Tower. Our driver, Peter, dropped us off while he circled in traffic until we had taken our shots. I took Carl's picture with his film camera, and then Carl tried to take my photo with my digital camera. As I sat on a wall in front of the Eiffel Tower, trying to look nonchalant about it all, I noticed that about 10 feet to my right was a very pretty young lady who was doing the same, posing for a shot for her mother. I don't know what came over me, it must have been the pheromones, but it seemed like a perfectly natural thing as I scooted over next to her and put my arm around her shoulder making a more interesting picture for both of our photo albums. She was a great sport, and thoroughly pleased with all of this. She told me her name was Maria Something-Very-Italiano and I told her my name was Michael Something-Very-McIrish. We posed for more photos, then shook hands, laughed and parted company with a smile. I hope her photo turned out okay because Carl didn't hold the button down long enough on my camera, so the shot from my camera was never taken.

That's one nice thing about digital cameras, instant gratification. In this case, it was instant disappointment. With this camera you can immediately view the photo you have taken. When we got back to the taxi, I displayed all the photos in the camera, but the lovely Maria was nowhere to be found.

Next on the list was the Arc de Triomphe, a little bauble of a monument that Napoleon had erected in his own honor. The elevators to the top were closed, so we climbed the 284 steps of the circular staircase. It seemed to be a Parisian version of the StairMaster exercise machine. The view from the top was *magnifique*. My favorite vantage point was the scene looking down the Avenue Des Champs Elysees toward the Louvre. The walk down was a lot easier, but for some reason it seemed to invoke a mild vertigo, possibly because of the much faster circular pace.

Back on the ground, I walked around the monument and measured in my mind to determine if it was possible to fly a biplane through its center. It seemed as if my Waco would fit quite comfortably. Carl agreed, but suggested that it would almost certainly be the last flight I would take — the gendarmes and the FAA would make sure of that. What an ideal last flight to make if you knew in advance that you were going to lose your medical certificate!

Here's a photo that Carl took of me atop the Arc de Triomphe:

I present this shot not for its photographic excellence, but as proof that I really was there. Some readers of my posts were skeptical that I was actually in Paris and were asserting that I was making this all up!

Another landmark we visited was the Notre Dame cathedral, situated on a small island in the middle of the Seine River. They were cleaning up the place when we got there. The facade was covered with scaffolding two-thirds of the way up. The top third, already cleaned, was a lovely shade of light beige stone. The bottom two-thirds were almost black with the pollution of the last century's automotive emissions. I think the finest features of the cathedral were the stained-glass rosette windows.

It was such a perfect day that we released Peter to find other passengers so that we could walk the Champs Elysees and mingle with the Parisians and tourists. We stopped for a meal at Fouguets, a sidewalk cafe at Avenue George V, and engaged in some serious people watching.

This is "springtime in Paris", and couples in love were everywhere, oblivious to everything around them. Another thing I noticed immediately was the sheer number of sidewalk cafes. There must have been at least a hundred of them on the Champs Elysees' between the Arc de Triomphe and the Louvre, a distance of about 4 kilometers (2.4 miles).

The sidewalks were very wide, at least 60', so they were not little intimate sidewalk cafes, but rather quite large affairs with only small indoor spaces.

The streets were filled with vehicles I had never seen before, some of them very futuristic. My favorite was a custom Harley Davidson with California plates that expired in 1995. I liked to think the owner came to visit and stayed. I also thought that it was considerably less expensive to ship a Harley to Paris than it was to ship my biplane.

Another thing that struck me was that the sidewalks were completely devoid of the sidewalk urinals that, for some reason, I had associated with Paris.

This famous street, the Avenue des Champs Elysees, was like Rodeo Drive in Beverly Hills, in that there were so many high fashion stores catering to rich women. There were many beautiful, well-dressed women on parade in the neighborhood. For this season, at least, it appeared that the navel was "in." There were more female navels on this street on this particular day than I think I had ever seen in my life to date. A fashion statement that I found to be interesting was the use of see-through plastic panels inserted into clothing at strategic spots such as over the navel, of course. It seemed to me to be a way of saying, "You can look, but you cannot touch, but even if you do I will be safe from your germs!"

Whether I was sitting quietly in a sidewalk cafe, or admiring the cityscape Paris, I found my thoughts drifting up into the sky, measuring the clouds and the winds and thinking of the day very soon when I would again fly my lovely biplane. Sixty days without flying is a heavy price to pay for the opportunity to fly the skies of Europe. Only a few more days...

We caught a taxi back to our hotel at Le Bourget airport to clean up and rest before we again headed back into the city. It was Saturday night, and springtime in Paris; I was sure that there was a bit of fun to be found. Since these postings are intended for "General Audiences" only, I will not go into the details, but you can surely imagine.

Day 5: The Calm Before the Storm

<u>Paris, France</u>

Today's big accomplishment was the move to a new hotel at Charles de Gaulle airport from our hotel of the same chain at Le Bourget airport. The rooms at the Le Bourget hotel were sold out (two years in advance). In fact, everything around Le Bourget was sold-out. The Paris Air Show had gobbled up everything for miles. Not only were the rooms not available, they were selling for four times the normal rate. The Law of Supply and Demand is universal.

My room at de Gaulle is a lot nicer than the one at Le Bourget. It has a window that opens to the fresh air (the other room didn't), and the best part is that it looks directly down the departure end of what must be Runway 26 Left. I was guessing at the runway number, as I used the compass in my watch to determine the runway direction.

The watch also contains a barometer (to calculate and display the current elevation/altitude), an air temperature sensor, gauge for determining underwater depth, stopwatch, calendar, alarm, and memory, as well as graphing capabilities for changes in altitude and temperature. Oh yes, it also tells the time! I use this watch as my backup instrument cluster in the event that I lose all electrics in the biplane. This event is not likely to ever happen, but backup is good. Just before leaving for this trip, my Breitling self-winding timepiece decided to become completely unreliable (compared to its normal characteristic of being just somewhat unreliable), so I was now wearing a monster Casio.

Tomorrow we plan to re-assemble the biplane. We need to attach the wings, the elevator, the wheel pants, reconnect fuel lines, antennae, electrics, then refuel and ground test the engine and instruments. If we're lucky, Carl might even get to test fly it. If everything goes well, we'll have a couple of days to go flying over the French countryside, exploring some grass fields for landing practice. Oh boy, good fun at last!

It has been WAY too long since my last flight. I need to fly again soon or I will surely explode. Only my pilot friends will understand this.

Tomorrow, I was off to try to find navigation charts of the local area, and to discover the procedures for flying in and out of the very busy jet airport of Le Bourget.

Two days ago, as we were unloading the Waco from the truck, there was a French jet fighter doing low-level aerobatics directly over the field. The traffic will only intensify over the next few days as airplanes of every conceivable description arrive from all over the world.

A low-pressure system is predicted to move across northern Europe later today and tomorrow. A thunderstorm passed directly over the hotel, dumping enormous rain showers and flashing lightning all around. The commercial airlines kept running in spite of it all. I was content to be on the ground. There's an old pilot saying that goes: "It's better to be on the ground wishing you were flying, than to be flying wishing you were on the ground."

Online some viewers expressed further skepticism regarding whether I am really in Paris. They claim that yesterday's photo did not show any noticeable Parisian landmarks so today I enclose a photo taken yesterday at the Eiffel Tower. I hope that this puts the issue to rest at last.

Day 6: Let There Be Wings!

<u>Paris, France</u>

Today was certainly a step in the right direction. Now that all four wing pieces have been bolted on, the Waco looks very much like its old self again.

We had a considerable amount of help from the very friendly and cooperative people at Euralair (whose mechanics and giant jet hangar we were using). At one time, we had as many as seven people assigned to various positions in the wing attachment process.

It was an amazing sight to witness. Imagine: one Frenchman who speaks no English, operating the fork-lift, holding the upper wing in place, while three other Frenchmen, who speak little to no English, manipulate the wing according to Carl's directions (Carl speaks no French, and in fact hardly speaks at all!), while at least two other Frenchmen fetching things, being ordered about by the only Frenchman who we could (barely) communicate with. All the while, I'm pacing around worrying that at any moment this zoo will produce an irrevocably broken biplane.

The only French I know seemed appropriate for the situation ("petite," "merci," STOP!). I speak English during emergencies since my French is quite limited, and yet I seem to slip in a few Spanish words among the few French words I knew, which confuses everyone, even me!

Here's a quick snapshot I took of Carl using sign language to direct the wing to its proper place:

There is still quite a bit to do. Carl is facing a real challenge with the fittings that attach the elevator to the horizontal stabilizer. He is a perfectionist (and so am I!) and it is unfortunate that he doesn't have access to his own tools, so the work is going a lot slower than it would at the Waco factory.

There were still a hundred other details that have to be taken care of: wires for lights, radio antennae, GPS, movie camera, control cables, inter-wing struts, flying wires, wheel pants, wing root fairings, brakes.... the list goes on. At some point, hopefully very soon, Carl will stand back, shrug and then climb in and go fly it!

We had lunch with Francois Bricheteau, the *Directeur General* of Euralair, and his friend Alain Strausz, a retired French Navy pilot and now flight instructor. They escorted us to their favorite local cafe and it was a good thing because this was not a tourist spot that had menus translated into English. The staff spoke no English either. Thankfully, our new friends translated everything and made suggestions and we had a great meal. Alain offered to accompany Carl on the first flight out of Le Bourget to a little grass field airport where we could buy navigation charts of the area. From the way Alain's eyes light up when he looks at the Waco, I can imagine him offering to go in the biplane if Carl were going to Antarctica!

All day long, as we were working on the biplane, groups of people came wandering over to "Ooh" and "Ah," pointing and looking it over, and talking quietly among themselves. It was almost as if they had never seen such an airplane before. In fact, they may not have. I have not seen another biplane of any kind since I arrived, and I was told that they are quite rare in Europe.

It seems unlikely that we will fly tomorrow because of all the work that remains, but possibly on Wednesday.

Day 7: Taxi Ride from Hell, Haircut in Heaven

Paris, France

While Carl was attending to the many details of re-assembling the biplane at the Euralair hangar at Le Bourget, I ventured out into Paris to find aviation navigation charts for Paris, Northwest France and Britain.

Yesterday, our new friend, Alain Strausz, had given me the address of a shop called General Aviation, in the south of Paris which could supply the needed charts. I called the hotel front desk and requested a taxi with a driver who could speak English. This was no small task because the clerk at the front desk could barely speak English herself, but we finally muddled through it.

It seemed that the French would not speak English if they could avoid it, and delegated the speaking of English to foreigners specially imported for the purpose of dealing with other foreigners. As a case in point, my taxi driver was Vietnamese, an ex-Army officer, a fact that came tumbling out of him almost instantly when I spoke my first words to him. He also was quick to say "My brother, my sister, my mother at Saigon Hilton." That was, it seemed, the extent of his English vocabulary, but I didn't know that at the time. I proceeded to verbally give him the address I wanted to go to on Rue Mademoiselle, he thought about it for a moment and then nodded enthusiastically.

I asked him several more questions as we drove along, but each of them was either ignored or he looked at me in the rear view mirror as if I was speaking Martian. On occasion, he would say something back to me in a language that didn't sound like French at all. This got me to wondering if we had ever really communicated at all, and would I ever wind up at the Rue Mademoiselle.

After 210 francs were counted on the meter (about $40), my concerns were proven correct. He slowed down and pointed to a huge building with a dome, what looked like a government building and said "General Aviation" (in French). This was ludicrous to me that a little pilot supply shop would be in such a place so I asked him "Rue Mademoiselle?" and he said "Oui" and looked at me as if I were mentally retarded.

That's when I took pen and paper and spelled it out for him. He took out a magnifying glass (I swear to you!) and looked it over suspiciously, not seeming to comprehend what I meant. I looked for street signs and saw that we were on a street that resembled "Mademoiselle" only in that it began with "M." I pointed to the street sign, then again at my piece of paper. That's when he took my paper and started to guess at each letter: "F?" (NO! "M"), and so forth, until we had gone through the alphabet several times and he seemed to have finally understood how to spell it. He then consulted a huge listing of every street name in Paris, and with the aid of his magnifying glass finally located "Mademoiselle", and then compared it to my paper, and then seemed to explode in a fury composed of despair, hatred for all Americans for ruining his homeland, and for me personally for being so stupid. For the rest of the ride, he seemed intent on killing all pedestrians, scooters, and any car smaller than his Mercedes. He weaved thru traffic like a madman, and I really thought that I had met my end. How ironic to have survived the Vietnam War (by joining the West Virginia National Guard) only to die 30 years later at the hands of a crazed Vietnamese taxi driver in Paris. Life is very strange.

But God was good to me today. Somehow the little shop called "General Aviation" appeared to me as we were speeding down the street and I yelled, "STOP!" which seemed to be an international word as he skidded to a halt amidst the honking of horns behind us.

I told him that I would not pay for the part of the ride that was his mistake, but then he started to come unglued, and I began wondering if this ex-Army officer might have some weapons under his seat. Discretion being the better part of valor, I quickly handed him the full fare and got away.

In hindsight, what did I expect? Most taxi drivers in the US don't speak English either!

The rest of the day was anticlimactic. I got all the charts that any pilot could ever want and I will study them in detail. The pilot shop was professionally represented by the English-speaking "Chris". I inquired of Chris if there was a place nearby where I could get a haircut and he pointed to a place just down the street, and even walked me there and helped to translate my needs ("Just a little off the top, not too short") and then returned to his shop.

Caroline was the only person in the shop, a lovely Parisian girl whose English vocabulary about equaled my French -- almost none. Coincidentally, it seemed we knew the same words in each other's language, so nobody learned anything. When I stumbled out a question regarding if there was anything she could do about my *"blanc"* hair, pointing to the few but ever-growing number of white hairs at the temples, she said "No, no! Is nice!" touching my temples with both hands and smiling sweetly.

I imagined coming back to Paris in my later years and taking a room on *Rue Mademoiselle*, across the street from the *"Coiffure"* sign, just to be convenient to this tiny salon, so that Caroline could reassure me that my white hairs were so nice. Here is Caroline:

The rest of the day was spent studying the charts. Carl called to say that progress was going very slowly on my biplane. There would be no flying today, and tomorrow is still in doubt.

I keep looking forward to the time when my wheels will part company with the earth and my biplane lifts up into the air for my first look at France from the sky. Soon, I hope...

Day 8: A Very Short Story

<u>Paris, France</u>

We got the plane flying after a very long day and a lot of hard work. Unfortunately, I didn't fly, but Carl did — he scored a test flight around the city of Paris. Lucky dog! It is now 11:30 pm. I have to get up early so we can go flying in the morning. I hope to fly north to the English Channel, check out the little airport at Le Touquet, and return.

I need to get clean, and get some sleep more than anything else in the world.

I am going to dream of fluffing down softly on grass runways and touching clouds and playing with the angels in the sky over France.

Day 9: Only Pilots Know Why Birds Sing

<u>Le Touquet, France</u>

The rose-lavender-peach colors of dawn filtered through my window this morning to invite me to go flying. I couldn't have been more ready to start the day.

Unfortunately, it was at least six more hours before we unwound all the red tape associated with 1) Normal preflight preparation, 2) Flying in France, 3) Flying out of Le Bourget airport, and 4) Flying an airplane associated with the Paris Air Show.

At last, I taxied out to Runway 25 and pushed the throttle full forward. For the first time in two months I was being pressed back in my seat, speeding down the runway, getting lighter all the time, lifting up into the headwind until that magic moment when the wheels finally separate from the ground and the wings take on the entire weight of the biplane, the moment when man becomes bird, the point in time when the dreams of all mankind from the dawn of history are realized -- I fly.

At only 1,000' I can see the skyline of Paris, the City of Light, with the Eiffel Tower as the "*piece de resistance*" prominently set out against the background. The countryside is green all around me, the highways leading out of town become narrower, the cumulo-nimbus clouds become more broken, and the day is so perfect I want to scream. There is no substitute for flying. It can only be appreciated by a flyer. Only pilots know why birds sing.

In a short while, I am crossing above *Pasan-Beaumont*, a small uncontrolled (there is no air traffic controller) airfield to the north of Paris, turning into a right downwind pattern for a landing on the asphalt runway, 28 Right. There is a grass runway just to the left of it, and I want to touch down on this soft natural grass, but I am saving it for desert. Right now, I want to do a normal landing, maybe a few of them, just to prove to myself that I can still do it. It has been 60 days since the last time I landed an airplane and I really needed to be sure that I could still do it. Is it like riding a bicycle? Is it impossible to forget how to do it? Will it come back to me in an instant?

The answer, dear reader, is yes. It came back to me as though my last landing were yesterday. It was not perfect, but then I have had only one *perfect* landing in my 1,544 landings so far (yes, I record and count every one). Maybe I will tell you about that one someday. For now, it is important only to say that this one was delightful in its own particular way. This was my first landing in France, so how could it be anything but wonderful. Oh, I admit it was a shade fast on the approach, and so I floated a bit long down the runway, and maybe I bounced just ever so slightly (not enough so that anyone would ever notice, but then I'm a perfectionist). All things considered, it was a very good landing.

I loved it so much I rolled out only a little bit and then firewalled the throttle and lifted off for another try. The second one was even better, but still had some imperceptible element of imperfection that just made me want to do it again, and then again, and then again, until I felt that my hunger was satisfied. And then I had desert.

The grass runway is directly next to the main asphalt runway, but it is much wider. I had heard that this particular grass runway was rough, a bit bouncy, but when I first touched down, it was as if pillows had been arranged for my visit. There was a slight direct crosswind of about 5 to 8 knots, but the grass let the wheels slip to the side ever so slightly, removing the faintest trace of squeak that would have occurred on the asphalt. Instead, there was just a quiet fluffy "Welcome Back" when my biplane traded sky for grass.

I had several helpings of desert this morning, and each was as tasty as the first, and I would still be there right now, gorging myself on the finest aviation experience a pilot can have (just ask any pilot you know), but today I had a higher purpose. I was on a mission. Today I was going to the English Channel. The airfield is called *Le Touquet*, on the north coast of France. The plan was to see the English Channel, to touch the other side of the Atlantic Ocean, to fly low over the beach and to return to share the experience with you.

The town of *Le Touquet* is a wonderful blend of English and French. It was the first time I had heard the English language spoken properly in the week I've been in France, but it was because Brits spoke it. The town of *Le Touquet* was chosen by English kings as a summer getaway, and the populace of southern England has been popping over here ever since just for a quick change of scenery. It's only 50 miles from England, across the channel. The town is right on the beach, an improbably wide beach of the most appealing sand. I had to take home a few seashells as souvenirs. The village is small in every respect. The streets were small enough only for one lane of one way traffic, the sidewalks were less than 5' wide, and the tiny shops were probably only double that in width.

It was a typical coastal day, a low overcast, and scattered light rain, so I had a quick meal and then headed back to the airport for an early departure. The return trip to Le Bourget airport, to the northeast of Paris, was uneventful, except for the occasional light showers en-route. The clouds hung low at just 1,000 feet above the ground, and that was just fine with me because I wanted to be close to the farms and villages just under my wings. In the 100 miles between Le Touquet and Paris, I passed over many little towns which must have been at least 500 years old, with huge central churches and tiny little houses clustered all around for protection from forces above and beyond. It was as if nothing had changed here, ever, at least not from my vantage point.

It was a superb flying day. It is amazing that it happened when it did, because it was the last possible day I could fly before the Paris Air Show. The moment I landed, I taxied to the special exhibition area and was towed into the parking spot where my lovely Waco biplane would spend the next 10 days among some of the most macho aviation machinery in the world. More than a million people will see my Waco, my incredible piece of flying sculpture. They will admire it, they will desire it, they will harbor secret fantasies about what it must be like to fly it... but could they ever imagine a day of flying as perfect as today?

Here is a photograph of the northern beach of France, along the English Channel, just to the west of Le Touquet, as seen from the cockpit of my open-cockpit biplane at 100 feet above the water:

Day 10: Friday the Thirteenth

<u>Paris, France</u>

And now for some not-so-good news: yesterday was so thoroughly excellent that I could not bear to discuss the less than positive aspects that evolved. Today, it seems appropriate to share it with you.

The first thing I noticed during preflight preparations was that the trim control was misbehaving. It operated the stabilator properly, but the feel was way off, seeming clunky and harsh. I made a mental note of it, and continued with the flight. In the air, the trim control was much more difficult to operate. It needed a lot more muscle to get the desired results. We definitely need to work on this back on the ground. Not a major thing, but...

As soon as I switched on the avionics, it was evident that the HSI (Horizontal Situation Indicator) was toast. This device is a gyro-stabilized compass that also gives me a visual CDI (Course Deviation Indicator) readout from my GPS (Global Positioning System) as well as a backup VOR (Very high frequency Omni Range). Now all of this alphabet soup of acronyms means that without this HSI critter, you can't tell where you're going! Well, there is a wet compass as a backup, and there is one other VOR on the panel, (I even have a VOR in my backup handheld radio, now that I think of it). So I wouldn't get lost without my HSI, but it is sure one of the sweeter instruments on my panel, and I will not be leaving Paris without getting this one repaired. Carl figures that it got bounced around too much on the train ride from Detroit to Montreal, before being loaded onto the ship to France.

There is also a problem with the tail wheel. For the first time ever, it shimmied on landing. I couldn't believe it. I have heard of other Waco biplanes doing this, but mine was always so smooth. Carl said he would have another entire tail wheel assembly shipped in from the factory, and he would put it on himself. He's a class act!

So the airplane has a few complaints after being mistreated and ignored and stuck in a box for so long. I suppose I would too.

But what's going on with *me*? For about a week, I have been noticing a slight tightness in my throat, which I attributed to the constant presence of cigarette smoke everywhere in France. I just figured I would get used to it and the scratchy throat would go away. Not so. Two days ago, it was really bad in the morning, and then got better at the end of the day. Yesterday, it was okay in the morning, so I thought I was on the mend. But it was not to be.

Yesterday's perfect day of flying took its toll. The air was chilly and wet, and my jacket collar was not tight enough to keep out the cold. By the end of the flight, I was very hoarse, almost inaudible without shouting on the radio. By the end of the day, I had lost my voice completely, and this condition has continued throughout today. For the first time in my life, I am mute. I'm a mime! If there is any consolation in all this it is that I cannot speak the language anyway, so why bother. Another consolation is that the biplane is locked up in the display area, so I couldn't fly it even if I could speak.

So my biplane and I are both suffering from some minor ailments, and we will work on getting fixed up over the next few days.

While I was out today, dealing with some of the red tape involved with the air show, I tried to get a little sleep in the back of the rental car while Carl waited in line to get exhibitor badges. My rest was rudely interrupted with the sound of some of the most powerful jet engines produced by man, flying just a few feet over the roof of the car. Then I noticed that we were parked at the approach end of the main runway at Le Bourget. Can anyone identify this fighter jet?

I hope your Friday the Thirteenth is going better than mine. Thanks for being there. It helps to have someone to talk to, especially when you have lost your voice!

Day 11: Who Is This Guy? Why Is He Doing This?

It's a gloomy, rainy day in Paris, a perfect day to catch up on my correspondence, do some writing, and reflection. One of my new e-mail friends has asked me a question that echoes a request made by other readers who have just joined into this journal, namely: "Who is this guy and why is he doing this?" My long-time friends will find some new tidbits among the following, so they will not be so bored, and all will find the seed of motivation that has lead to this adventure.

I was conceived on the "Day of Infamy," the attack at Pearl Harbor, December 7, 1941. Precisely nine months later, I arrived as the second of six children (three boys, three girls). We were not an overly large family for Irish Catholics, but sizable enough for me to develop an instinct for self-preservation, especially at mealtime.

I was a beautiful child, my mother's favorite, as she told me many times in private. However, my siblings make the same claim, which, if true, indicates my mother's wonderful sense of humor, that she would kid them that way.

I attended a boys-only Catholic high school, and a boys-only Catholic college, so girls were always somewhere else. My advantage was that I had wheels. It seems that it's impossible for a guy to date if he has no wheels, and I had the good sense to choose to be born into the brood of Charles F. McCafferty, who would become Philadelphia's largest Ford dealer, and therefore my access to cheap transportation was assured.

I never got free cars, but I could buy them wholesale and get them repaired at a discount. I could also "borrow" my father's car-of-the-moment without it being a criminal offense, so I had a youth filled with late night adventures in such incredible automobiles as his 1959 Jaguar XK-150/S roadster, which I raced to speeds in excess of 120 mph at 3 am with the top down, in a mad dash to escape the police. I remember turning my lights off (to more clearly see the lights of any oncoming traffic) and passing a milk truck on the curve of an old country road. I was an idiot when I was young.

I went through a lot of cars because I was so rough on them. I loved to experiment with how they would behave in various situations (wet, snowy, icy, sand, bumps, hills, etc). I remember doing 'donuts' in snow on a one-lane road, with cars parked on both sides, just to show off for a friend. Surprisingly, I had few accidents, but one in particular happened right in front of high school just before classes started for the day. Everyone was out front catching a smoke just in time to see me hit the brakes and skid into the back of a car which had stopped to parallel park. My target car then hit the guy in front of him, and then he did the same, etc, until we had five cars destroyed in a pileup that is still a favorite topic of nostalgia at reunions. And I can still see the hood of my car crumpling up in slow motion, as it did that morning, just before my face was bloodied on the steering wheel. I tell you all this only to underscore what you have by now determined: I'm lucky to be alive! And aren't we all?

Cars were a major focal point of my life, being born into the business. I used to hang out at my father's car lot, directly next to the famed Langhorne Speedway, where all of the most famous stock car (pre-NASCAR) drivers of the time would come to race. Ford Motor Company sponsored the best teams and they used my father's dealership as a staging and repair pits in preparation for the races. I wandered in awe through the maze of racing machines, tires, tools, and legendary drivers, thinking that someday I would do this.

And one day, I did. When I finally graduated from college, a minor miracle in itself because I never achieved academic distinction (except for achieving the lowest end of the scale!), I seemed to go through a metamorphosis. My first job, with IBM as a sales rep, was so interesting to me that I buried myself in everything I could read about computers, and I became a very good salesman, using a combination of innate sales talent (Irish blarney), technical know-how, and total focus. This combination led to an excess of cash at an early age, which I spent on (you guessed it) fast cars. I raced my own car in weekend races on the East Coast tracks, and performed very well, and had some amazing experiences.

From early childhood I was fascinated with flying, but I was always told that it would be impossible because I had such poor eyesight. I believed them, until one day I discovered a magazine about flying that contained an ad selling remanufactured Stearman biplanes. It was at that moment that the thought finally hit me that I could buy my own airplane and fly it without needing the military or the airlines to provide one.

Buying one of the "normal" (single wing) general aviation aircraft available at the time (Piper Cub, Cessna, etc.) was completely uninteresting to me simply because they just looked so normal. If I was going to fly, it was imperative that I would fly something that looked extraordinary. This was just the natural extension of my philosophy concerning the selection of cars, either for racing, or for everyday use.

Immediately upon seeing the ad for biplanes, I phoned to inquire about price and availability, in spite of the fact that I had never even sat in a small plane before. From that point on, my sole focus was to sell enough computers to get the biplane. Unfortunately, the price of the plane went up rapidly due to the demand. When, after six months of selling and saving, I had the original purchase price, the new price dictated another three months of selling, and then when I had that in hand, the price had escalated again.

During this period I took flying lessons, in a very normal airplane, a Cessna 150 that I disliked immensely, a Volkswagen of the skies. I took only eight hours of lessons, just enough to solo and prove to myself that I could handle an airplane. It was also during this period that my boss at IBM, George Roper, showed me the ultimate price one must pay for poor judgment in the air. He was a new pilot too, and he got lost in a fog, lost situational awareness, lost control and found his own untimely demise.

There was really only one thing that could have kept me from flying and racing cars at that point in my life, and as luck would have it, that one thing came along in the form of a lovely and spirited young lady with whom I fell in love, and her priorities included a home and a family, and therefore these goals became my priorities. This was the end of my racing and my flying for the next quarter of a century.

The results of that union were threefold: 1. I learned about Love and Marriage, and, 2 & 3: My two incredible children Mike and Kendra. Everything in life is a matter of choices and I feel that I made the right choices, because I would never go back and change any of it.

Success in business came to me as the result of lots of work, which somehow seemed not to be so hard, as I was obsessed with the challenges of computers and starting and running my own businesses. This involvement in computers and business ran for the next 25 years, and provided the backdrop for some other growth experiences as well, including divorce, bankruptcy, and malignant cancer, all of which I seem to have recovered from well enough. The business career culminated in my inventing, writing, developing and building a company to sell my software TeleMagic, a contact management and sales automation software product for sales and business people. This last chapter in my business career consumed seven years of my life, and ended with the sale of my company, my retirement from business, and the rebirth of my flying career.

In the early TeleMagic years, when I was still working out of my small apartment in Del Mar, California, atop a cliff overlooking the surf, I would be working on my computer when occasionally I would be visited by a biplane flying low along the waterline, that would then pull sharply up, reverse direction, dive down again and then disappear back up the beach. I was so moved by those moments that I imagined that one day I would do this.

And one day I did. It took seven years. At 50 years of age, I finally had the freedom to do what I wanted, and one of the first things I wanted to do was fly. Within a few months of the sale of my company, I started taking flying lessons in a Stearman. With only a few hours in this vintage biplane, I literally fell in love with a Waco YMF-5 at an air show and was astounded to learn that these planes are built brand new, from scratch, by a little company in Lansing Michigan. I was stunned by the beautiful lines of this Waco, and on the flight back home in the Stearman, all I could think about was the Waco. On the first day of business after the air show, I called the Waco factory, and after a brief conversation, sent them a deposit to reserve a biplane for me. This time, there would be no delays, no price increases. This time I would have my biplane, and I would fly it. Little did I know how costly it would become.

I was completely filled with the enthusiasm of flying, and the excitement that soon I would have my very own open-cockpit biplane. I just had to share this wonderful experience. I asked my flight instructor, the son of a writer of some of aviation's more popular books, to give rides to some of my closest friends. I would have preferred that I do the flying, but I was still a student. And I would have preferred that it would be in my own biplane, but it was not yet ready for delivery.

It was on the first day of spring, March 21, 1993 that a small group of my friends went for rides, one by one, in the biplane I first flew, a pumpkin-colored 450 Stearman, with pilot Rob Bach at the controls, while I stayed on the ground and awaited their return. One by one, they got a small taste of the joy I feel each time I take to the sky. One by one they returned to a gentle landing, except one.

My son, Mike, was the last to fly that day, and when I strapped him into the cockpit before takeoff I was thinking how much I love him, and what a wonderful person he turned out to be. The pilot looked at the gas gauge and mumbled a few words about having enough. But he didn't. The plane ran out of gas and crashed into a small hill near the runway, destroying the plane, and breaking Mike's back, paralyzing him from the waist down. I was on the scene before the paramedics lifted him out of the wreckage, and I could hear him telling them that he couldn't feel his legs. He was incredibly lucky to be alive. My only thought from that point on was that we would do whatever it took to overcome this setback. I was convinced that he could prove wrong the doctors' prognosis of life in a wheelchair. And he did.

It was not without Herculean effort on his part that he did this. If there is any message that I want to share with you, dear reader, it is that Mike is my personal hero. During his extended hospitalization, and rehabilitation, he never once complained of the pain, he never once railed out against me for getting him into this mess, and he never once gave up the fight for recovery. If I did not see it myself, I would not have believed that it is possible to fight so hard and so long and still maintain a delightful sense of humor and be a loving, lovable person. As I write this, Mike is walking with the assistance of crutches, definitely beyond the point where the best doctors had ever thought he would be.

The pilot received only a small cut on his forehead, and a six-month suspension of his license.

For several days after the accident, I could hardly walk myself, a condition that most certainly was psychosomatic, partly in sympathy for my son's condition, and partly because it seemed that I could not possibly *deserve* to walk under the circumstances. For the next several months, any more flying was unthinkable. My sole focus was on helping Mike through this crisis. It was only when he started showing signs of improvement that I could give my own life any thought.

It was then that I had to decide if I would ever fly again. If I did not, it would send the wrong message to Mike: that it was okay to quit when things don't come out as planned. If I did not fly again, I would have backed away from a great personal goal. I figured I had no choice in the matter. I just had to fly.

The ancient McCafferty clan's coat of arms is emblazoned with the Latin phrase "Justicia et Fortitudo Invincibilia Sunt" (Justice and Fortitude are Invincible). I nailed that coat of arms on the wall of my son's hospital room and told him that it was true Justice that he would walk again, and that if he had the Fortitude, he would be Invincible.

So it was then that I re-ordered my Waco from the factory and started again in earnest to achieve my wings, and to overcome the midnight devils that would visit me and fill me with fear and doubt. My son became my hero. If he could overcome his devils, then I could overcome mine. (And so can you!)

Mike. My son, my hero.

Now that you have some historical perspective, you may understand my current motivations. During the last few years, I have learned something about the nature of Spinal Cord Injury, and how scientists are working on finding a cure for paralysis, and just how close they are. A condition that for thousands of years had been considered to be a death sentence is now giving way to the inexorable advance of technology and human will. If we can put a man on the moon, we can surely find a way to repair a few nerve bundles, can't we? In my experiences with my own challenges in life, and those of the people close to me, I have witnessed that we are quite capable of doing virtually anything that we truly believe and persist in going after with total focus.

I wanted to help with the search for the cure for paralysis. Yes, it was a biplane that Mike was riding in when his paralysis occurred. Could my biplane help somehow to find a cure for those who are paralyzed now or in the future? It seemed to have a ring of Justice to it.

My work now is simply to do what I can to help with the search for the cure for paralysis. I will fly my biplane, and with my writing, I will share these adventures with others, and I will donate 100% of the profits from these adventures with those who are dedicated to the search for a cure for paralysis. I am not going to beat on you for donations, but I will point you in the right direction if you are so inclined: http://keck.rutgers.edu/SCIP/scip.html

I believe that our actions cause our results. I believe that we have some personal responsibility to contribute to the common good. I believe that if our actions are congruent with our beliefs then we live a good life. I fly a biplane and I write, this is what I do right now, and I do this for me and for the common good.

I heard this advice for writers: People will love you if you get them to think that they are thinking, but they will hate you if you really make them think. At the risk of offending you, dear reader, I ask you to consider what it is you are doing that is for the common good, and if by some chance that element of your life is not currently active, then would you consider joining me in this worthwhile cause? Would you simply click on the website above and learn more about what can be done if the resources were available? And then follow your heart?

My message is over. Thank you for reading this far.

Tomorrow, we go to the Paris Air Show!

Day 12: The Paris Air Show

<u>Paris, France</u>

In French and then again in English, the loudspeaker welcomes us to the 42nd <u>Paris Air Show</u>. This show has been held every two years for most of the last 84 years (a couple were missed due to WWII).

Le Bourget airfield, the site of the Paris Air Show, is the place where Charles Lindbergh touched down on his historic first solo flight across the Atlantic. They gave him a warm reception, and I have heard that the French are very friendly to American aviators, so I am hoping they like my biplane. I would soon learn that they (almost) liked it too much.

We set up shop early, before the crowds are let in, and do finishing touches to the Waco, wiping off minute specs of dust, so that it is in perfect shape for display. We are not even set up yet when it seems there is a crowd around the biplane, looking in and under and all around it. And then the gates open!

Soon we have people everywhere around it, and there is just no way we can deal with them all. There is a fence in front of our display, to keep the people back, but somehow they are getting in from the sides and the back. Soon it was utter madness.

Kids and dogs and ladies with baby carriages, pilots and journalists and photographers are all jockeying for position. And they all find it impossible *not* to touch it, to run a hand over the beautiful natural wood prop, or to push a finger into the wing fabric to test its strength, or to rap a knuckle on the cowling, to kick a tire, pinch the leather, climb up on the wing, to lift the aileron or elevator, to push on the rudder, test a trim tab, or lean on the side of the plane while looking in the cockpit... "STOP!" I yell at last when I see an exuberant father holding his young son up to look in the cockpit, unconscious to the fact that the son is kicking away at the fabric on the fuselage. It is just too unbearable to watch the desecration of my lovely flying machine. I freaked!

Within minutes, we had jury-rigged a makeshift barrier out of tie-down ropes, and this kept people from standing too near the fuselage to get a look inside the cockpit. Next we had signs made up, in French and English, with the very stern "DO NOT TOUCH" (no "please," no "thank you") and hung them on the wings. And we had people stationed at the back, front and sides to be sure that people heeded the signs.

It was as if by magic: almost immediately the crowds were keeping their distance and treating the plane with the respect it deserved. Now I could relax and enjoy the people watching while the people enjoyed the Waco watching.

Most people didn't believe it was *not* restored. They could not comprehend why someone would go to the trouble to build a 62-year-old biplane from scratch and then try to sell it new.

The Waco factory was represented in force here today. Don Kettles, the world's greatest (albeit only) Waco salesman, with his incredible good energy and patience tried his best to sell in English to people who spoke something else. Of course, the world's greatest Waco biplane pilot, Carl Dye, who speaks very little English (because he speaks very little, period), was here to deal with technical issues. And the new guy on the block, Mitch, the new owner of the company, came by the display right after arriving from a long flight from the US. But best of all we had Antoine, our secret French weapon to deal with the legitimate prospects. Antoine is the son of Bernard Chabbert, our friend in France, who helped us with our problems with customs. Antoine is the only one among us who can speak French, so he was very busy. If it were not for him, we would have looked like four American monkeys (See- Hear- Speak- and Understand-no-French). Here's a photo of the team, along with an unusually pretty French lady who seemed interested in buying a Waco (or was it just my imagination?):

Some of the older visitors to our display would stop and smile and quietly remember good times long past when these were the airplanes of their day. The language barrier prohibits a lot of talk so there are few long conversations about the planes they flew in their youth. But it doesn't matter. I have heard these stories before at other shows in the US. The spirit of flying is the same in any language. The gleam in their eyes says it all.

The Waco is positioned immediately next to a Russian MIG-AT trainer to the right, and opposite a Romanian Air force MIG-21, upgraded with the latest systems. Nearby, the very latest "Eurofighter", and all around are a variety of attack and rescue helicopters and two enormous space rockets, an amphibious kit plane, unmanned drones and a paramotor (fan and parachute), the Airbus 319, and the entire Dassault line of military and civilian aircraft. All this was visible in the immediate outdoor area. There are several HUGE exhibition halls and many, many, many more aircraft on display farther down the line. There is much more here to see than anyone could cover in a week.

At 1 pm the air displays start with an aerobatic routine by a vintage biplane (of course!), a Belgian designed Stampe from the Breitling aerobatic team. Next comes an attack helicopter doing loops, followed by demonstrations by the Airbus 319 and 340 commercial airliners showing their stuff in steep climbs, turns and slow flight. Then the big guns: The Mirage 2000-5 Single Engine fighter jet, the current inventory of the French air forces, followed by the Dassault Rafale twin engine jet fighter, due to be in service in another five years. There were two displays by the Rafale, one fully loaded with bombs and rockets and fuel tanks, and another one stripped and flying for fun. Then there were corporate jets, whisper quiet displays to give your ears a break from the thunder of the fighters, but soon there were more of the crowd pleasers: a MIG-29, a MIG-21, and the Americans displayed the F-18 and F-16. The Stealth fighter wasn't there (or was it?).

The sound of these big fighters interrupts all conversation. It is more than deafening, it is a heavy physical force that beats against your entire body, not just your ears.

In the midst of all this eye candy, in this smorgasbord of visual treats, I would have to boast that my lovely little biplane was unquestionably one of the most photographed airplanes at the show. People would pose their children, or girlfriends in front of it, with the big wood prop and round engine creating a nostalgic background. With billions upon billions of dollars worth of high tech mass transportation, spying and killing machines all around, it seems as if people can still appreciate the inherent "rightness" in an airplane built solely for fun.

Day 13: The Air and Space Museum

I tried to sleep late this morning, hoping it would help clear up my laryngitis that has persisted over the last few days. Still having much difficulty speaking, my plan for today was to see the Air and Space Museum, assuming that I would not have to use my voice for anything in a museum, and I could give my throat a rest. It was definitely on my list of things to do, better than staying in bed.

I admit to feeling like it was going to be a dull day because I have been to quite a few air shows and air museums in the US, and I figured on seeing a lot of the same stuff. Wow, was I wrong!

The French call this place *"Musee de l'air et de l'espace"* and it is located at Le Bourget airport, the site of the Paris Air Show. It consists of seven buildings that house aircraft segregated by type. In one building there is only spacecraft, including a real Suyoz T6 command module which still shows considerable re-entry scorching. All the rest of the approximately two dozen spacecraft are mostly replicas of various satellites, including the first one ever in space, the Sputnik I, as well as the Vostok I capsule which carried Yuri Gagarin to become the first man in space. It looks like some Jules Verne underwater diving helmet right out of "20,000 Leagues Under the Sea." There was even a Russian lunar land rover.

A separate building was devoted to prototypes, and my visit gave me a whole new appreciation for the extraordinary variety of aircraft that the French have developed. And with such style! I wish I had the words to describe the most unusual, eccentric, and yet undeniably lovely shapes that they gave their aircraft. They surely did not spend their time waiting to see what the Americans were doing so they could copy it!

Another building housed a collection of aircraft from 1919 through 1940 (between the wars). One of my favorites was the huge twin engine Farman Goliath F-60 that looks like a flying streetcar, and carries 12 passengers seated in wicker chairs (which seem not to be bolted to the floor!). The passengers are comfortable inside the plane, but the pilot must endure the elements flying in an open cockpit. There was no tail wheel, only a skid. The wheels were held in place only by bundles of bungee cords.

My true favorite among the planes in this building was the Potez 53, a 1933 monoplane with retractable main gear and a tailskid. It achieved 380 kph at the time. One of the most curious things about this plane is that the glassed-in area for the pilot's head is only about six inches across, an incredibly tight fit that seemed like it would be impossible to turn your head even a little. I liked this airplane because it just looked so good, so I share a photo of it with you here.

The largest of the buildings showed off the Concorde prototype #001. It was possible to walk through it and inspect it in detail. I toured it twice. For me, it was a great memory because I flew on the Concorde from New York City to London about 10 years ago. I remember barreling down the runway with the entire airplane shaking like crazy and wondering to myself "My God! How fast are we going? This plane should have taken off by now!" I finally got my answer from one of the museum tour guides. The rotate speed is 250 mph, which is certainly faster than I had ever gone on the ground in any type of vehicle. I also remember being impressed with just how small the airplane is inside. The passengers' windows are tiny, just barely bigger than a pack of cigarettes. It holds only 100 passengers, but it achieves twice the speed of sound, and has been doing this for more than 30 years. It is the only major commercial airliner that has never had a fatal accident.

One of my fondest memories of my trip on the Concorde was inviting myself into the cockpit while flying at 59,000 feet at Mach 2, and standing there having a very calm conversation with the pilot and engineer. Since it was a foreign airline, there was no restriction on passengers in the cockpit during flight. It was awesome!

Someday soon, you will be able to tour this fantastic museum from the comfort of your favorite chair and be able to fully understand everything about them in English (I had to figure it all out with my limited French). Soon, all the museums in the world will be on the Internet. Won't that be good news for your feet!

One of the highlights of my visit was a 3-D movie that showed an old biplane (I think it was a Bucker Jungmeister) flying low over the countryside, and in the Alps, over lakes and cities. It was spectacular photography, and it really made me feel very lonely without my lovely biplane. I watched it three times!

Tomorrow I'm going back to see the rest of the museum, especially the building that highlights the earliest stages of flight. If the weather is good, I will find the exact spot where Lindbergh touched down when he first crossed the Atlantic.

Taking a break from the museum, I stopped by the Waco display to see how my biplane was getting along. Of all the airplanes in that museum, I still like my Waco the best!

My timing was a bit off. As soon as I got outside the museum, it started to rain. I got to stand under the wing of the Waco for a couple of hours while the storm moved through. During all this, Carl took some time to install a new tail wheel and a mechanic from Euralair removed my HSI for inspection and (hopefully) repair. Bernard Chabbert introduced me to Catherine Maunoury, the 1988 Aerobatic champion. We arranged that she would fly me in her plane and I will give her a ride in mine, when we are together in Megeve, in the French Alps, (only 10 minutes by air from Mont Blanc) in mid-July.

Now, that could be some interesting flying!

Day 14: Another Rainy Day in Paris

Paris, France

I'm wearing out with all this rain. It's been raining just about every day for the last week. Cold and wet is not my idea of a fun combination, and it's not doing my laryngitis any good either.

It was a perfect day for finishing my tour of the Air and Space Museum. Today, I inspected the largest building, the one reserved for the earliest flying machines, up through WWI. This was definitely the finest part of the museum.

The only word I can think of to describe these early aircraft is exquisite. It is evident that early aviation pioneers took their inspiration from birds. The wings of some of these machines are so delicately shaped that you would think that they are, in fact, part bird.

Some of these machines, however, are comical! It seems that almost every conceivable shape had been tried to figure out what it would take to fly. There were machines with two, three and four wings, some with circular wings, some with the empennage in front, some with two wheels, no wheels, four wheels, floats or skids. Some had gas engines, some had steam and some were part balloon.

I particularly liked the one with a fuselage shaped like a boat, but it wasn't designed to be a seaplane. Down the sides of this craft were long rows of copper tubes that seemed to be designed to cool the water for the engine. It was one of the most unusual designs I've ever seen, and this model was perfectly constructed. I just had to take a photo of it:

The French are absolutely in love with aviation. Even their money reflects this. I was delighted to discover that my favorite aviation author is featured on the 50 Franc note (front and back). Antoine de Saint-Exupery (1900-1944) was an early mail pilot, flying open-cockpit biplanes across North Africa and through the Andes in South America. He wrote some of the finest books about these experiences, and one of the world's most popular children's books, "The Little Prince." If you ever get a chance to read any of Saint-Exupery's books, do it! They are wonderfully written, almost poetic.

When I think back to these early days of aviation, and the great hardships that these pioneers endured, I feel very fortunate to be benefiting from their efforts. They had to fly without weather reports, navigation aids or radio, and their machines were notoriously unreliable. Isaac Newton said: "If we achieve great heights, it is because we stand on the shoulders of giants." These men were the giants of aviation. It is a humbling experience to walk through such a fine collection of the earliest flying machines, and to learn about the people who designed and flew them.

There was a Wright Flyer replica in the collection, but it wasn't treated as anything special, just another piece hanging from the ceiling.

For the first time since I've been in France, I really wished I knew the language. There were no translations into English, and I could make out some of the display text from my familiarity with Spanish and Latin, but it would have been so much better if I could read in detail about these early heroes and their machines.

I visited my Waco at the display area today. Seeing it there, enduring a light rain, made it appear quite lonely. I know it wants to fly, and to feel the tickle of grass under its fat tires. I know it wants to be free of all these people, and get out from behind that metal fence. I sure want to set it free!

People are very nice here. Several people have invited me to visit them on my tour. Francois Michiels has invited me to a very nice airport near St. Tropez in the south of France. Philippe de Segovia has invited me to visit his airport at Lognes, to the southeast of Paris. He is a writer for *Aviation & Pilote* and wants to do a story on the Waco. And Pietro Maffioli has invited me to visit his place in Venegono, in the north of Italy. I am very ready to go flying.

Day 15: An Old Irish Prescription

Paris, France

I searched the entire Paris Air Show for a photograph that would interest me, and could find only one. As you can see, it is the cockpit of my own biplane, a fact that you can be sure of because it has my name inscribed boldly thereupon. As you will also be quick to notice, the cockpit is empty. That is, it does not contain *me*! This is the basis for my less than euphoric state of mind.

One solidly positive thing that happened today was that the sun appeared. In fact, it was a perfectly delightful sunny day. I spent the entire day at the Air Show, basking in the sun and listening to the many show attendees who came by the display.

The five weekdays of the show are reserved entirely for aviation professionals (pilots, aircraft company personnel, corporate aviation people, etc.). The general public is excluded from the show during the week, and allowed in only on weekends. So today I met all kinds of pilots. Test pilots, commercial airline pilots, fighter pilots, general aviation pilots, aerobatic pilots, military transport pilots... you name it. You can generally tell the pilots who stop by. They all have that same smile, and that same light in their eyes. It comes from recognizing a *real* airplane, finally, in this sea of high tech hardware that responds only to the on-board computer that takes only general cues from the pilot. In my humble Waco they see an airplane that can truly be flown by the pilot, with a real stick, instead of a steering wheel. It's an airplane that demands to be flown every minute because it has no autopilot; an airplane that allows the pilot to feel the air in which he flies.

I sit there in the shade of my wing, and watch these world-class pilots come to admire my biplane and to run their hand over a real wood propeller, and to marvel at the sophisticated gadgetry on the instrument panel. Most of these extraordinary pilots have never flown an airplane such as this, and they dearly wish to change that.

I have no official duties at this show. I am not there to help the Waco factory people sell biplanes, not even to answer questions or hand out brochures, or sell t-shirts or hats. I listen to pieces of conversations going on in different languages, and I can hear the same questions endlessly repeated:

What kind of an airplane is this? How do you say Waco? What kind of engine does it have? How many horsepower? When was it built? Is it restored? Is it new? May I have a closer look? How fast does it go? How did you get it here from America? Blah, blah, blah, blah...

I am drifting in and out of awareness of the details of what they are saying because I am watching the air show going on almost directly overhead. Aerobatic routines continue for almost four hours each afternoon, performed by the latest military fighters as well as small single engine championship aerobatic airplanes. The questions around me grow faint as the sounds in the sky grow louder, and I am no longer on the ground in the shade of my wing. I am in the air pulling G's, going over the top of that loop.

"Hey Michael, come meet this fellow from Denmark (or Germany, or Switzerland, or wherever). He would like to meet you and invite you fly to his airport." This kind of question breaks into my reverie many times during the day, and I am forced back to reality. Today, I have met lots of great pilots, some legends in this part of the world. It is unfortunate to meet them under these circumstances. It would be far better if we could jump in the biplane and go for a tour around Mont Blanc, or fly low over the Loire river, or play with a light crosswind on some sweet grass field. But here we are standing on concrete, out of our element.

All they can do is to simply say something like "Nice airplane" and ask if I will be flying near Zurich this summer, hoping that if possible they could share some time in this great machine. There is not much I can say except that my plans are to go wherever the sun is shining, that there is no schedule or plan. At this their smile returns, and they nod their understanding. They will give me a card with their contact information, then we shake hands, wish each other good luck, and they disappear into the crowd.

It is sad. We should be flying. A biplane like this should be flying.

When I am President of the world, I will arrange for every person to be given their own open-cockpit biplane, taught how to fly it, and then there would be no wars.

The HSI (Horizontal Situation Indicator), which was removed from my biplane two days ago, has been found to be in perfect working order. Therefore it must be the gyro that is faulty, and it was removed today for testing. If it is the gyro, it will be expensive. I am fortunate that they have one available for replacement.

Living at a hotel at Charles de Gaulle airport has been a sterile experience, so tomorrow I'll move into a hotel in the center of Paris (actually in the 7th district). This will give me a chance to spend some time in the neighborhoods of this great city, and do some sightseeing.

Day 16: Observations From A Sidewalk Café

Paris, France

Although I was only moving to a different hotel, it was good to be packing my bags again. It gave me a feeling that I was actually going somewhere. This was a short-distance move, from an airport hotel at Charles de Gaulle airport on the outskirts of the northeast side of Paris to a very small hotel in the heart of Paris. They call this the 7th district, a very nice section, habituated by intellectuals, according to the taxi driver who delivered me there.

The room is claustrophobic; it is so small. I can deal with that. Maybe I'll get out more often. There are no English-speaking channels on TV. That's okay; maybe I'll meditate more. The phone system is primitive, only rotary dial phones. Remember them? I have tried every possible method, even an acoustic coupler, to use my computer to dial out from the room to no avail. The only way I can get my e-mail is to take my computer to the front desk and plug my phone adapter into their fax line, which bypasses their switchboard. That's okay with me too, because my room is on the first floor, only a few inches from the front desk. (It's a *very* small hotel!)

The hotel is owned by three very nice French women: Danielle, Sophie and Catherine. They are quite small too!

The rain stopped soon after checking in, and the walls of my room were closing in on me, so it was a good time to escape. I took a tourist map of the center of Paris with me and found my way on foot to the Boulevard Saint Germain, heading in the general direction of the Notre Dame Cathedral, using the compass in my watch as the primary navigation instrument. Paris is a maze of streets that change names abruptly, streets that are only one block long, and intersections of five or more streets that seem to come together, but not continue out the other side. I'm sure city planners have learned a lot from the mistakes made in Paris.

It wasn't long before the rain started again and I ducked into a sidewalk cafe and took a table by the window so I could examine the city as it passed me by.

The streets were busy. Even with this inclement weather, there were people everywhere. Tourists, students on vacation, unemployed, homeless, beggars, police.... pedestrians of every sort fought their way along narrow sidewalks and across streets clogged with traffic moving along fitfully, honking and cursing each other while scooters weaved among them all.

Smoking is omnipresent. They smoke as if it were good for them. Could they have got the news wrong? I have never seen so many people chain smoking. They smoke when they eat!

And they do love their baguettes! It seems that everyone is carrying a baguette or two, conspicuously sticking out from its too-short white paper bag. The people who aren't openly carrying a baguette, I suspect of having the remains of one tucked away in a handbag, or stuffed in their knickers, or else they are on their way to get one.

I think maybe national flags would be more identifiable if they dropped the abstract colors and replaced them with more generally recognizable icons of life in the nation they represent. I'm thinking, for example, that the baguette would be ideal for the French flag. The US would have a Big Mac, a guitar (for rock 'n' roll) and a '57 Chevy. Italy's flag would have a big steaming meat-a-ball, and a Ferrari. Germany would have a big fat sausage and a stein of beer. Ireland would have a shamrock and a pint of Guinness.

Women are at least 30 pounds slimmer in France than in America. There is just no question about this. And from my observations from this sidewalk cafe, there are more redheads here than in America.

The trees along the Champs Elysees are a soldierly lot, standing tall and straight, and very well trimmed along the sides. I get the feeling that if a single leaf were to overhang more than the others, a Parisian would report it to the Gendarmerie who would trim it immediately. The streets are clean, and graffiti is rare.

My 'mixed' (ham and cheese on a baguette, of course) sandwich is finished, and the rain has stopped, so I'm off again to walk the few remaining blocks to Notre Dame. The cathedral is on the *Ile de la Cite* (Island of the City), a very small spit of land in the middle of the Seine River, which was used in earlier times as a prison (the island, not the cathedral). Soon, the ambiance of the locale takes on a more somber tone, and I round a corner to see this magnificent cathedral with its enormous flying buttresses, an architectural characteristic of the times.

I toured Notre Dame about a week ago. This time, I'm here for another reason. I find a place to kneel, close to the altar in the center of the church, bathed in the filtered colors of two of the largest stained-glass windows ever built by man, and strike up a conversation with my Maker. (The thought occurs to me that St. Peter is up there saying something like: "Hey guys, look at this! There's McCafferty down there in Notre Dame! The last time we heard from him was that night he was speeding around a curve with his lights out, passing a milk truck, outrunning the cops! That was a long time ago. Wonder what he wants now?").

It's a humbling experience to kneel in this great historical church, which survived everything, even the Nazi invasion, and has been the source of so many prayers sent to heaven, that it seems impossible not to do the same. My prayer is simple: safety for my passengers and myself, a successful tour, and the hope that my writing will inspire some people to join in the search for a cure for paralysis. I light a candle, and leave.

Barely visible over the rooftops in the distance is the most recognizable landmark in Paris, the Eiffel Tower. I haven't had a good walk in two weeks, so I decide to go for it. I follow the Seine the entire way, passing the *Bateaux* (river tour boats) that sell a more comfortable way to get there. In a park along the *Champs Elysees* there is a statue of a man on a horse, sword held high. The inscription reads "Erected by the school children of the US, in honor of Lafayette. Statesman, Soldier, Patriot." Without the aid of Lafayette and the French, we'd still be a British colony.

It is a very long walk, as it turns out. The weather turns rainy again, cold and windy, but I press on. Not the best weather to be nursing the remains of laryngitis. I must be crazy, but I'm on a mission. By the time I get up to the top of the Eiffel Tower, the rain is blowing horizontally and it's impossible to stand on the windward side of the open deck. I descend to the enclosed level one flight down and look out over the city of Paris, a long way down. The photo below is facing south, and in the distance is Santiago Chile, 11,625 kilometers away, according to the sign above the window. You probably can't see Santiago because of the clouds and rain, but in the foreground you can surely see the Seine.

A digital display informs me that 169,092,917 people have preceded me on this tour since 1889. Monsieur Eiffel built a very durable piece of work.

At this altitude, the conditions are raw. I take the elevator down to an indoor cafe on the second level, only 30 stories up, and get a cappuccino and apple tart amid a throng of highly animated schoolchildren from Spain. How delightful to hear another language, one which I can almost understand.

Barely warmed up, and mission accomplished; I find a cab waiting in line at the base of the tower (imagine, finding a cab in the rain!) and head for my cell at the hotel.

Now I'm really hungry. Sophie recommends the 'very good' restaurant just one half block away, but when I arrive at 7:15, I am turned away. They don't start serving until 7:30. The French are very precise about when you may eat. It is virtually impossible to get a good meal until after 7 pm. Lunch stops at 2 pm. Breakfast stops at 10 am. If you are late or early, you go hungry. Maybe that is why they are slimmer.

Dinner presented a challenge. No one spoke English and the menu was entirely in French, but I secured a wrinkled, typed translation from behind the bar. One must be careful in these foreign countries. Some of the menu items were intestines (yuk!), snails (hardly any better!) and other stuff that was untranslated and probably indigestible. I played it safe and ordered the chicken.

It was fantastic. It was prepared baked on a bed of spinach and capped with a flaky pastry surrounded by a mustard/cream sauce that was extra-terrestrial. That's when it hit me: This was my first professionally prepared French cuisine since I've been in France! Everything else I have eaten was institutional hotel food, air show food or sidewalk cafe food. It was hardly *haute cuisine*. But this was the real stuff. Vive la France!

Day 17: The Loose End of a Long Red Tape

Upon awakening from a late sleep, I was pleased to find that my voice had returned. Not a bit too soon, for I would be in need of it this afternoon.

But for now, it's food I have on my mind, and for brunch I am directed to a cafe called the Babylon, just down the street, on the corner. Although it is not raining at the moment, it is cold and gray with a solid low overcast. I choose to sit inside by a window. I am a voyeur of the scenes unfolding in front of me. Across the street is a tree filled park. On another corner is Le Bon Marche, a large upscale department store.

I ask the waiter if there is a no-smoking section. He turns to say a few words (in French) to the bartender and they both have a good laugh. I think that the joke is that there are probably no smoke-free sections in all of France, and that I must be some veggie-eating environmentalist-bleeding-heart American who needs a no-smoking section. I join them in their fun, and say, "Okay, I'll sit here and eat, but I won't inhale!"

The "mixed" (ham and cheese) omelet is absolutely superb. And yet it was prepared very quickly and delivered without fanfare on a simple plate with a crude piece of lettuce as the only garnish. The French must have some unique food chromosome that gives them this special gift in the kitchen.

Another gastronomical miracle has occurred. I thought originally that I would miss my cherished cup of Starbucks Gold Coast each morning. But the French coffee has grown on me. It is outstanding. Startlingly strong and thick, but with whipped milk and sugar it becomes quite civilized, and very tasty.

The Bon Marche department store is extremely well done: very clean and stocked with high-end fashions for men and women. My destination was their bookstore in the basement. I was looking for an English/French dictionary, and finally wandered randomly until I bumped into the proper section. What I found, however, were dictionaries for people who speak French but who want to know English. Which is understandable, of course, but no good for me. A true Catch 22! I bought one anyway, figuring I could stumble through it.

By the way, my initial reading indicates that the French have two different words for "lover": *maitresse* (for a sexual partner) and *amoureuse* (if she is enthusiastic about it). Just wanted to share that with you.

Now sufficiently armed to deal with almost any linguistic situation that occurs to me in this country, I wander the streets to see just exactly what kind of trouble I can get into. After an hour of random walking, I turn a corner and am stunned by what I see before me. It is a statue of a figure, half man and half horse, but this is no ordinary Centaur. This one is only partly covered with flesh, and the rest reveals a skeleton made entirely of machine parts (long screws, rods, angle-iron, etc.). His entire body is composed of such stuff, and most incredible of all is the very impressive array of tools that seem to be exploding from his butt! There is a shovel, a very large screwdriver, a rake, a pick and who knows what else. I thought of climbing up on this 25' high statue to get a better look, but then scrapped the idea. Were these tools really exploding from his butt, or was he just keeping them in a convenient place for when he needed them later? Or had he suffered some nasty industrial accident? It was tough to say. The brass plate on the pedestal indicated it was put there by the Ministry of Culture, so I guess only the artist knows for sure. Nobody in the immediate area seemed at all curious about it, and they didn't seem to mind at all that I was curious about it. I know that my camera was not capable of getting the detail that I would like to share with you, but here is something that you will not see every day in the US:

I was soon attracted by a small clothing shop called Ireland Way, and thought to myself that here indeed would be a little island of the 'auld sod', and that they might be able to tell me the weather in Ireland at the moment. I was eager to learn if it is good for flying. In the least I expected to hear the English language with a lovely Irish accent. NOT! No one spoke English at all. I found a cashmere scarf I liked, and thought it would be just the thing for some biplane flying, but learned that it was made in Scotland! All of a sudden it seemed too expensive, and I left it there.

Stopping back at the hotel for a break from the streets, I received a call that brought me back to reality. The shipping agent who arranged for the clearance of my biplane through customs wants me see some official at the Le Bourget airport and sign a document, but no details were available as to what this document is all about. The only thing they know is that since the biplane was imported for the Paris Air Show, on a temporary basis, they need to be sure that it is removed immediately after the show. If I do not return the biplane to America with the same shipping agent, then the shipping agent will have to pay 1,000,000 francs (divide by 5 for dollars) and all kinds of hell will break loose.

I remind the shipping agent that it was discussed ahead of time that the biplane is here for three months for a tour of Europe, and the Paris Air Show was just the first stop, but somehow it seems to have gotten all turned around. They are suggesting that I could not possibly expect to fly my biplane all over Europe without dealing with all the Customs people in each country. They say I must call each of them ahead of time and find out what arrangements need to be made. They are suggesting that I should contact some (unknown to them!) special kind of person who would be able to help me with all this.

Well, this is where the telephone marathon starts, and for the rest of the day I am dealing with shipping people, the Waco factory people, and our contact in France, Bernard Chabbert, and on and on. This is not my happiest news of the day, of course, and I can imagine myself being engulfed in endless red tape, huge customs duties, penalties and having my biplane confiscated. I visualize myself locked in leg irons and thrown into the dungeons of some rat infested French prison with deviants who may have seen, and gotten a few ideas from, that statue of the Centaur.

But hey! It's Friday afternoon, payday the world over. I refuse to wallow on the horrible things that *could* happen, when I can go out and make them happen! The last time I was in Paris, about eight years ago, I spent a few hours in a place called Rosie O'Grady's, an Irish pub of course, and downed more than my share of pints of Guinness in celebration of my whirlwind visits to London and Paris to sell the foreign rights to my TeleMagic software. It was thus that I had found myself in Rosie's with checks in my pocket for $186,000, just enough to pay my debts and survive in business for another month or so. And buy a couple of pints of Guinness while waiting for the plane home. I woke up the next morning with one of those pint glasses, empty, in my raincoat pocket. I still have that glass, and it's one of my favorite souvenirs.

Tonight I'm going to get another!

Day 18: Meditations at the Babylon Café

<u>Paris, France</u>

Paris is a fantastic city with more to see and do than ten lifetimes could consume. Incredibly sophisticated, yet terribly common, it is still a city, and for that, I cannot endure it much longer.

Give me some remote stretch of beach, even without sun, and my spirit soars. Get me away from these teeming millions; give me peace in isolation. Let me breathe pure fresh air. Let me see a tree in its natural place, view the sky without man's obscuring stones. This is the music in my soul.

The words come back to me easily. From a poem, by San Juan de la Cruz, reprinted at the beginning of Carlos Castaneda's "Journey to Ixtlan," it is about the mythical solitary bird.

> The conditions of a solitary bird are five:
> The first, that it flies to the highest point;
> The second, that it does not want for company;
> not even of its own kind;
> The third, that it aims its beak to the skies;
> The fourth, that it does not have a definite color;
> The fifth, that it sings very softly.

That solitary bird is within me now. (However, I think tonight the "party animal" will replace him, but for just a little while!)

Sean Curtis came over from London later this afternoon. Sean was the very first person to buy my TeleMagic software, even before it had a name, in 1985. Over the years, we have become good friends.

He will be flying along with me for the next couple of weeks as we tour Europe. We are hoping that we can fly to England, Scotland and our shared ancestral home, Ireland.

Day 19: A Street Party of Epic Proportions

Paris, France

After a most sumptuous and delectable dinner last night, Sean and I took to the streets to walk off what surely must have been a week's worth of artery-clogging fats, cholesterol and other tasty stuff. This was one of those times when, if you are not expecting anything in particular, the most incredible things happen.

We walked slowly toward the Boulevard St. Germain, the main street close to our hotel. As we got closer, we could hear music and shouting, and were pleased to find a reggae steel drum band playing at a sidewalk cafe, and stopped to listen for a bit. It was only when we looked beyond this spot, and further down the street did we even begin to comprehend what was happening.

The Boulevard St. Germain is a wide four-lane street with a wide sidewalk. The entire width of this street, and as far as the eye could see, was filled with people of every description, and they all had only one thing on their minds: PARTY!

We turned away from our little band and headed for the main crowd, diving into their midst, and walked among the throngs for at least two miles! There were several different bands on each block we explored. The traffic had been re-routed and there was just this enormous, mad street party. It was not only on the Boulevard St. Germain, but it spilled out for many, many blocks in each direction! In fact, we could not even determine the outer limits of this madhouse, and we tried. It seemed that the entire city of Paris was one incredible party.

It was a combination of Woodstock along with everyone's personal memory of the biggest party in high school. People were standing on the tops of street signs, newspaper stands and telephone booths, trying to get a better view of the bands.

Sean and I were mesmerized. Never before had either of us seen this many people in one place. I have been to St. Peter's Square when the Pope was giving mass, and it was nothing compared to this. I have been to Indianapolis for the 500-mile race, and it seemed boring compared to this. The only comparison I could make would be to Ft. Lauderdale on spring Break, and even that event could not compare in sheer size to this zoo.

We walked for miles, still incredulous with the enormity of what was going on around us. Stupefying, jaw dropping, mind-blowing and more. It was tough to get over just how big this party was, and to get into it, but somehow we did. It was a party of epic, even cosmic proportions, and it would be impolite not to join in with gusto. So we did! We never did find out what the occasion was, at least that night. It was inconceivable that they could do this every Saturday night!

The next morning (Sunday, 22 June), we learned that the previous night's festivities were in celebration of the first day of summer. This mother of all parties was the brainchild of a French Minister of Having-a-Good-Time 15 years ago, and in fact this kind of revelry happens all over France. I'm beginning to like it here!

Today began somewhat late in the morning, due to the need to recover from the monster party. We had some of that excellent French coffee along with an apple torte at the Babylon cafe. Then it was a brisk walk for several blocks to check out the Musee d' Orsay, which is a renovated train station of magnificent architecture, and now houses the prize possession of the Ministry of Culture, a collection of 19th century art, especially the Impressionists.

My high school Fine Arts class came out of the cobwebs in my mind, and here again were the paintings of Renoir, Degas, Monet, Manet, Gaugan, Toulouse Lautrec and many more. Even my favorite sculptor Rodin was represented with his Gates of Hell and several other pieces. A sculpture that I have never seen before was the polar bear by Pompon. It was so real you were compelled to reach out and touch it (strictly forbidden). It was incredible to see hundreds of Impressionist paintings hanging on the walls within reach of the considerable crowds. These pieces would easily bring millions of dollars at auction, and yet, they were perfectly accessible to everyone.

On the way back to the hotel, we stopped at a nearby fruit stand and picked up some cherries, peaches, cheese, crackers, yogurt and some Evian. It was a great meal!

In the early afternoon, we attacked the subway system, the "Metro," and found our way to the outskirts of Paris, then a very quick taxi ride to Le Bourget for the last day of the Air Show. A most extraordinary treat was the Russian Su-37, with vector thrust, which displayed aerial maneuvers I have never seen before. One is the "cobra," which involves the plane pitching nose-up while in level flight, still continuing in its original forward motion, then returning to level flight again. Another maneuver shown for the first time was a complete flip, which starts with the cobra, except that the nose goes past the vertical, continues right around past the tail upside down and comes out into level flight again, all the while maintaining the original forward direction. It's a true "flip." Unbelievable!

Sean was very impressed with all the attention the Waco was getting, but he was completely awed by the enormous power of the fighter jets in action.

We ducked into the American Pavilion just in time to escape a major downpour. (More rain!) My mission there was to enlist the help of the US Commerce Department with my negotiations with French Customs. I'm not sure if that will reduce or increase the mountain of red tape, but at least it's worth a try.

There was a break in the rain and we took advantage of the interlude to jump on a bus to the Metro, then with the aid of a lovely young lady named Sophie, we found our way back home. It was a major achievement: We descended into the bowels of Paris and came away with our health, our knickers and our possessions. Emerging from underground, I used my compass/watch to find the way back to the hotel.

We sat under cover in a local cafe, sipping an excellent Port wine, watching the wet world go by.

Tomorrow I must deal with the red tape of the French Customs Department, find a solution for the broken HSI, get the right wing adjusted, and maybe, if the gods are with me, I just may FLY!

Day 20: Anticipation

Paris, France

The morning started with *cafe gran avec creme* and a *tarte de pomme* (a coffee with cream and an apple tart). The pastry is beyond extraterrestrial. I had two, with two coffees. It's a good thing because this was the last food I was able to eat until dinner at 8 pm.

After a quick breakfast, I was back into the Metro, the subway system in Paris, headed for <u>Le Bourget</u> airport. My mission today was to get my biplane out of the display area and into safe harbor at Euralair at the other end of the airport. This was the first day after the Paris Air Show and every one of the 1,600 exhibitors would be tearing down their displays and chalets and flying their airplanes back home. I was expecting a zoo. And that's exactly what it was.

It looked like a war zone. Debris was everywhere, cranes were lowering dissected helicopters into huge crates on top of flatbed trailers, forklifts were speeding everywhere, thousands of workers milling about, police, show officials, and total chaos as far as the eye could see. Somehow, I had to find someone to speak English and determine how I get a tow out to the main ramp so I could start the biplane and taxi to the other end of the airfield to Euralair. The phone company was, for the first time in history, too efficient. There were only empty places where there used to be payphones.

That's when it struck me. (It's been so long since I have flown, that I almost forgot). I have a radio! I jumped in my biplane, flipped on the avionics switch, keyed in the Ground Control frequency, and asked them to send a tug to tow me out to the ramp. They said no problem; there would be one right along. I should have known it was too easy. An hour later, still no tug. So I call again. This time they say that there is a Boeing 707 that is holding everything up. It is stuck, in the way of everything trying to get to the taxiways. There is a double semi Volvo truck that seems to have been abandoned in place and it is just too tall for the wing of the 707 to get over. This I've got to see.

I take a walk several hundred yards down the display area to check it out, and sure enough, everything is stopped waiting for this impasse to end. But it seems to me that my little biplane just might be able to make it past, if I could get it part of the way under the wing of the 707, real close to the outboard jet engine. If I could do that, then I could just barely make it past the other airplane, and a truck, and then freedom. I paced the distance off. It was exactly 10 paces, 30 feet. My upper wingspan is 27 feet, leaving 18 inches on each side. Hopefully.

I call Ground Control again and inform them of my situation, negotiating for the approval to attempt something, which if it fails, will clog up everything until the next Air Show in two years. They go for it and send a tug that arrives in 15 minutes, but without the ropes I requested for towing. Just another detail that I had to improvise my way out of, and finally borrowed one that was just barely long enough. Getting underway at last, we crawled past the big jet stuck there with all the traffic waiting behind it, the envy of everyone, not just because we were the best looking airplane at the show, but because we were moving, and they were not.

Reaching the taxiway, I disengaged the ropes and fired up the engine for the first time in nine days and taxied the mile up to Euralair's big hangar. The doors opened as if by magic just as I cut the engine, and I pushed the Waco to dry safety just a few minutes before the sky opened up for a torrential downpour. If I had not been so persistent or resourceful in getting a tow, I would have been sitting in the open cockpit out on the ramp getting soaked to the skin. Lucky me!

The folks at Euralair were very helpful in getting my right wing adjusted. It was flying just a shade low and all it took was a turn and a half on the rear "N" strut, and some minor adjustment to the aileron connecting rod. I could have gone flying, if it weren't for the weather.

Then I visited Customs, and they promised to have some paperwork for me tomorrow. I also got the information about the place I have to go to get the HSI replaced, if it still looks like it needs it when I finally get to fly. Next, a little bit of cosmetic black paint to repair a gouge that occurred when someone ground his or her heel when attempting to look into the cockpit. And last, but certainly not least, I visited my hosts in management at Euralair, and thanked them profusely for their hospitality and professionalism, and promised to come back in September so we could do all this again, except in reverse!

Walking back into the hangar, and looking at my Waco in its state of readiness, I was struck with just how beautiful it really is. I was aching to fly.

The plan right now is to see if Customs will allow me to fly it after they give me the paperwork tomorrow. If I get past that hurdle, then I will go for a test flight to an airport just outside of Paris, where the HSI was tested and where they have a spare if needed. I'll go there and do some landings and test my navigation equipment. If everything checks out, then the next day I'll go wherever the sun is shining, and I haven't got a clue where that will be!

There is no photo in today's e-mail because it was a gray, gloomy, overcast, rainy day. There was nothing pretty or interesting about it, except how great the Waco looked sitting in the hangar, ready to fly. And you have already seen a picture of it, so now you and I can just imagine it!

Day 21: Another Day On and Under the Ground

<u>Paris, France</u>

Awake early, I made some phone calls to see if I could find someone to fly with, but the two professional pilots I know who are familiar with Paris airspace both had other plans. As it turned out, it didn't really matter. Later, I called Sean's room, waking him for a quick breakfast before I took the Metro/taxi trip to Le Bourget to see if I could fly.

The weather at the airport continues to be pure yuk. Low overcast, cold wet air. The good news is that it didn't rain for the first time in what seems like weeks.

I had a very good visit with my biplane today. I cleaned out the baggage compartment, and rearranged everything. It had become completely fouled up with all the people in and out of it at the Air Show. This was a good meditative time for me to become reacquainted with my beloved biplane. I went completely through both the front and rear cockpits checking out and making sure everything was in its proper place. I removed excess stuff and put it in a long-term storage box for when I return in September. I set up the cockpit with my log book, hand held radio, kneeboard with checklists, pens, flashlight, and all the other little goodies that are needed in the process of flying. I checked the floors and all around the controls to be sure there were no loose items (I found several packets of photographs in the front cockpit left by the Waco factory people). This process of going over every possible thing in the biplane is something that I do to make myself comfortable with taking it into the air. I like to know that the machine is in perfect working order. With all of this done, I was now ready to do some flight planning.

The Le Bourget airspace is quite complicated. Unlike most of my flying in the US, where I just jump in and go, at this airport it is mandatory to file a flight plan, even if you are going VFR and staying in the country. In addition, one does not just take off and fly direct to the destination. Here at Le Bourget one must leave either to the east or to the west only, because Paris is to the south and Charles de Gaulle airport is to the north and you have to stay out of those two spaces. Immediately after taking off, regardless whether it's east or west, one must fly through two different reporting points which can only be located by the intersection of radials from two different <u>VORs</u>. These reporting points are not on my moving map database, so I really must use the VORs, a procedure which I haven't dealt with in years! Today was spent with my navigation charts, planning my exit from Le Bourget and getting all the radio frequencies documented and visualizing how I would deal with both the departure and arrival airspace. I have been accused of actually spending too much time in preflight planning. It is a visualization process that gives me the confidence I need to feel comfortable. After a couple of hours of this, it was now time to tackle the red tape.

I spent some time dealing with the Customs situation, and finally received permission to fly my biplane. I signed a document (without a clue as to what it says), and they tell me that it's okay now to take my biplane to the UK. I'm living in denial. I figure that if the weather ever does clear up and we ever do get to fly toward England, then I'll deal with their customs when I land and maybe tell them that the plane is inoperable so I won't be able to fly it back out of the country right away.

With the government paperwork cleared up for now, I then went over to the operations office of Euralair and picked up some weather forecasts. The morning forecast said it would rain in the afternoon, but by the time the afternoon forecast came out, it said it would not rain. I called the airport to the southeast of Paris where I had planned to fly to check out my directional gyro, and they said it was low ceilings and low visibility. As the ceilings lifted in the afternoon it seemed as if I could have flown, but the air was still cold and wet, so I passed on flying for today and returned to Paris to buy that cashmere scarf that I saw last week, which at the time was too expensive. After several days of being cold and miserable, I decided that it was now a bargain!

So now my biplane is ready, the government will let me fly it, I have a scarf to keep me warm, the weather is forecast to be flyable (but just barely) tomorrow, I have meditated and visualized, and now there is nothing left in my way at this time. Tomorrow, all I have to do is fuel the biplane and go.

I am getting quite capable with the subway system. I have been able to emerge in the desired place with consistency. I have also developed the requisite mannerism of not having any direct eye contact with some of the loonies who inhabit the underground trains. There is one particularly interesting method of begging I have noticed: A fellow gets on the subway car, and makes a short, but loud speech (I haven't got a clue what he could be saying) and then goes through the car collecting handouts. It doesn't appear to be very effective, but it's novel.

As good as I have become in navigating the subway, I was a complete failure above ground. I went for a walk on the Rive Gauche (Left Bank) today and got so lost that I thought I might just have to send up a flare. I forgot about my compass watch, but as disoriented as I was, it may not have done me any good. The positive news about all this is that I stumbled on some really great little places. *Rue Bonaparte* is a street so hidden that only the lost could find it. I found a rare bookstore window that totally captivated me. It's a good thing the shop was closed or I could have lost control and started a collection of very old books in languages I can't read.

I met up with Sean for a late afternoon lunch. His plan was to run several miles through the streets of Paris and top it off with a run up the Eiffel Tower. (Yeah, right!) He called me later and confessed that he had also gotten lost! Never did get to the Eiffel. He got so lost in fact that he took a taxi back to his hotel. Amazing coincidence.

Tonight, we plan on taking in the Hard Rock Cafe, just to be able to say we were there.

While I was working on my biplane at Le Bourget, a Gulfstream IV landed and parked next to Euralair. There were dozens of photographers waiting for it. The airplane was painted the most disgusting black and red with the Batman logo and a sign "Batman and Robin, World Tour." I didn't recognize the people who got out, but the photographers sure went wild! Who do you think it was?

Day 22: To Fly Is To Be

<u>Nangis, France</u>

Last night, I used my Internet connection to The Weather Channel to look up the forecast for today, and I was pleased to see sunny skies predicted. I went to sleep fully expecting to fly in the morning.

Jumping out of bed early to check the sky, it actually did look promising. Although it was cloudy, the clouds appeared higher than during the previous weeks and I even imagined that I could see some hint of blue color above.

"I'm going to *fly* today!" were the first words to escape my lips, to no one in particular, to the World in General. This was said with great gusto and with heavy emphasis on the word *fly*. In fact, I even sang the word!

I rushed through a breakfast and ran outside, quickly looking again at the sky to confirm my belief that surely the sun would shine today, and then headed again into the subway for the trip to Le Bourget. When I emerged at the end of the line at *La Chapelle*, it was raining! Now a positive thinker, such as I am, immediately thinks that this rain is just a light shower, and that it is very localized, a freak event that is not at all indicative of the general conditions in the area. In fact, a very accomplished positive thinker could even look into that raining sky and still see some blue. And I think I did. When the taxi dropped me off at Le Bourget, it was still raining, but I was convinced that it would stop. And it did. And then it started again.

I visited the operations office where I had to file a flight plan and got the latest weather forecast. The conditions it forecast were absolutely horrible. In another couple of hours the sky would be throwing all kinds of garbage my way. Thunderstorms, ice, low ceilings, cumulonimbus down to 1,500 feet, high winds with gusts even higher! Not a pretty picture by any measure, and certainly not flyable. But outside, right at that moment, it was relatively decent, with high clouds, and the winds were only about 15 knots. Sure it was raining, but not that hard, and visibility was not all that bad. It was the kind of day that normally I would never even consider flying. It was the kind of day one would choose to stay home with a good book, by a fire, with a glass of Port wine and some Mozart.

But a positive thinker, who woke up this morning with a song in his heart and flying in his soul, would not even consider that these conditions were not flyable. In fact, I have flown in worse, but never by choice. Conditions like this occur to you when you are already in the air and it comes as a surprise. But it was flyable. The only thing I didn't like was the fact that it was raining. But a little rain never hurt an airplane, and so what if I was going to be sitting out in the open cockpit in the rain. Many an early pilot flying the mail sat in much worse conditions. My flight was relatively short, so it couldn't be all that bad, could it? And besides, I *really* needed to fly. This is what I do; this is who I am. To fly is to be.

The decision was simple. Fly now in the rain, or don't fly at all today. And with the way the weather has been, who knows when I would ever fly again. So I filed my flight plan and headed for the biplane.

The gas truck took forever to arrive. And when he got there he took a nasty scrape out of my right wheel fairing with a ladder he used to reach the upper wing. Not a good omen, one could think, but not for a positive thinker like me.

Finally, I strap into my seat, wrap my new lucky scarf around my neck, put on my kneeboard, organize my maps, fire up the big round engine (so good to hear it again!), dial in all of the radio frequencies I am going to need to get out of Le Bourget, contact Ground Control and advise them that I am indeed going to fly, receive clearance to taxi to runway 25, and slowly move out of the ramp area of Euralair. As I turn back for a last look, there is a throng of mechanics and office workers who have assembled in the open hangar door to watch this extraordinary airplane take off. My wave is returned many times over, and I am sure they are wondering who is this crazy nut that wants to go flying in the cold rain in an open-cockpit biplane. I know that's what they were thinking, because I was thinking the same thing.

I find runway 25 and while holding short, do my run-up checks and announce to the tower that I am ready to go. The tower now advises me that the wind has shifted considerably (as well as increased in strength) and would I like to take another runway, 21, more aligned into the wind. I agree that 21 would be better under the circumstances, thinking that it would be wonderful if I could just as easily choose a runway that would be in the sunshine!

Throttle full forward, the plane charges into the wind, rolling a very short distance before surprising me that all of a sudden I am in the air. Things start to happen very quickly now. Tower directs me to turn left immediately, stay under 1,500 feet and report when I have arrived at "Echo One," a place that exists only as the intersection of two radio beams and is indicated in my cockpit by two different instruments. The only problem is that one of those instruments is not functioning properly. In fact, that is the reason for this flight in the first place, to go to the airfield where they can repair it. This leaves me in a bit of a predicament of course, but I have prepared to meet this situation. It has worked throughout the ages in all manner of difficult situations, and I'm relying on it now. I beg for mercy.

"Le Bourget Tower, this is Waco biplane November Two Five Zero Yankee Mike, I am not familiar with your area, and I would appreciate your assistance in locating Echo One." I could have told him that I had an inoperative instrument, but then I would have been stupid for taking off without it working properly. No, it was better to be ignorant than stupid. And what are they going to do to me anyway, shoot me down? Make me come back to Le Bourget and write something on the blackboard 100 times? No they would rather help me get out of their airspace as quickly as possible and into someone else's airspace. So they steer me where they want me, probably having a good chuckle among them in the tower. (Crazy American, flying that old biplane in the rain, getting himself all wet.)

I'm reminded of an old saying: "It is better to ask forgiveness than it is to ask permission." It usually works!

Soon comes the tower's sign-off: "November Two Five Zero Yankee Mike, you are clear of our area, proceed to your destination on your own and you may change radio frequency. *Bon Jour*." (Translation: "Good riddance")

Well, I know exactly how they feel. I like dealing with air traffic control as much as they like being interrupted by people like me. I prefer to go flying in silence, without being given orders about which way to turn, which runway to use, to speed up, or slow down, to climb or descend. Birds don't take orders from traffic controllers, and they do just fine, thank you.

Finding the airport at *Nangis* was easy with the help of my GPS. How did people fly without the help of a couple of dozen orbiting Global Positioning Satellites? They flew with the aid of a compass and a clock, and many times they got lost, or worse, but a GPS is a miracle. I have flown without it, but I surely prefer to have one.

Nangis has a hard surface runway and a grass runway, and I chose the hard surface only because I had no way of knowing the condition of the grass. With all the rain lately, it could be partly underwater, which could bring my beautiful Waco to an untimely and unattractive turnover on landing. My approach was just the littlest bit high, but I burned off the extra altitude with a sideslip, then straightened out just before touching down for a very nice landing, if I do say so myself. But then there was no one else there to say it, and it really must be said, or it wouldn't be as much fun. So there!

Nangis is a tiny airport. No tower to go bossing you around. There were only a few hangars, a flight school and Aerodima, the shop that would fix my HSI. As I taxied up in front of Aerodima a group of about eight people were waiting for me with smiles all around, and the biggest smile in the crowd was Helene Brillant-Gavard. I talked with Helene a couple of times on the phone before coming here, about the field and the weather. She is the only one there who is fluent with English, so she was elected to deal with me.

Here's a photo of Helene, her husband René, and Mr. Brillant, her uncle.

I had arrived just in time. Everyone was just leaving for lunch and I was invited to go along. French food is just wonderful, of course, but it is even better when you have someone who really knows the food and can translate the menu for you and recommend the right things.

At lunch, I learned from Helene that the very interesting looking plane I saw in their hangar was a Vampire, the first French Army jet aircraft, built in 1950. The main section of the body of the aircraft is wood! Helene's father is a big fan of the P-38 Lightning, but there are none for sale, and even if they were, it would be way to expensive. So to ease his hunger for a P-38, he bought 4 Vampires. An interesting tradeoff. John Travolta owns and flies a Vampire, so it's got to be cool. Here's a photo of the one in their shop, getting an annual inspection. What you can't see is the twin boom design very reminiscent of the P-38.

Soon after we returned to the airport Mr. Brillant, Helene's uncle, located the problem with the HSI. He removed the gyro unit from the Waco, and holding it in his hands, gave it a gentle shake to demonstrate that there were some bogus noises coming from inside. It sounded like a kid's toy the day after Christmas: broken. Within minutes he had it taken apart on the bench, identified the problem as a ball bearing that had come unstuck, stuck it back where it belonged, and everything checked out again. (This is my very un-technical translation of a very technical French explanation.)

Just as they were re-installing the gyro, the skies dumped more rain, so we pushed the biplane into the hangar for the night. It then occurred to me that I have no idea how I'm going to get back to Paris and my hotel room. But for some reason the universe always takes care of the details. Helene and her husband were going to drive into Paris that very afternoon, for an appointment that Helene had there, and it would be no problem to take me back with them. In fact, René dropped me off at the front door to my hotel. Am I living right, or what?

Day 23: Of Corsica!

<u>Porto Vecchio, Corsica</u>

The rain in Paris has become so relentless that we have been working on a contingency plan: Go to the closest place on the planet where the sun is shining, and wait there until it clears up in Paris.

Sean consulted the local travel agent with the idea that we would go to Ibiza, a small island south of France, in the Mediterranean, which we understand to be the party capital of Europe this time of year. He came back with the news that Ibiza is already booked with celebrities and that there is no room for two more. However, Corsica is available.

Corsica? Where is that? It is also an island in the Mediterranean, but it is off the west coast of Italy. A French possession, (Napoleon stole it fair and square in 1750-something) with a decidedly Italian flair, it is less than two hours by air from Paris, and the sun is shining there, guaranteed.

I called my new friend Helene Brillant in Nangis and was informed that the weather there was horrible, and that my biplane was snug and safe in a hangar, and that it could stay there as long as I wanted. There was nothing to stop me now.

So this was how we have found ourselves in Corsica. When I woke up this morning I would never have imagined that we would be in Corsica in the afternoon. In fact, I could not have located Corsica on a map, not even on a bet. And now we are here. Life is amazing!

We landed at *Figari*, a very small inland airport in the Southeast of the island. Quickly, we rented a Peugeot cabriolet, dropped the top to soak up the last warm rays of afternoon sunshine, and headed over ancient mountain roads to Porto Vecchio, a harbor village on the southeast coast of the island.

We were booked into the Hotel Roi Theodore, owned by a Swiss gentleman who decided to retire here and bought the hotel just four years ago. It was perfect, with a large pool, lush vegetation, and clean rooms, quite reasonably priced compared to the astronomical prices in Paris.

Dinner that night was at an outdoor cafe just across the street from the marina. The food was far below Parisian standards, and the service was awful. We were accompanied by great quantities of mosquitoes that did not wait to be served; they just helped themselves to me, Sean, and everyone else in the place. We tried a local Corsican red wine, which was probably a mistake, because I woke in the middle of the night with a raging headache.

The mosquitoes were everywhere, even in my room that night. I figured that the only way to trick them was to leave the TV on, with the sound off so I could sleep. They were attracted to the light from the TV, and stayed away from me.

Yet, with all of these negatives, it was the first time in weeks that I felt warmth. It was delicious. Tomorrow, we explore more of the island, heading south to *Bonifacio*, a larger village that is supposed to be the action capital of Corsica.

Day 24: More Than Just A Pretty Face

Bonifacio, Corsica

As we were checking out of the Hotel Roi Theodore, just outside Porto Vecchio, Sean met a couple of guys who immediately identified him as a Southern Californian. After a brief conversation he found that one of them was a pilot, and mentioned my biplane trip concept (that's about all it is right now, a concept!), and then brought them by my room so they could see a photo of the Waco.

We all had a great conversation about Europe, the horrible weather in the north, Corsica, and the local attractions. It was when we turned the talk to flying that our new friend and I really hit it off. He kept me spellbound with stories of north and south transatlantic crossings, his Beechcraft D-18 which he keeps at Santa Barbara, his working to certify a new composite seaplane, etc, etc. He was here in Corsica for the wedding of a friend, but he had homes in Madrid, Santa Barbara, the Philippines, and somewhere in Germany. He suggested that the best flying in Europe would be in Spain, because of the weather, and even offered to let Sean and I use his home in Madrid. What a generous gift!

It was only when we were parting, and exchanging e-mail addresses did I learn that this extraordinary person is none other than Iren P. Dornier, Chairman of the Board of Seair, Inc. Now for anyone who knows the great names in aviation history, the name Dornier is right up there at the top of the list. It was difficult not to like him immediately because of his youthful enthusiasm for flying, even though he has had many years of it under his belt.

A short drive down the southeast coast of Corsica from Porto Vecchio is the southernmost village of Bonifacio. This little town is much more lively and picturesque than where we were yesterday.

The weather could not be better. It is in the low 80's, with a blue sky sprinkled with little cotton-ball clouds, and just the slightest breeze to keep you from being too hot. It is *sooooo* good to be warm and dry again. Now, if I could only have my biplane with me, it would be a perfect setting.

My room is on the fourth floor of a very old hotel situated at the inland end of the harbor. From my room I can look out over the narrow U-shaped harbor and see all the small shops and cafes and boats. It's peaceful, with the slow pace of a seaside village. There are tourists, certainly, but not so many of them to crowd the place. In front of the shops is a one-lane, one-way street. On the harbor side of the street are the sidewalk cafes. On the other side of the street are the little shops. Occasionally, from the street below, I can hear outbursts in Italian (almost certainly cursing and derogatory language, from the sounds of it), a refreshing change from the French of the last few weeks. Every once in a while, however, there will be a very French "Ooh-la-la" from a dockhand as a shapely tourist passes by. It's a great scene, and I want to get out in the middle of it.

Sean went for a run to work off some souvenir inches he picked up in the Paris restaurants. I stayed back in my hotel room to enjoy the view and the weather without strain, to catch up on my mountain of e-mail, and to write these few lines to share Corsica with you.

Now I'm going to go out to explore the ancient fort that dominates the skyline at the top of the hill near the mouth of the harbor. Later, I'm sure the natives and the tourists will be restless, and the several 'discotheques' will be jumping. There is one called "Amnesia" which sounds, by its name alone, to be perfect!

I think of my lovely biplane and hope that it is not too mad at me for leaving it in France. I hope that it does not hate me for being warm and dry while it is shivering in some unfamiliar hangar. Maybe my friend Helene will look in on it and reassure it that soon it will be warm, that I will come back, and that we will fly again, and that the dream we set out with will surely become real.

As I write this, a small plane flies low, past my window, in a tight left bank, looking down on the harbor of Bonifacio, as if to say, "Be patient. It will be better than even you can imagine."

Day 25: Mono-kinis

<u>Ajaccio, Corsica</u>

There are two distinct dimensions to the town of Bonifacio, and when I wrote yesterday I had only experienced Bonifacio as the harbor village. For dinner, we walked up a steep old cobblestone street to the top of the hills overlooking the harbor. It is at this vantage point that a great walled city and fort were built, sometime around the 12th century, and today it is much the same as it has been for hundreds of years.

Entry to the fort on foot is across a drawbridge, designed to be raised in time of attack. Past the main gates, the city is a maze of extremely narrow streets, and very narrow doorways with unbelievably steep steps leading to the upper floors of the dwellings. Some of the buildings are now restaurants, and many of the buildings are still inhabited by the locals.

The entire city is built on the peak of the hill between the harbor and the Mediterranean. Much of the perimeter of the city on the Med side overhangs precipitously over the waves that are eating away at the supporting rocks below. This process has been going on for hundreds of years of course, but the place is still standing, although when you look at it from the side it seems that the whole city is going to collapse any minute.

It's the kind of place that, when your dinner is finished, it starts to seem prudent to go back down to the harbor village and have desert, where it might be a bit safer!

This morning we packed up and said sad goodbyes to the very friendly and helpful receptionist, Valerie, who brought even more sunshine to our visit.

We drove north, along the west coast of Corsica. The road is a tortured stretch of about 100 miles that reminds me a lot of the drive along the coast of California between San Simeon and Big Sur. Each turn in the road presents you with a spectacular view of the Corsican coastline or else a view of the interior forest or farmlands. Every few dozen miles, there is a small town that has been held in suspended animation for hundreds of years, including the people!

At one turn in the road, the view was so awesome that I just had to stop at the roadside restaurant, have lunch, and take some quiet time to absorb it all. There were just a few people enjoying the beach below us. The day was sunny, and very comfortably warm. For the first time on this trip, I noticed that the European preference for sunbathing topless is favored also here in Corsica. Here's a picture of Sean, enjoying the local scenery!

Our destination today was Ajaccio, the largest and most cosmopolitan town in Corsica, its administrative capital, and the birthplace of Napoleon Bonaparte. It was only a short walk from the hotel to the beach, so we headed there first and found considerably more evidence of Europeans' complete disdain for the American need to wear both parts of the bikini. Having amassed considerable visual experience on the matter, and after having virtually non-stop discussions on the topic, Sean and I are both in agreement that the Europeans have achieved superiority in this area. I would present detailed photographic evidence for your further consideration, but I'm concerned that my next e-mail might originate from a Corsican jail. You'll just have to use your imagination.

We found an English newspaper that announced that Britain was having the rainiest June in 15 years, and is expecting it to be the worst in 100 years. The weather forecast is for more of the same. There is a huge high-pressure area off the west coast of Ireland, but it is stuck in place by the low-pressure area sitting over Western Europe.

We all know that the rains have got to stop sometime, and when it does, I will be flying the biplane again. This is very similar to the time during last year's tour of the US, where we were stuck for nine days with rain and low ceilings in Lansing, Michigan. I am focusing on the more positive aspects of this trip, finding sunshine in areas where even in the best of weather the Waco would not be going.

Patience is the key. In the meantime, when I am driving along these coast roads, I am not really driving. I am flying my open-cockpit biplane. And in the moments before I fall asleep at night, I am touching down on a soft grass field.

Day 26: The Global Perspective

Ajaccio, Corsica

Slowly seeping into my consciousness is the awareness that I have been asleep for a very long time, and just now I am waking up to a world much larger and more varied than I ever imagined.

I was 40 years old before I ever applied for a passport, and even then it was only because my good friend Joey Stewart, a citizen of Ireland, when he learned of my deficit, was so incredulous that I felt as though I might as well be missing a limb and not have been aware of it. Until that time, my "international" travel had been limited to a couple of islands in the Caribbean on brief vacations. There just had never been any "reason" to go elsewhere. I had more than enough opportunity in my businesses in the USA.

It was the gross unemployment in Ireland and the natural focus of Ireland in the European community, which forced Joey to leave his little island home, and take a job selling candles to churches throughout Europe, then Canada and the US. When we met, therefore, he had significant appreciation for the benefits of international travel, commerce and a global perspective. I, on the other hand, was blissfully unaware of my ignorance.

He was amazed that Americans, for all their global power, for the most part were so provincial and uneducated, so self-centered and unaware of the diversity of the planet. His extensive travels had shown him just how much more he had to learn. Fiercely Irish, he was astounded that I, with a name like Michael McCafferty, had never been to Ireland, and in fact could not even point to the place on the map where my ancestors were born. Oh, of course I could point to Ireland, but I had no idea where in Ireland they were from. This embarrassed me greatly, and after a quick call to my father I felt much better that I could at last point to County Donegal, on the northwest coast of Ireland. But I still knew nothing of it, nothing of the history of Ireland, the troubles my ancestors were made to endure, the famine and oppression which finally forced them to leave their home, the beauty of the land, and the people who live there now, their thinking, their hopes and fears.

Reflecting on all of this, it seemed to me at the time that while I had lived well and had succeeded in business, I was woefully uneducated. At his insistence I finally applied for a passport, took my first trip to Ireland, and started my elementary education as a citizen of the world.

My business at the time was focused on the huge market for software in the USA. There was more than enough to deal with in the domestic market. At early trade shows, people from Europe, Asia, South Africa, and Australia all wanted to buy my product, but I resisted dealing with foreign countries because I wanted to stay focused on the main vein of gold in my home market. It was only when I needed the money badly did I finally relent. I grabbed my passport, jumped on a plane, and swapped digital bits for francs, pounds sterling, and other suspicious-sounding coin of the realms that I visited.

The urgent need for the money cut my travels to an absolute minimum. I had no appreciation for where I had been. It was treated as a gross inconvenience to have to leave my comfortable apartment by the Pacific and breathe the smoke filled air of the planes, live out of a suitcase, try to communicate with people who didn't even know English. What could possibly be wrong with their education system that they didn't even teach their children English? What a disadvantage!   How could they survive in the world today?   How could I have been so naive?

Over the next several years, there was more international travel, virtually all of it on business, and with similarly profitable but sterile results. It was only just barely seeping into my being that there was something out there, something going on, that is compelling. Australia, Singapore, India, South Africa, Switzerland, England, Ireland (again), France, Netherlands, Portugal. In just a few years, I had been to more places than most people I knew, but I had only "gone to places." I had not really traveled. I had no real depth of understanding, no appreciation for where I had been.

And now I am here in Corsica, with its wonderful mixture of Italian and French culture, but with a heart that beats only "Corse," its placement at the crossroads for vacationers from all over Europe, its history measured in millennia, a climate and a people just perfect for relaxation, open discussion, and learning. Here I am awakening to the richness and diversity of our planet. I am a global infant, virtually unable to communicate, barely able to move about without assistance, innocent of everything good and evil, a sponge soaking it all up with enthusiasm.

In some reading just before leaving on this trip the words leaped off the page "There is no educated man who has not traveled widely." At the time, I rebuffed the author as elitist, but now I find myself agreeing.

This afternoon, in a walk through the town of Ajaccio, we met a seller of souvenirs, and because of an extended rain shower (the weather in Europe has followed us here!), we enjoyed the protection of his shop from the storm, and learned of his country. We heard him speak of the forces within, which are much like the IRA in Northern Ireland, who fight for independence and the true Corse identity. There are the occasional bombings of public buildings and the "discouragement" of overdevelopment of the natural beauty of the island. This answered our wondering about why there were not more international first class hotel chains represented on the beaches, why such a paradise was not more commercially developed.

The Corsican flag flies proudly above the French:

A large cruise ship was in port today, so the town was filled with more tourists than before, and there were more English, German and Spanish languages in the mix of French and Italian.

This afternoon we visited the Museum of Cardinal Fesch. It contained some paintings dating as far back at the early 13th century. Most of the works depicted famous saints being martyred, the crucifixion, last supper, and other topics that a Cardinal would find appropriate for his private collection. The stuff was all very dark and dismal, so we bailed out into the sunny streets after a quick tour. Later tonight, there will be an outdoor Italian film festival in the courtyard of this museum. That sounds like a must-see!

The persistent low-pressure system over Western Europe is moving east, and the giant high-pressure system should be over Paris by Tuesday, so we are returning to Paris on a mid-day flight tomorrow. If all goes well, we'll be flying on Tuesday afternoon. Wish me luck...

Day 27: Please Stand By: We Are Experiencing Technical Difficulties

<u>Porto Cervo, Sardinia</u>

With every resolve to return to Paris this morning, based on The Weather Channel's forecast of partly cloudy for the next few days, I called Helene in Nangis, France to be sure the weather and the plane were okay for flying. Don't believe The Weather Channel. The weather in France was awful: rain, low ceilings and cold. We tuned in to CNN International for their latest weather forecast and they forecast the nasty weather for the next 7 to 10 days. I called our hotel in Paris and they said that everyone in Paris was depressed and sick and desperately waiting for summer to come. It has been terrible for weeks, without stop.

There was no reason to go to Paris and be cold, wet and miserable. The only question was where to go? Sean wants to go to Scotland as soon as the weather gets better there, but it is still yucky, so pass on that. Majorca seems like a good bet. But Sardinia is just a one-hour ferry ride south from Bonifacio, just down the road from Ajaccio.

We checked out of our hotel in Ajaccio, drove south to Bonifacio, and took the ferry to Sardinia, then drove southeast to Porto Cervo. Here's a parting shot of the ancient walled city of Bonifacio, taken from the ferry.

To me, this is what an adventure is about. When I woke up this morning, I thought I was going to Paris to fly, but instead I've taken a ferry to Sardinia to stay warm and explore a new place.

Sardinia is a part of Italy, so we had to show passports to get on the ferry, but there was no Customs at the Sardinia end. It's a very relaxed atmosphere. There is no mixed identity of French/Italian/Corsican as there was in Corsica; here it is pure Italian. I love to hear Italian spoken. It is just so expressive, lyrical and emotional.

Laundry is high on our priority list. The hotels in Corsica didn't have any laundry facilities, so we are down to our last clean clothes. They will pick it up tonight and have it back tomorrow night, so we will have to stay here for two days. After that, who knows?

The hotel we stumbled into is probably the nicest one I have stayed at on this entire trip. And that's not saying a lot, really. But it is good to have some nice, thick towels for a change. And Varushka (Russian name but very Italian) has been friendly and helpful. The money is very different. I'm not used to paying 160,000 of anything for a room for the night, but here the lire trades at 1,500 to the dollar, making it all seem like Monopoly money. Even the smallest denomination paper note has three zeros. It takes some getting used to.

Connecting to the Internet has been a challenge. The hotel in Paris had a rotary phone system and no matter what I tried, even an acoustic coupler, I could not get my computer to dial out properly from my room. The solution was to bypass the PBX and use the fax line at the front desk. This same approach was used in the hotel in Corsica. It was inconvenient, but effective. The only thing I needed was an adapter to get the US style phone plug to work with the French style outlet. I knew I was going to be in France, so I brought this adapter with me from the US. Now that I have found myself unexpectedly in Italy, and I have no adapter for this country, I'm scrambling around trying to find a store that would have it. This is no small problem.

Computer communications has always been fraught with challenges. Getting dissimilar hardware and software to talk to each other is never an easy thing. Considering the added difficulties associated with foreign countries, not just the adapters required but also the PBXs, the phone company hardware/software, the time zone differences, the local Internet connections (if any), I'm surprised that things have been going so smoothly.

There will be times when my daily e-mail just doesn't get through, and it may even happen for several days in a row. So don't be overly concerned if it happens again. It's probably not a problem on your end.

Day 28: There Is No Language Barrier!

<u>Porto Cervo, Sardinia</u>

This starts out slow, but bear with me and I think you'll agree it gets better. I have been planning this tour of Europe for six months, and I could have prepared myself by learning to speak the languages I would encounter. I didn't even try because it seemed such an overwhelming job. I needed French, German, Italian and Dutch... It seemed impossible to become conversant in any, let alone all, of these languages, and I gave in to the temptation to believe that most of the people would know English and that I could get by. And it is true that you will not starve, go without shelter or be able to find your way home if you don't know the local language. You can survive.

It is easy to believe that a language barrier would exist. What I have found is that ANY barrier we perceive, in ANY aspect of life, is negotiable. That is, any barrier we perceive is put there by us. We choose to perceive a barrier, for whatever reason, because it suits us. Just as easily, we can choose to perceive NO BARRIER. This philosophy is at the core of my beliefs. Our reality is the result of what we have chosen for ourselves. Our present state is the result of our continuing to choose that state. Our future will be the way we choose it to be.

Returning to the subject at hand, "The Language Barrier": it does not exist except that we choose it to exist. What I am learning is that the best way to deal with the "problem" of not knowing the local language is also the best way to communicate in one's native language:

1. Eye contact. This is essential for personal communication.
2. Smile. Creates positive physical changes and receptivity.
3. Tone. The tone of your voice is more important than the words used.
4. Generous and sincere spirit.
5. Sign and body language. Occurs naturally in all languages.
6. Universal words, such as: "Okay," "Champagne," "Yes," "No," etc.
7. Use of a common third language when needed or desirable.

The practical aspects of what I have learned about communication were very clearly demonstrated to me last night. I found myself dealing with an Italian person who spoke absolutely no English, and of course I speak absolutely no Italian. It was of the utmost desirability for me to communicate and I also perceived that there was a very high desire on her part to communicate, but the deadly imagined "Language Barrier" initially blocked us both.

We had both successfully passed through steps #1 and #2 above and thus had created the mutual state-of-being for further successful communication. It occurred to me that Tone (#3) was essential so I just started talking English using some of the best tones I could create, some of which have unquestionably universal understanding. You may laugh at just how ridiculous it might seem, but we were having a full-blown conversation in two different languages, neither of us understanding a word spoken by the other, and yet the tones were unmistakable, so the words were irrelevant. We were in a local disco at the time, so it was simple and obvious to demonstrate my generous and sincere spirit (#4) by offering, using sign language (#5), a gift that would help ease her thirst. We continued to converse with lots of #3 and #5, which was facilitated by music and dance (#7). After several more demonstrations of #4, and lots of #1, #2, #3, and #5, we were finding that there were a surprising number of universal words (#6) that were creeping into our otherwise completely unintelligible vocabulary exchange. It was about this time that I discovered the use of a third common language (#7), even though neither of us knew very much Spanish. However it brought a new richness to our dialog. We could now understand about one word for every several hundred spoken. It was about this time that I noticed a gold ring on the third finger of her left hand, and from the depths of what little I remembered of my high school Spanish class, I asked "Esposo?" (Husband?). When she replied with two universal words (#6) "No Problem," I was struck with the thought that in these Latin countries crimes of passion (murdering a spouse's lover and/or the spouse) are not very seriously punished, in fact, they are even expected in some cases. From that point, my desire to continue this very successful communication faded, and I found other handy opportunities to experiment in linguistics.

To summarize, I can assure you that based on my own personal experience, it is not necessary to study the language in order to communicate in a foreign country. And I wholeheartedly encourage you to try these fun experiments for yourself as soon as you have the opportunity.

For your viewing pleasure today, I have enclosed a photo of Porto Cervo, as seen from my hotel room balcony.

Day 29: The Animal and The English Lord

<u>Porto Cervo, Sardinia</u>

The hotel where we are staying, as well as this entire corner of Sardinia around the town of Porto Cervo, was created out of raw dirt about 30 years ago by none other than The Aga Khan, one of the most incredibly wealthy individuals in the world. Needless to say, everything around here is first class. Some very large private yachts are in the harbor now, with more arriving each day to celebrate the beginning of the season that starts this weekend. Today, the smallest ship in the Aga Khan's private fleet of luxury motor craft arrived in the harbor. His smallest is still the largest boat in the local waters!

Along with such first class digs comes a first class staff. We have been befriended by two of the staff at this hotel, and they have gone way beyond the call of duty and shown us very personal attention and favors that have made our stay exceptional.

One is Alesandro ("The Animal"), and the other is Dario ("The English Lord"). I'll leave it to your own common sense to distinguish from the photo below which one is which.

Alesandro is the nightly entertainment in the hotel lounge. He is very talented, a complete one-man band, singing and playing the keyboard accompanied by his computerized sound system. When I needed the special adapter to hook up my modem to the Italian phone system, it was Alesandro who took time out of his day to drive me in his car the two-hour round-trip to the nearest city.

During the drive through the narrow Sardinian mountain roads, Alesandro told me (in his very limited English) of his love for music, and how he cannot bear to play the same routine each night, he just must do something different each time, because he is a creative person. He told me of the Italian man's order of priorities (1. Women, 2. Wine, 3.

Food, 4. Sport, 5. Work), and confessed that maybe he only had the first four in his list of priorities, and that #1 far overshadowed his interest in any of the others.

He was driving at high speed, passing on turns and all the time he was talking with the assistance of very Italian sweeping hand and arm gestures. For some strange reason, I never really feared for my life. It was clear that he was in his element. Even when he told me "I am Animal" (referring to himself, of course), I easily could see that his self-image was completely accurate. He is 29 years old, and has experienced Europe's best luxury resorts because of his talent. He cannot possibly imagine ever being married, and has no plans for the future beyond next weekend. When I agreed that he did indeed seem to be an animal, he corrected me quickly: "No, I am not AN animal, I am THE Animal".

Dario is quite the opposite in many regards. His English is quite good. His business card identifies himself as a "Barman." He works the poolside bar during the day, and the bar next to the lounge where The Animal entertains at night. The two of them are good friends and have worked the season at this hotel before. Dario is the epitome of "The English Lord." He is quite refined, wears a double-breasted suit when he tends bar in the evening and his manners are impeccable. When I mentioned that I needed the phone adapter for my computer, and that the people at the front desk were clueless and unable to help me, he was the one who took the time to understand my needs and phone around to find the needed part, and then asked Alesandro to drive me to make the purchase. Although different in many respects from Alesandro, Dario's priorities in life seem to be identical.

It was Dario and Alesandro who guided Sean and I to the local discos and made sure that we were treated well, and introduced us around. Without their assistance with the language and the customs and the right places to go, our visit would have been much less interesting.

Today, we toured the local private yacht club, which would have been off limits to us if Sean had not had a letter of introduction faxed from his club in San Diego.

Some observations on the cultural differences between Italy and Southern California: There is no focus whatsoever on health except to have a good tan. There are no health food stores, no vitamins, no low fat foods, or reduced cholesterol foods. There are virtually no non-smoking sections in the restaurants.

However, the Italians are much more enlightened than the French in one respect: they do not allow you to bring your pets into the restaurants. I remember vividly one restaurant in Paris where a well dressed man and woman came in to dine, accompanied by their huge, longhaired dog. The dog was almost bigger than the man's wife! It had been raining, and of course the smell of wet dog is unmistakable, especially in a small, crowded restaurant. It was an exuberant animal, probably pleased to be out of the rain and smelling some good food, and demonstrated its pleasure with large sweeps of its tail, brushing patrons on both sides of the aisle. The French were quite unperturbed with all this, but I just couldn't believe it!

Day 30: Sensory Overload

<u>Paris, France</u>

I just couldn't take it any more! I just had to get out of the sensory overload of the disco scene in Porto Cervo. Maybe The Animal and The English Lord can take it every day, but Sean and I were in complete agreement that it was just not for us.

The weather is perfect there, but if you aren't into the disco scene, or lying in the sun all day, there is just nothing to do. In fact, there's just no intellectual stimulation at all.

And besides (my father says that when somebody says "and besides," what follows is the *real* reason), what I really, really want to do is to fly.

I figured that the only option is to go back to France and sit at the airport with my biplane and wait until the weather gets good enough to do some touch and go's. No matter how long it takes.

These are the thoughts that were going through my head when I woke up this morning, and then Sean called to say that he was completely bored with Porto Cervo and we came to the agreement that it was time to get out of town.

Within an hour, we were checked out of the hotel and driving north to St. Teresa to catch the ferry back to Bonifacio, Corsica. Immediately upon landing in Corsica, we drove north to the airport at Figari, and with only a minute to spare, we returned the rental car and jumped on the plane to Paris, then a taxi to the hotel. Rental car, boat, plane, taxi; three countries in five hours. Everything went like clockwork.

We are staying at a Swedish hotel here in Paris, and the phone system here is one of Alexander Graham Bell's early models, and not at all compatible with computers. The typical way of dealing with this is to plug into the hotel's fax line, bypassing the PBX. Unfortunately the night clerk at this hotel is a very frightened old Swedish man who can only say "No-no, no-no, what if problem? No-no." And so one more e-mail was delayed. Add one more element to the list of problems to communicating using a computer: night clerks.

My plan right now is to take the train to Nangis tomorrow around noon, get a hotel there and fly whenever the ceiling lifts higher than 1,000 feet. I must get some air under me: get some landings. I need to fly so bad I can taste it!

Day 31: Good Friends and Good Flying

Nangis, France

I awoke to the splashing sounds of cars plowing through the rain-soaked streets of Paris. It was a day like all the others in recent memory. The sky was filled with great swirling, billowing clouds, swollen with uncountable tons of water lifted up from the sea hundreds of miles away. All over northern Europe it has been raining for weeks.

No biplane pilot in his right mind would have thought to go flying on a day like today. But, sometimes, if you want something badly enough, and believe it with your entire being, and simply move in its direction, and gently, persistently assume that it will be... it will be. Sometimes.

But if you assume that it will not happen, it almost certainly will not.

This then is the great magical mysterious law of the universe. Positive thoughts can create positive events. Negative thoughts cannot.

So if a certain biplane pilot wants so very much to fly, he must persist in visualizing and projecting a reality that defies all logic. He must hold in his mind a picture of perfect flying weather when all around him is the most perfectly unflyable weather as far as they eye can see.

I have a certain technique, which I have used from time to time, and for reasons unknown to me now I have not used for several years, but today I tried it out. I find a peaceful place, quiet and comfortable, and begin to think only of my breathing, how the air fills my body completely. Each breath I take I try to completely fill my lungs, far beyond what a normal, unthinking breath would do. I breath in one long breath for a count of ten, hold it for a count of ten, release it for a count of ten, hold no breath for a count of ten. Then repeat. And repeat this process for perhaps two or three dozen times, until I feel a great energy rousing in my body. It is an amazing feeling that I feel no other way. When this feeling comes to me, I then think of the event that I want to happen, and I 'send' that thought into the universe, letting it go from my mind. Then I repeat the breathing process a couple more times, and then stop the process and go about normal life.

I can't say that the process is infallible, but I can say that many times the event that I have created in my mind has happened in reality. I have no explanation for how it works, but it seems to work more often than not. I learned about it from a book called "Psychic Energy," referred to me by a friend when I was going through some difficult times, about 15 years ago.

I worked through this process while still in bed this morning, the sounds of rain falling on the window of my hotel room in Paris. Then I got up, and called my friend Helene in Nangis, where my biplane was still hangared out of the rains. I told her it was my plan to come to Nangis, get a hotel room and stay there for as long as it took for the weather to clear, and then fly my biplane, even if just around the area. She told me about the rain there, but said that her husband René would be driving to Paris this morning, to deliver some papers to his lawyer, and he could pick me up and drive me back to Nangis, saving me the inconvenience of taking the taxi and train.

Sean stayed in Paris and planned a trip to Dublin for a few days to visit relatives and friends there.

René came to my hotel, and the rain was coming down even harder than before. On the hour-long drive to Nangis, the rains increased, becoming angrier and heavier, hurling more and more ridicule on my plans with each mile we passed. But still I believed I would fly today, because that was the event I created in my mind. I had seen it, so it must be real.

When we got to Nangis, it was still raining, so we joined Helen and her father for lunch. But I could hardly eat. I was preparing, in my mind, to go fly. Still, the rains came down.

When we left for the airport, just a few miles away, it was still raining, but I sensed it was giving up. When we arrived at the airport it was still raining, but I could see it would soon stop. When I walked into the hangar and saw my plane for the first time in a week, I was struck again by how lovely it looked, a work of art. My first touch of it was a familiar touch, and I knew that it too wanted to fly. The sky grew lighter, the clouds lifted higher, and it was now only very lightly raining. I prepared my plane and my charts and my checklist, and my mind. And the rain did indeed stop.

I pulled the biplane out onto the ramp in front of the hangar and went slowly through the preflight inspection. This is always a very private time for me. It is the time when I look at, and touch, virtually every part of the plane that could possibly affect flight. At this time, I go into a semi-meditative state. I want to be alone.

And for this flight, especially, I want to be alone. This will be only the third time I have flown in almost three months. I need the practice. I want to do some touch and go's alone. I most certainly do not want to subject another human being to my imperfection at the controls. I am wishing I could fly away and practice at another airfield, but there is nowhere else to go. It is raining in all of France, only here it is not. I know the entire airport will be watching me.

And so is René. He is standing back about 20 feet, watching me preflight the plane. He is a professional pilot, an instructor, an Airline Transport Pilot, and he knows what I am going through right now. He does not interfere, he just watches. He knows better than to ask if he can go fly with me, but I can sense that he does. I am torn between my desire to fly alone, and his desire to fly with me. But I know how he must be feeling. I know how I feel when I see this plane. It draws you in.

"Would you like to fly?" I ask. And just as quickly he is in the plane!

The first couple of circuits of the field were uneventful. I struggled to regain my comfort and smoothness with the controls. My landings were adequate but undistinguished. It was the third takeoff that would make even an atheist speak the name of God.

We had just lifted off the runway only a few feet, and I kept the stick forward, staying low and level to build up speed. At the end of the runway, I pulled back and climbed fast in a left hand turn, heading toward the downwind leg for another landing, when at about 700 feet above the field, for some reason, René looked up and back over his left shoulder and saw the other airplane headed for the same piece of sky we were aiming for.

At this time, René was not operating the controls, but he is a professional pilot and an instructor, and he knew in that instant that if he had tried to explain to me that we had traffic at 9 o'clock high and on a collision course, that it would have taken more time for him to say it, and for me to process and locate the bogey, and react, than we might have had left. So he grabbed the stick and yanked hard right, and pushed down. At that same instant I also saw the traffic, but we were already safely away. I took over the controls again, and landed behind the traffic that should never have been there in the first place. We got out and he talked with the other pilot to understand what had happened.

René knew the other pilot. It was the man who taught René how to fly! This other instructor was training a student, who had not set his altimeter properly, and that was the reason why their airplane was so low as to be at pattern altitude. It was a simple mistake. Aren't they all?

René quite probably saved several lives today. But he didn't make much of it. He just did what he trained to do: Fly the airplane, do whatever it takes to make the plane do what it must do under the circumstances.

It wasn't until much later that I reflected on how it was that René was even in my biplane at all that day. Remember that I was determined to fly alone today. What came over me to invite him along? If I didn't invite him to come with me, would I have seen the other plane in time? Would I even have been so close in the first place? It is impossible to say, of course. But René' was there, and he did the right thing. Some people who have had similar experiences might suggest that my guardian angel was looking after me today, and may have whispered in my ear that it would be a nice thing to do to offer to take Rene' for a ride, as a way of thanking him for driving me from Paris to Nangis.

Soon after I parked the biplane, the clouds grew darker, and a chill returned to the air. I knew it would rain again, so we pushed the biplane back into the hangar, and very soon the rains came again, even heavier than before.

It was enough flying for one day, under normal circumstances, but my spirit was saying, "I have not yet had enough. Let's go flying again!" Looking out the window from inside the office, no one would have believed that it would be flyable again today. There was a full raging storm outside, the rain slamming down with a fury. It was only 4 o'clock, I thought, and it doesn't get dark until 10 pm. We have plenty of time. And soon, the rains let up, and then it stopped. And the sun actually came out!

Once again we rolled open the hangar doors, and pulled the Waco into the light. This time, as I walked around my plane, checking it over for the flight to come, it was Helene who appeared, wearing a leather flight jacket, and a smile. "Are you coming this time?" I asked. But I didn't have to ask, really. Just a couple of hours ago she had stayed on the ground and watched her husband René play in the sky in this beautiful bird, and now it was her turn.

This time everything was perfect. Not "perfect" in the sense of the word that it went well, without flaw, but perfect in the sense of the word that it is inconceivable that it could have been better. There was NO wind, yet you could feel the perfection of the air. Each breath was like inhaling the cool clean sweet juice of life. The recent torrential downpour had scrubbed the air so thoroughly that nothing remained except the clearest, most extraordinary, crystalline ether. It was as if every local blade of grass, every leaf, every plant had just breathed its great gift of oxygen for my biplane to fly in.

Another pilot, Stephane Patrigeon, was standing by this time, watching me prepare the Waco for flight. He owns a red Pitts Special, a little aerobatic biplane, sitting in the hangar right next to mine. It's getting late; he has family waiting for him and he really shouldn't go flying right now, he says, wistfully. But the sight of my Waco, the perfection of the weather at just this instant, it's all just too much for him, and he pushes his Pitts out. A biplane pilot for sure, he has his priorities straight. A man could live the rest of his life and not have conditions this good ever again.

I did three or four touch and go's, each landing was so sweet and smooth and gentle that it was as if my guardian angel was still in the air with me, showing me how he lets down on his favorite cloud in heaven. Was I really flying this time, or was he? I would be bragging if I were to tell you that I made three or four of the best landings ever made by a biplane pilot, so I will just tell you that I had help from a higher power.

Helene was ecstatic the entire flight. It was her first time ever in an open-cockpit biplane, and she loved the feel of the fresh air on her face, and the freedom of being out in the open. On one trip around the pattern, we flew through a little cloud that drifted into our way. On another circuit Helene saw a rainbow. Another time around, she took this photo of Stephane in his little red biplane as he came flying close in formation.

Here is another photo of Stephane's Pitts Special, with mine in the background. Stephane arranged the two planes very carefully and had me take this photo from just this exact perspective. Notice how his much smaller biplane appears to be the same size as the Waco.

When perfection has been achieved, more is not possible. So we landed one last time, taxied back to the hangar, tucked the biplanes away for the night, and Helene brought out a bottle of Champagne for a celebration of life. We lifted our glasses in agreement: "Good friends and good flying."

Day 32: Testostérone Alley

Ever since I have been in France, a full 30 days today, every pilot has told me that I MUST visit La Ferté Alais. Actually, it is the second thing they say to me. The first is in the form of the question: "Have you been to La Ferté Alais yet?" It is expected that any pilot who visits France will soon go there. When they find out that I have not yet been there, they look at me sadly, as if I have nothing in common with them, and then they say "You MUST go there."

It is Mecca for French pilots, and I can see why. It is a wonderful little airport in the countryside just south of Paris. There is no hard surface runway, only grass, and the grass is well tended and the surface is quite smooth and plenty wide.

My visit there today was finally achieved with the assistance of my new friends René and Helene. Since it is a private airport, it is necessary to call ahead to get permission to land, and René handled this for me. He and I were both surprised that the people at La Ferté Alais were already aware of my Waco being in France, that I would soon be going to Megeve (in the French Alps) and that I was a friend of Bernard Chabbert. They were looking forward to welcoming me to their airport!

René and Helene crowded together into my front cockpit and we lifted off from Nangis for the less-than-30-minute flight to La Ferté Alais. The sky was very cloudy, with a ceiling at about 1,200 feet above the ground, but it was not raining, and it looked as if it might clear later in the morning. The wind, while straight across the runway, was less than 5 mph. There was a slight chill, so I kept warm in the air with my new lucky blue cashmere scarf.

Approaching La Ferté Alais from the air we could see a big DC-3 with WWII Normandy "invasion stripes" painted on the wings sitting beside the grass runway, with other very interesting airplanes (not so easy to identify) parked all around, and there were lots of good sized hangars which promised other goodies inside.

Whenever I approach a new airfield I am always very cautious, looking for any traffic on the ground or in the air, looking for the windsock to figure the wind speed and direction, which runway is in use, trying to determine any special conditions which might exist, etc. I was concerned that the recent rains might have caused puddles of standing water, or muddy areas, but it looked to be in good condition.

So all the physical conditions were good, but the mental conditions were still being resolved. My mind is processing the fact that I am about to land at a most famous, possibly the most famous, airfield in all of France, a place held in high esteem by them, a place where surely there would be many good pilots on the ground watching my approach and judging my landing, and my overall performance as an aviator. Yes, I would have an audience of some very critical people, and they knew I was coming. I had to give it my best. I had to be worthy of my beautiful airplane, and I even imagined that I would be representing all American pilots among the best pilots from France.

All of this weighed heavily on my mind as I crossed over the runway at pattern altitude and cut left downwind, then base, then final. René handled the radio, calling my position and intentions in French. On final approach, I was a little bit high and burned off some altitude with a slip, which I'm sure must have looked nice from the ground. I flared a bit high and the plane dropped in from a foot or two, but the wet ground was very soft and the drop was not rough at all. In fact, it was really very pleasant. The best part of it all was that it was a perfect three-point landing. I felt that I could have done better, but it was not completely graceless. On balance, America was well represented this morning.

The rollout was very smooth and I taxied back to the parking area, taking care to avoid the wet areas on the advice of René. As a final flourish, I unlocked the tailwheel and powered up slightly while holding the right brake, swinging the plane around in a tight 270-degree arc, to park facing the runway. I was aware immediately of the many people who were watching, and the several who were walking toward my biplane for a closer look.

Soon we are greeted by Mr. Jean Salis himself, the owner of this great place. Helene translates for us as he welcomes us and invites us to have lunch at his special table in the airfield restaurant for lunch, where he will join us later.

Suddenly, I realize that I am ravenously hungry, and since it is lunchtime, we head directly for the restaurant, and are seated at the biggest round table in the center of the room. The table seats about ten, and there are already a few men seated there. Since I know no French, Helene sits next to me and translates the remarks going around the table.

The table fills up quickly, and now we are all men of aviation (Helene is the sole female) gathered for lunch and to exchange the news of the day. One of the topics, I can tell without translation, is this American fellow who has come in his Waco, a nice craft even if it is American. Some of the other remarks I can also tell simply by the tone of voice and the gestures, are the stories of flying, men bragging about their deeds, some showing off for the lady present, others outdoing each other for the sport of it, some putting others down in order to build up their own inferiority complex.

Helene translates it all, even the fellow who remarks that I couldn't be a real biplane pilot because I am eating no meat, only vegetables, drinking no wine with my meal, and I don't smoke. He remarks also that I would be better off back in America with its black people (not the term he used). I am taking it all in, smiling politely at this boorish fellow as if his humor is pleasant to me. He is cutting his meat with a large and menacing folding knife that he has taken from his pocket, and I am not about to pick a fight with a man with a knife and bad manners.

Hanging on the walls of the restaurant are paintings and photos of great airplanes and great aviators, and one of the great Mermoz hanging higher than all the others. Only slightly lower is the photo of Mr. Jean Baptiste Salis, the fighter pilot from the First War, and the father of the current owner of La Ferté Alais. There are pictures of great fighting machines such as the P-38 Lightning, Mustangs, Yaks and other warbirds. There is even a great photograph of a very old Bleriot flying toward the white cliffs of Dover, the first airplane to cross the English Channel in 1908.

The bar at the end of the room is limited to only about eight seats, and behind the bar there hang aviators caps from many wars and many airlines. I wonder what great feat of courage it took to earn the privilege to have one's hat hang behind this ancient bar. And I wonder what fantastic stories this bar could tell of the men who drank here over the years.

Back at our table, my new "friend" with the knife is drinking more and behaving poorly, but he gets no rise from me. When he cleans his knife and folds it away, feeds the last scraps from his plate to his dog sitting by his side, rises to wrap his white silk scarf (I swear it's true!) around his neck, puts on his aviator sunglasses and flying jacket, and looks in my general direction as if to see if I have had enough abuse, I rise and offer him my hand, with a smile, and speak "Bon Jour." I have learned over the years that it is important to deal with one's enemies with pleasant behavior. It confuses them wonderfully! I was told later that this fellow had already wrecked two airplanes.

All around were the spirits of legends, living and dead: men and flying machines. This place had seen so very much of the history of aviation. And these living men knew it. The place was awash in testosterone!

After lunch, Mr. Jean Salis joined us briefly and invited us to tour the hangars. What a wonderful collection of airplanes! I can't begin to tell you of the great aircraft he has there, you just have to see them for yourself. Only two were familiar to me, the F4-U Corsair was my favorite, and the big yellow Stearman was Helene's long time favorite. I asked her if she had ever sat in one, and when she said no I asked an official standing nearby if it were possible for Helene to get in the cockpit, and "Voila!" — one happy lady in her dream machine! See photo below:

The assistants at the museum were very helpful, and even let me sit in the cockpit of the English De Havilland Speed Dragon, a wonderful WWII twin-engine transport that had such great looks I was mesmerized by it. There were probably more than 50 airplanes, most of them flyable, most of them original. There were several one-of-a-kind aircraft from the very first days of aviation, such as the Bleriot, Breguet, Morane and Caudron. Some were replicas specially built for movies, such as the Spad and the Fokker Triplane used by the German multiple ace Baron von Richthofen (who was finally shot down not too far from here). The place is a national, no a global, treasure.

Too much to see in one afternoon, we had to get back before the gathering clouds closed in. When I started up the Waco, one of the faces in the crowd gathered around was my "friend," whose smile and thumbs-up seemed to me to be genuine, a sign that my beautiful biplane had made another convert. We rolled out onto the grass runway, and lifted effortlessly into the air, climbed to pattern altitude, turned left downwind, then rounded off the turn to base and final, descending sharply on final for a long low pass for the admirers below.

On the way home, René guided me to Fontainebleau, the extraordinary summer palace for Louis XIV. Louis had style, for sure!

Back at Nangis, I chose the grass runway this time, and just loved it of course. America needs more grass runways, especially in California, near my house.

Day 33: Just Playing

<u>Nangis, France</u>

I spent the morning catching up on my journal and waiting for the weather to improve to the ideal conditions I knew would be achieved later in the day. Sure enough, at around 3 pm, the wind dropped to almost nil, the sky became blue with small white clouds that looked painted in place.

René helped me roll out the biplane and we taxied to the pump for fuel. They don't take credit cards for avgas at many of the smaller airports in France, so it's important to keep lots of francs on hand. During the refueling process, we attracted a lot of attention. There were probably more than 30 people milling about checking out the biplane, and plenty of complimentary comments. I wish I could speak French. I know that they felt as uncomfortable as I did, not being able to communicate their feelings.

It's Sunday, and the most ideal flying day in many weeks. It seems that there are more people out flying today than I have ever seen for such a small airport. And the variety of aircraft is even more delightful. There are the normal training single engine aircraft, of course, and aerobatic planes, and there are ultralights, and lots of gliders, and even a jet Vampire comes by for a low pass. We are talking a really, really busy little airport. So I'm definitely going to be bringing René along for the ride, so he can help spot the traffic in the pattern, and handle the radio in French.

I did a few touch and go's, the first couple of which were marginal (for a perfectionist such as myself, that means that they were okay). The third one was quite nice. Then we took off and left the traffic pattern to go play in the sky.

This is the third day in a row that I have been flying (only three hours in the last three months), and I am just now starting to get the feel of it again. I climb up to 3,500 feet and do a few wingovers and some tight turns and now I am feeling immensely better, so I turn the controls over to René. He does some even tighter turns, and a few even nicer wingovers and turns the controls back to me. So I just had to play a little bit more and then took the biplane back to the field for a final landing. I really wanted to land on the grass, but with all the gliders using the field (they have priority on the grass), I had to use the hard surface.

We were in the air only about 40 minutes, but it was heaven! We played in the sky like children.

Actually it wasn't total play. Some of the time, I was checking the accuracy of my HSI, which performed flawlessly. I needed to be sure it worked properly under radical heading and attitude changes. I am going to need it tomorrow.

Helene was waiting for us when we pulled up in front of the hangar and shut down. She could tell that we had been having more than our share of fun, probably from our ear-to-ear grins.

At this time of year, and especially with all of the low-level flying and grass landings of the past few days, we collected a lot of bugs on the cowl, landing gear and leading edges of the wings. Helene suggested that we should take some time to clean the plane, and René also wanted to pitch in, so my natural laziness was outvoted and we all grabbed a rag and worked for an hour to put the Waco back into pristine condition. Helene took a break long enough to photograph René on the ladder debugging the top wing. I'm more safely sitting on the ground cleaning the landing gear.

The hotel I stayed at my first night in Nangis is closed on the weekends, so Helene invited me to stay at her house last night. Since she has been following my adventures via these e-mails for a couple of weeks she knows that I am always short of clean clothes, so she made sure that my laundry was taken care of.

It's starting to sink in. I have met some really super French people with René and Helene. Let's recap here: René saves my life by avoiding a mid-air collision, they invite me into their home to stay for a couple of days, grace me with free breakfasts, do my laundry, give me free hangar space, and even insist that they help me clean my biplane! I ask you, are these French people great, or what?

Day 34: The Blue Wizzard

Bourg en Bresse, France

Today is the end of my stay in Nangis. It's time to say goodbye to my new friends Helene and René. They promise to visit me when they come to the US and to keep in touch by e-mail. René helps me with last minute preflight planning to Bourg en Bresse, at the foothills of the French Alps.

The mission today is to meet up with Matthias Zuellig, the owner of a Waco biplane identical to mine, except that it is a very handsome dark blue. He calls it "The Blue Wizzard" (photo below). He lives in Zurich, Switzerland, and will be flying west to meet me at Bourg. From there, we will be flying around Europe for the next month.

I plan my flight as meticulously as possible, drawing my course line on my charts, checking for obstructions, making notes on a separate piece of paper with the checkpoints and their frequencies, runways, pattern altitudes, etc. (The separate paper is needed as a backup in case the primary navigation chart blows out of the open cockpit. It hasn't happened to me yet, but it could. It's also a lot easier to read my own notes than the printing on the charts.)

My plan is to leave after lunch. I use the time until then to top off the fuel tanks and load the baggage. I also remove the front windshield and cover the front cockpit with a snap on cover. This makes the biplane look much different, longer in the nose, stronger, much more like a vintage fighter plane (possibly because it is now a single place aircraft).

The big advantage to me is that the visibility is greatly improved with the front windshield removed.

Helene's father Serge joins us for lunch. There's a good bit of light and friendly small talk, but it's like we are really just trying to forget the fact that we will soon be parting, new friends who will not see each other again for a long time. I really like these people, and I would like them even if they didn't do my laundry, clean my biplane, give me hangar space, save my life, etc.

Back at the airport, Serge helps me pull the Waco out of their hangar one last time. René helps me with some radio frequencies I'll need to get through some low-level military training routes. Helene gives me a hug and one of those two-cheek French kisses. I fire up the Waco, taxi out to runway 6, lift off into a light left crosswind, turn right to a heading of 150 degrees and I'm gone.

This flight was 171 nautical miles (about 200 normal miles), as the crow flies. There was a scattered to broken layer of cumulus clouds at about 2,500 feet, and I stayed below them for the entire trip. The turbulence was really not bad at all.

When I got to the military low-level jet training areas, I tried to get Dijon tower on the radio, but they didn't answer, maybe because I was flying too low, so I just kept on going, but kept my head on a swivel, looking for traffic coming at me at 450 knots. Yeah, right! If I could spot traffic like that, they would be past me before I (or they) could react, so I just kept lower than they would probably be flying, out of harm's way, and turned on my transponder, hoping they could pick me up on their radar. As it turned out, I never saw any military traffic the entire flight.

The French countryside is a pure delight. Everywhere below me were gently rolling hills covered with farms and pastures for goats and cows. All of the farms seem to have been there forever.

For the entire duration of the two-hour flight, I never talked to anyone on the radio, except at the last minute when I was descending into Bourg en Bresse. They have a hard surface and a grass runway, and I had announced my intention to use the grass, but a voice came back over the radio that the grass was wet and soft and that I should use the hard surface. The wind was probably over 15 knots, but it was right down the runway, so the landing was easy.

When I taxied up, there were already a small group of curious locals waiting to check out this alien craft. One fellow said that there has never been a Waco at this field.

In France it is normal to have to pay a landing fee at airports. When I signed in at the main desk, the official waived the fee, because "you have such a beautiful airplane." A new friend, Karim Jarraya, a young pilot of 26 and of Tunisian descent, was very helpful with the language challenge. We sat on the patio and sipped Cokes while waiting for Matthias to appear in the pattern with his blue Waco. If the locals thought it was great to have one Waco here, they must have flipped when they saw TWO all of a sudden.

Karim tried to get us hangar space, but it was not available, so he lent me some screw-in tie-downs to keep my Waco safe from the raging north wind (called "Mistral" in these parts). He also helped push our biplanes into the grass for the night, and then drove us into town to a hotel. What could I do to repay him for his kindnesses? I offered to treat him to dinner with Matthias and me, and he jumped at the chance. I guess young pilots everywhere are eager for a good meal!

And what a meal it was. I can't begin to describe it all, but each forkful was sublime. Matthias chose an awesome wine, a St. Emilion. For desert, I had an apple tarte (tarte Tatin) with an oversized bucket of fresh mildly whipped heavy cream, and a cafe gran creme. I was completely stuffed, incapable of eating even just a little wafer. After a meal like that, I am overtaken with a sense of delirium, and my body moves about led by my belly, much like a large ocean going tanker. I hope I leave France soon. I can't keep eating like this or I will surely explode. Or I will need a bigger airplane.

Tomorrow, the French Alps!

Day 35: Oh! Are We Stylin' Now!

<u>Cannes, France</u>

The hotel where we stayed last night in Bourg en Bresse was built in 1853, and I think I slept on one of the original mattresses. One side of it had a very large depression in it, and I woke up in the middle of the night dreaming I had fallen into a hole and couldn't get out. This was about the worst hotel I have stayed at so far this trip. When I checked out, I resolved to upgrade my standards for future accommodations. I had no idea what was about to happen.

Matthias and I got together for breakfast and discussed the plans for the day. One option was to fly into Megeve, a small airport at an elevation of 4,800 feet. It was a rather tricky airport, a very short runway with only one way in, with no go-around possible and a steep uphill runway. It requires a special logbook endorsement to fly in there, so the only way we could get in would be to land at a nearby airport and get two instructors to fly with us, show us the ropes, and get us legal. The reason for all this trouble was because I was invited to attend a weeklong gathering of some high-level aerospace people. I wanted to attend because Bernard Chabbert, my French connection, had invited me, but I was not at all excited about landing the Waco at this airport, and Matthias was not interested in spending a week in one place. When I called Bernard about our concerns, he got all bent out of shape and hung up the phone on me. Well, that sure eliminated the Megeve option from our possible destinations today.

Matthias suggested that he would like to fly to the Mediterranean, and especially Cannes. The route would take us through the French Alps, similar to the Megeve option, but we would be going south instead of east. It was a no-brainer for me because I love to fly the coastline, and I was really looking forward to flying in the Alps, and if I could have both in one flight, count me in!

From Bourg en Bresse we flew southeast for less than an hour to Chambéry and landed for lunch. The airport is situated at the south end of a long lake, and bounded on both sides by high mountains. There I met another pilot, Henri Gavet, who took a liking to our biplanes and told me about his days of flying an old Kinner-engined Fleet. A thoroughly decent fellow, he invited us drop in if we were on the west coast of France where he "had some vineyards" and we could be sure of a nice bottle of wine. After lunch, we continued south past Grenoble, the site of past Olympic winter games. It was right around Grenoble that the scenery became unspeakably spectacular.

We flew down a valley that followed a series of lakes winding through the mountains all around us. Not just mountains, but Alps, a completely different kind of mountain than I have seen before. These are monsters—massive, rugged mountains with sinister shapes. One reminded me of a spiny-backed dinosaur, another one looked like the Sydney opera house, another one was like something I saw in Monument Valley New Mexico, but it was much larger with its top hidden high in the clouds. The place consisted of mountains on top of mountains, still snow covered, which disappeared into the haze and clouds so that it was impossible to tell just how tall they were. Sometimes, the sides were sheer drops of pure rock for thousands of feet. A waterfall seemed to hang motionless, suspended in space, as it plummeted so far down it dissipated into nothing but vapor. I was spellbound.

My biplane transported me in slow motion as I wound through this earthen church, a place where God must surely be most pleased with his handiwork. I became aware that I was actually getting choked up about the experience of being in the presence of a power beyond anything that we mortals can comprehend. This day the air was peaceful, and we slipped through these hallowed halls with grace and beauty, but we knew that another day this place could produce storms of such fury that our meager craft could be splintered in a flash.

I passed over lakes that were a startling turquoise color that I had never seen. I thought it could not be real, that there must have been some additive, some pollution to make it that way, but if the water in this remote place, from these sacred mountains, were polluted, then there is no hope for this planet. Is this what real water looks like?

Over one particularly breathtakingly beautiful valley, I thought that I could easily live here for the rest of my life. I would sit on my front porch, rocking in my chair, with a smile that would last forever.

All too soon, the mountains faded, the valley widened, and we were headed out into the flatlands, and toward the Mediterranean. Through the haze we could see the blue of the sea and the orange tiled roofs of the houses by the shore. What minor turbulence we experienced in the mountains disappeared as we reached the coast. The air became so still that it was only the vibration of the big round engine that brought home the reality that I was really flying an airplane.

Matthias slipped ahead of me, according to plan, and called the controller at Cannes, receiving permission for a flight of two Waco biplanes to land. We turned left over the sea for about five miles, then headed back toward the shore for a left downwind entry to the pattern. The wind was about 15 knots, and only about 30 degrees crosswind, so the landing was uneventful. We parked the biplanes on the grass, tied them down and headed for the terminal.

We bought a bottle of champagne and celebrated life, two of this world's luckiest guys, biplane flying and the good life in Cannes, and when the bottle was gone, we caught a taxi to what has got to be the finest hotel in town.

This is the high season in the south of France, and therefore the costliest, and this being a top of the line 4-star hotel, they are taking a real pound of flesh for the rooms. But the way I look at it, I'm just paying them some of the money I saved by staying in all of those dingy, dirty, old hotels for the past month. We are on the beach, of course, and the rooms look out over the Mediterranean and the private yachts anchored offshore. The lobby is alive with the comings and goings of some of the most beautiful people in existence. If we are going to build a master race, here is the place to collect some DNA. I would love to hear some of the stories of these people. One does not come to a place like this without having done something interesting to earn it.

I could go on and on about what a fine hotel this is, about all the amenities, the service, the cleanliness, etc. But the thing that really struck me was the fact that the same person who registered us at the front desk walked us to our rooms, and when I saw the two single beds in my room, I expressed my preference for a king-sized bed, and without missing a beat, she said she could have the bed changed out right away, and she did! And this was the first time I have seen a washcloth in a hotel in more than a month. There was also a real shower, with automatic temperature control and more control handles and water spouts than I have been able to figure out what to do with. And terry cloth robes! I am in heaven!

We like it so much here we're going to stay another day. Tomorrow, we figure that we'll fly down the Italian coast and back. But then you never know! That's why it's called an adventure!

Day 36: And We Didn't Get Arrested!

<u>Cannes, France</u>

Have you ever flown a biplane low over the coastline of the French Riviera? Have you ever slipped through the air just a few feet above a transparent turquoise sea? Have you ever done wingovers through a Mediterranean cloud? Raced a Donzi speedboat out of a harbor? Waved your wings in reply to the appreciative wave of a young lady sunbathing aboard a tycoon's yacht?

Well, I hadn't either, until today.

Matthias and I rolled down Cannes' runway 17 together, lifted off in formation and climbed out over the Mediterranean. Our mission was to fly east along the coast to Italy, then turn around and retrace our path to Cannes and continue farther west to the controlled airspace of Marseilles before we headed back to Cannes again.

The flight lasted 150 minutes from startup to shutdown, and I would have to search my memory hard to find when in the last 54 years I have more thoroughly enjoyed the passage of time. It could only have been when I was falling in love.

The fantasylands named Cannes, Antibes, Nice and Monaco appeared out of a light haze, each a magical apparition coming into focus and resolving itself in the bright sun, and then passing under my wings and back into the haze behind me. Villas and castles, villages and cities, solitary sun worshipers on isolated islets and throngs of beach goers on long sandy strips; sailboats and super-yachts, jet skis, swimmers, paragliders, helicopters, banner-towing airplanes, commercial jets, private jets, all these people and their toys, their vacations and vocations, their comings and goings were all a humdrum backdrop for two of the loveliest sculptures ever to take to the air: two open-cockpit biplanes, passing in review for everyone below to look up, breathe in and sigh. An inspiration we were, I know it. We touched many lives today, I'm sure of it. I know we touched mine.

Here's a shot I took of Matthias and his Blue Wizzard, near Monaco:

When we returned, we lunched at the Club Bar at the airport, and drank champagne and reflected on a great day of flying. From time to time during lunch, I would have the thought that any minute some French aviation official would tap me on the shoulder and say, "Come with me," and handcuff me and send me to some dark dungeon where I could never again see the sky, my penalty for having so much fun. It must be illegal, I think. There must be some obscure law that is dragged out when someone is discovered smiling just too damn much.

Will I then be able to prove I really earned it? How can I prove the 30 years of hard labor I've served in the preparation for these moments? What can I say when it is not enough to work hard and long for these rewards because so many others work harder and longer and still not get a break? Will I then be able to point to cancer and divorce and bankruptcy and say, "See? I have endured!" Will the answer be that still others have suffered far more?

These are heavy philosophical questions. The only answer I have been able to come up with is that we are all doing whatever we are doing because it is supposed to be happening. It was more than 15 years ago when I was working at my computer by the window of my apartment by the Pacific; when I looked up to the sound of an open-cockpit biplane flying low over the surf, then pull up hard in a climbing turn and head back out of sight. I had never seen or imagined such a thing in my life, and on that day, I was inspired. I barely breathed the promise to myself: "Someday!" Great beauty is put in this world to inspire us. On that day 15 years ago, that pilot was doing his job, and today I was doing mine. Today, I did my job very well.

Day 37: Riding The Edge Of The Storm

<u>Ascona, Switzerland</u>

The preflight weather briefing predicted heavy weather moving in from the west with a 40 percent chance of rain and thunderstorms at our destination within the next several hours. Our flight would take 2.5 hours. There was an alternate airport near the destination, but it was on the other side of a mountain. If the weather had already moved in when we got to our first choice, the low ceilings might already have closed the alternate. Matthias knows the terrain, and he said even under normal conditions there would be low visibility along the route. Go, or no-go?

With all the other considerations involved, and especially a full load of gas and the possibility of retracing our steps back to safety, we decided to give it a try.

We departed the Cannes airport with a formation takeoff to the south, then turned east and along the shoreline, following the directions of a succession of controllers in Cannes and Nice, until we were past Monaco and left to our own navigation into Italy. The voices on the radio turned from French to Italian (my favorite!). There was heavy haze along the coast, but when we turned north at Savona it got awful, and I was thinking seriously of turning back. The conditions seemed worse because of the low broken cumulus hanging just inside the shoreline and the mountains we had to pick our way through until we arrived at the Bormida river valley, which we followed until we broke out into the clear at the huge Po river basin.

All the while, we could see the big cumulus clouds to the west, building up with the heat of the day and the up-slope air currents over the mountains being pushed toward us with every mile we travelled. It was a race to see if the weather would beat us to Switzerland.

The Po valley, in northern Italy, is one of the most fertile regions in the world. There was nothing but green farmland for as far as the eye could see in every direction. Not a square inch of land was unproductive. Keeping Torino's restricted airspace on our left and Milano's Malpensa airspace to our right, we threaded our way north to the other side of the Po valley and the higher elevations before dropping down to Lago d'Orta and our target Lago Maggiore. The photo below is Lago Maggiore, taken from just under the cloud deck.

We flew this long, wide, and thoroughly beautiful lake for 30 miles with 4,000 to 6,500 foot mountains lining both sides. Clouds were hanging in the valleys and on the peaks, and there was still a light patchy morning fog lying on the water.

There are two airports at Ascona, but only one had Customs, which was open at this time. Matthias has been to this field before, and it is definitely challenging. He told me about it ahead of time and let me decide if I wanted to tackle it. The downwind leg starts over the lake and at about mid field, the ground rises up very quickly until you are only a hundred feet or so above the trees. The base leg is where you lose sight of the runway completely, and you must fly as close as possible to the very high mountain staring you in the face. When you are so close to it that it seems you are going to be devoured, you turn right for final approach and regain sight of the runway. It isn't over yet because you have some power lines very close to the approach end of the runway, and you must come in high and drop fast, get on the ground quickly and get on the brakes because it is a short runway.

Sounds easy, right? Maybe for someone who practices this kind of thing, but my trick-landing skills are a bit rusty with so little flying over the last three months. But Ascona's challenging airport allows for a go-around and that's why I figure I'll give it a try.

I followed Matthias in the pattern, and he landed without incident.

My approach was too high at the base turn and when I was looking at that monster mountain coming straight at me, it was difficult to lose altitude, just a natural reaction. When I turned final and saw how high I really was, I put the biplane into a very strong slip to burn off the altitude, but there was just no way I was going to land short enough to stop before the end of the runway, so I called over the radio that I was going around.

On the second attempt, I was braver on the base leg and got a lot closer to the mountain, and a lot lower, and when I turned final I was still high, but with the help of a strong slip I was able to get over the wires and onto the runway with plenty of room to spare. It wasn't a particularly pretty landing, from where I sat, but it was effective.

The controller had us park in the tall grass by the side of the runway. The grass is mixed with white, yellow and purple flowers, and clover, with a distinct aroma of mint. It was such a delightful parking place; I had to take a picture.

Matthias came over to me while I was still in the cockpit and congratulated me on the landing, and said "Welcome to my country, welcome to Switzerland," and we shook hands. Then, he told me that he just found out that our alternate airport was engulfed in rain at the moment. We just made it!

At lunch, in a restaurant on the edge of the Lago Maggiore, I reflected that we heard French when we left, Italian en route, now they are speaking German and the menus are in German and Italian. Matthias is Swiss and he speaks all of these languages and English with ease. I've got a lot to learn! When the bill comes for lunch, I realize that we're dealing with a whole new monetary system. I have only French francs and I need Swiss francs. And a new phone adapter for my modem! A lot can change in a two-hour flight in Europe!

The hotel is even better than the one in Cannes, but less expensive. That was a 4-star; this is a 5-star. We had a choice of staying at another 4-star, or this one, and the question was settled when I asked Matthias how many stars he felt he deserved! His answer was the same as what I was thinking: Six!! Here's the view from my room: (Matthias' room faces the town.)

For the first time since I have been in Europe, I feel comfortable with the airport spec sheets. Yesterday, I bought a complete set of Jeppesen books for all the airports in Europe, and they are all in English as well as the language of the country. The ones I had been sold in Paris were all in French, so all I could really decipher were the numbers (runway number, length, width, radio frequency), and that didn't make me feel that good. Now, I can really understand what's going on!

We are about 90 minutes by Waco from Zurich where Matthias lives. If the weather is good tomorrow, I'll get a chance to visit with him and his wife Nici and their

17-month-old son, Hendrik, for a couple of days. I've been looking forward to this for a long time. I also want to get an authentic Swiss Army knife with all the "stuff" in it! And some chocolate!

Day 38: The Gods Must Have Been Sleeping

Zurich, Switzerland

The weather forecast indicated that we might make it over the mountain pass into Zurich. The cloud bases were at 8,000 feet, and the minimum recommended altitude for crossing the pass is 8,000 feet. So maybe. It's another one of those situations where you just go take a look. As long as you keep the back door open, and have enough fuel to get to an alternate airport, it's worth a try.

Matthias was taking a passenger on this leg. A good friend of his, Geo, had never been in an open-cockpit biplane before. He arrived at the airport with his camera and a face full of smiles. He had been looking forward to this for a long time.

We took off in sequence from the tiny airport at Ascona, turning left in a big circle to gain altitude before we crossed the airspace over Locarno and headed east down the narrowing valley. The mountains soared out of sight into the clouds and beyond. We continued our climb until we were only a thousand feet under the clouds and picked our way through a valley that climbed up to meet us. Soon, there were mountains all around us, the ground was only a thousand feet below, and the cloud bases were just over our wings. Ahead, it seemed as if there were impenetrable walls of granite with no way over except into the clouds. Not an acceptable solution.

I saw no way through, but Matthias knows these mountain passes, and he kept flying straight ahead. Soon, what looked like one wide mountain face split into two peaks, with a narrow pass between them. We flew to the edge of the pass, and could see that the way was clear. We had just enough daylight under the clouds, and above the ground, to make it through.

The air was completely still. The flying was silky smooth. With the sheer immensity of the Alps all around us, the clouds, the snow, and the incredible formations of granite that reached out for us, all of these elements seemed to give grave warning of great danger. But the air was so still that we slipped through this awesome place without even a bump.

I am not used to this sort of thing. To me, mountain flying is turbulent, filled with bone-jarring thumps that take you by surprise, and rapid lifts and descents on fast moving columns of air. But not here, not today. It was as if the gods who live here were asleep, or else they were feeling kindly today, and let us pass without incident. If they wanted, they could have splintered our fragile little wood and fabric winged toys with a puff of Alpine wind.

We let down through the pass, each turn more wondrous than the last, until we finally broke out over the lower ground around Zurich, a very welcoming sight. The entire flight, Matthias and I had hardly spoken a word on the radio. There's not much one can say at moments like these.

I know I have been to a very special place on this planet. The feeling will be with me forever.

Day 39: Wingovers for Nici

Liechtenstein

Matthias and his wife, Nici, have a lot in common. They are both dentists, work together and they love flying. They took flying lessons together on a vacation to California several years ago and on another vacation to Hawaii, they took a ride in a Waco biplane, fell in love with it and decided that they would have one of their own. We met at the Waco factory four years ago when we were there to take delivery of our new biplanes.

Today was Nici's day off from the office, and Matthias stayed home with their 17-month-old son, Hendrik, so Nici and I could go flying together. It had been about two weeks since Nici had done any flying in their Waco, so she was really looking forward to it. And it had been about two years since Nici and I had gone flying in my Waco, in California, where I gave her a tour of the San Diego coastline. Now, it was her turn to show me around her country.

After I took off and got a little bit of altitude, I turned the stick over to Nici and she took me south along Lake Zurich, then east to the tiny little country of Liechtenstein, northeast along the Rhein river valley (overflying pieces of Germany and Austria in the process), then back northwest to Lake Konstanz (Bodensee), and west back to Birrfeld airport, keeping just north of the busy Zurich airspace. It was a great counter-clockwise tour of the lowlands of Switzerland.

For Nici, it was a chance to show me some of her favorite places: Castles and monasteries, lakes and waterfalls, the church where she and Matthias were married, the town where she was born, the town where she grew up and went to school, an island covered in flowers, a place on a lake where ancient stick houses stand over the water, the town where her mother lives, high up on a hill. Nici made several turns around her mother's house hoping she would come out to wave, but she must not have been home to hear the sound of the engine.

I enjoyed flying over Liechtenstein. It is such a small country that it doesn't have an airport or I would have landed to check it out more closely. On the navigation charts, it isn't even identified as a country. Nici pointed out the modest castle where the big guy lives. It's good to be king.

When we got to the little town where Nici grew up, Nici asked me to take the stick and to fly out over the lake and do some wingovers. Oh boy, would I! It had been more than an hour that Nici had been flying (and doing a wonderful job of it too!), and I was thoroughly enjoying the tour, but the minute she suggested that I take the stick I realized how much I missed the feel of the controls, and to be asked to do a few wingovers... well, I just jumped at the chance.

A wingover is a very graceful maneuver, and with a little bit of practice it can be a lot of fun. I like to enter a wingover with a little bit of a dive to gain more speed than level flight can provide. Then I pull back on the stick and climb until the engine starts to slow, add full power to keep the climb going until the power fades. The biplane slows, hanging almost motionless in the air, and then I give it some left (or right) stick and rudder and point it downhill again in the opposite direction. I repeat until satisfied. Dives and climbs and turns all combined in a ballet in the sky.

I made a few wingovers to the left, then the right, and then some tight turns left and right, until I felt so good I flipped into a hard-left high-speed spiraling dive down to the lake surface and flew past the school were Nici learned about the laws of Physics. Now here she is, high above her old school yard, using the laws of Physics to invent new games that would amaze her classmates, then and now. Life has such interesting turns.

Later that evening we all went to a birthday party for one of Nici's friends. We were all surprised when two guys showed up with some of the biggest horns you've ever seen:

I have not been able to connect to the Internet to send e-mail for the last two days. The modem seems to be faulty. I bought a Swiss phone adapter in Ascona and it worked there, but I can't make it work at Matthias' home. We drove into Zurich to a computer store to get a replacement modem, but it won't work without the software that is on floppy disks, and I didn't pack my floppy disk for this computer, because I was trying to save weight and bulk, and I had no probable use for it. Until now! Tomorrow, the stores are all closed. Maybe Monday we can get this issue resolved.

Day 40: Lost in the Alps

<u>Birrfeld, Switzerland</u>

The weather was forecast to be excellent today, and rainy for the next several days. With such perfect weather for flying, and it being a weekend, everyone was in the air today. The airport at Birrfeld is usually extremely busy with gliders and tow planes as well as the normal general aviation powered aircraft, and today was no exception.

Matthias and I took off in sequence and headed south into the Alps. The air was warm and still, and there were broken cumulus at around 8,000 to 10,000 feet. It was a wonderful day to fly. The views were absolutely shocking. Each mountain pass brought some new impossible-to-believe vista of granite, snow and valleys below. Matthias and I were quiet on the radio for a long time. It was if we were in church. We would fly very close to rock formations at 7,000 feet, green with grass and trees and a solitary farmhouse, and watch the ground fall away dramatically, straight down to the valley floor. How can people actually live here? It's so scary, for me, to think of walking around at such heights, and yet, here I am flying through it all. Strange.

At one point, Matthias called my attention to a hotel on the side of a 12,000-foot mountain peak. We were at about 8,000 feet at the time, so I looked down and saw a building that looked a lot like a hotel, at about 7,500 feet, and was suitably amazed. I didn't find out until later that I should have been looking up, much higher, at the 11,000-foot level!

It was right about this point that Matthias and I flew under a dark gray cumulus cloud. I was following him by about half a mile. He was flying directly toward the side of the mountain. It was a granite face that started at ground level and extended straight up into the cloud.

The dark gray/blue cloud and the dark gray/blue granite face of the mountain blended together as I watched Matthias' dark blue biplane fly directly into the face of the mountain, and he disappeared. The mountain/cloud just gobbled him up. No more flashing strobe lights, no navigation lights. No more easily identifiable biplane wings. He was gone. I waited for the explosion, but there was none. He was just gone. I looked around for several minutes, and found nothing.

"Matthias. I have lost you. Say your position." I radioed, without hope.

Silence.

"Matthias. Where are you? I have lost you. Say your position." Again I radio. And again there was silence.

I look for pieces of Waco tumbling down the face of the cliff, but the mountain is still. How is this possible?

I keep searching. "Hello Matthias. Matthias do you read me?" Nothing. I wait a long time, planning my next move. I have plenty of gas. I have a GPS, so I can't get lost. I can find my way out of this mountain pass easily enough; just retrace my path.

"...ike... ...... bld... read ... ..." the garbled radio transmission is faint, but sounds like Matthias' voice. Am I imagining it? I saw him fly right into the mountain.

The way to get better radio reception in the mountains is to climb, so I add another thousand feet and try again: "Matthias. Do you read?"

"Yes, Michael. Where are you?" Thank God! But how did he escape the mountain? And if he did, where did he go? He is asking me where I am, but what I want to know is where he is! In fact, I haven't the slightest idea where I am except that I know I am 32.5 miles from Birrfeld on a heading of 150 degrees, but if I look around all I see are Alps all around me. I put the biplane into a hard-left bank and look down for a reference point. There's a lake below, a small one. Not much help. A lake in the Alps is like a cornfield in Nebraska. I radio to Matthias to give me a GPS fix from Birrfeld, but his reply is scratchy and broken. He is gone again. I climb again and pick up his transmission. "Michael. Do you see the paragliders?" I look up and see two paragliders floating above me! Incredible! What are these guys doing all the way up here at 9,000 feet? And there's a plane. Probably the one they jumped out of. I radio back that I can, but as we found out later, he and I were looking at different jumpers. We were separated at that time by about 20 miles.

We traded radio calls for about 10 minutes, trying to piece together broken transmissions and identify where we were in relation to each other. I flew in a direction toward our home airport and eventually arrived at a spot that I recognized. It was easy from there. I was over an airport located between two lakes, and there was another airport in sight at the end of the lake to the north. From my chart, I could see I was over Alpnach. I radioed my position to Matthias and he replied he would come to meet me. He arrived in about 15 minutes, appearing out of the cloud and mist and haze the same way he disappeared as if by magic.

We continued to fly together for another hour and a half. This time I kept him closer, and never lost sight of him again. We stayed out of the mountain passes and kept low over the hills and valleys to the north. We explored valleys and lakes and little towns. We played at dog fighting and flew formation together. It was a great day to fly and I didn't want to stop but when a really nasty-looking rain shower appeared out of nowhere and looked as if it might cut off our path back to the airport, I decided I had enough for one day, and headed back for a landing.

Over Cokes at the airport restaurant, Matthias and I went over the details of how and where we got separated, and how several of our attempts to resolve our situation were foiled because of missed or unclear radio transmissions. We agreed that from now on, we would both keep a fix on the same GPS position, and that if we ever got separated again we would say our position first with altitude, then with distance and bearing to the GPS fix. One of the big problems today was that Matthias didn't bring his hand-held GPS, because he knows this territory so well he didn't need it. Since I didn't know the territory at all, the only thing I could use to identify my position was the GPS. It was as if we spoke different languages.

It was another learning experience; another great day of flying.

Day 41: A Day Without Alps

Zurich, Switzerland

It is now late at night, and outside severe thunderstorms rage all through the Alps. I can barely imagine the kind of fury going on in those granite mountain passes right now. I am thinking again how lucky I was to be able to fly through there in smooth air.

The lightning flashes have cut off my phone connection several times before I get the idea that maybe I should disconnect the computer from the phone and the electric outlet before my equipment (and me!) get fried beyond all recognition. I guess I stayed on-line so long because it has been more than three days since I have been able to connect. Today, I finally got the problem resolved.

As it turned out, I had the wrong adapter to connect a USA modem cord to a Swiss phone plug. The adapter I bought in Ascona (Switzerland) worked, but only because the phone in Ascona was wired wrong! One of those rare, but interesting, cases where two wrongs make a right. Of course, the wrong adapter didn't work in Zurich at Matthias' home and that's why I thought my modem was FUBAR.

This morning, I took my notebook computer (Toshiba 660CDT) to the Toshiba authorized repair center in Zurich, and got the problem resolved. The genius who figured it all out was Urs Glattli, and he did it in less than ten minutes, gave me the proper adapter, and did it all for free! What a class act! So, if you are ever stuck in Zurich with a computer problem, now you know who to call.

Today was not a flying day. The weather was forecast to be yucky, and it delivered as promised. There was a break in the mess during dinner and the skies cleared up over the Alps, revealing a most spectacular skyline. I would have taken a picture, if I had my camera with me, but then you have probably already burned out on seeing Alp photos by now.

In addition to the weather problems, it seems that Nici has got some kind of bug, so it has been one of those bummer days all around. Matthias will take her to the doctor tomorrow morning. Nici has been an absolute angel during my visit. Last night, Nici and Matthias teamed up to make one of the finest meals I have had on this trip. What made it so special, I think, was that it was the first real home-cooked meal in 45 days on the road. What a treat!

We have set out a plan to fly again on Wednesday to Geneva, where Matthias will pick up Nici (who will drive there with little Hendrik to turn him over to a sitter for a week or so) and then we will all fly to Germany the same day. From there we will tour north through Germany, then along the north coast of Europe into Netherlands, Belgium, Denmark and Sweden, and whatever else there is up around there. This is the country that Nici wants to see most, and she will only be able to fly with us for a week or so, then has to come back to Zurich to keep the dental practice running until Matthias returns around August 11. After Nici returns, Matthias and I will try to tour England, Scotland, and Ireland.

All of the foregoing is completely dependent on the weather, of course.

Here's a photo of Nici and Matthias' son, little Hendrik, 17 months old and a bundle of energy. He has about three words in his vocabulary right now, so he and I can speak the same amount of German. However, I think he understands more than I do.

What really impresses me is that their dog Cora understands a LOT more German than I do, but has only slightly more trouble with speaking it.

Day 42: Lunch in St. Moritz

<u>St. Moritz, Switzerland</u>

Nici had a miraculous recovery from her illness of the day before, so Matthias and I were free to go flying. Aviation is like that: Sometimes you think you will fly, and you don't, and sometimes you think you won't and you do.

The weather is good, other than the haze that hangs over the Zurich area. The mountain passes are all open, for now anyway. So where to go? The only direction we haven't gone yet is southeast. And the prime destination in that direction is St. Moritz. You may have heard of it, the playground of the rich and famous skiers. It is buried deep in the Alps, and the airport is at the highest elevation in all of Europe, for jets, 5,600 feet. This means that the air will be much less dense than at sea level, and therefore ground speed will be much faster on landing, and controllability will be an issue on takeoff and landing, and the plane will not climb anywhere near as fast as at lower elevations. We will have to climb to 8,500 feet to get over the highest pass into St. Moritz.

There is nothing difficult in any of this. It's just that these are some of the more unusual circumstances surrounding this particular flight.

The first part of the flight goes without incident. We take off from Birrfeld Regional Flugplatz (airport) using runway 26 and turn right to 292 degrees to avoid making too much noise over the houses near the airport. From there, we head out over Lake Zurich and fly the length of the lake southeast into the Alps.

The clouds are hugging the peaks of the highest mountains on both sides of the valley, and as we go deeper into the Alps, the cloud bases fall lower down the sides of these incredible granite walls. We fly on, and the clouds are now hanging in the air at several different altitudes, hanging low over Alpine pastures, and falling down into the valley below, looking for all the world like some gray Spanish moss dripping from unseen branches.

We were at about 7,500 feet and cruising close together when my TCAD (Traffic Collision Avoidance/Detection) sounds an alarm that there is traffic in the vicinity. It rang three pings in rapid succession, the signal that traffic is very close. I immediately called to Matthias that we had a bogey in the area, but as the words are coming out of my mouth a red-tailed Swiss military fighter jet slips past Matthias' right wing with less than 200 feet to spare. I'm sure that jet jockey never expected to see a couple of rickety old biplanes up here, if he even saw us at all. Military jets seldom travel alone, so when I saw another one coming straight at me, I snapped this photo as he blasted right over my head, probably less than 10 feet!

(Actually it didn't happen exactly like that. In fact, it didn't happen at all, not the second jet anyway. I can't tell a lie. Pretty good joke, right? I figured you would be ready for a good gag photo right about now. This photo is a doctored picture (using Paint Shop Pro) of a Vampire that sits on the ground, welded to a pole, at the St. Moritz airport. The first jet that nearly hit Matthias was real, an F-5 Tiger, current inventory in the Swiss Air Force.)

Climbing slowly up to 8,500 feet, in stair-step fashion to keep above the rising terrain, we pick our way through valleys and passes until we are met at one turn with clouds that seem to go down to the ground. It looks to me as if we have met with an impasse, but Matthias keeps on flying. He is on the right side of the pass, and I am on the left. From his vantage point, he can see around the cloud in front of me and sees that the pass into the St. Moritz valley is clear.

This last mountain pass is the narrowest one I have yet flown. There seems to be no way a plane could turn around in here. Once you have committed to enter this pass, you better be right that the other end, which you can't see from the entry, is clear! We press on, and after the final turn in the pass, we are greeted with rain. At first it is light, and nothing to be concerned about. Matthias is flying ahead of me. We can see St. Moritz to the left, but he decides to turn right to show me a spectacular lake and then he turns back again toward St. Moritz.

I wasn't directly behind him going over the lake, I was more to the left, in the center of the valley, and as I went deeper into the valley, I was completely surprised when the rain became much heavier. The water was curling around my windshield in sheets and dripping all over me and my charts. The weather was moving in very rapidly so I executed a quick 180 and got out of there immediately.

At this altitude, the temperature was in the 40's, there was lots of moisture in the air, and we were descending 2,000 feet to pattern altitude for St. Moritz, so I added some carburetor heat to avoid icing. I kept warm with my lucky scarf.

The approach into St. Moritz is a lot like the one into Ascona. I had to fly downwind very close to a mountain on my right, keeping the runway on my left, at 6,600 feet. Field elevation is 5,600 feet. The trick is to keep as far to the right as possible, but stay out of the trees, which are only a hundred feet under the wheels. Further downwind there are some power lines that need to be crossed over, then a left base turn in the widest part of the valley. There is so little room to maneuver that the turn to final has to be made way beyond the runway centerline, and then make a right base/final approach to land. Very, very interesting!

We had a nice hot lunch to warm up from the flight, but we ate indoors because the rain was now passing over the airport. From the restaurant, we could see both ends of the valley, and it didn't look good for getting out of there today, but with a lot of optimism, we refueled in the rain and left the biplanes covered while we hedged our bets by making arrangements for hangar space for the evening. Then, we went back to the restaurant to wait and see what the weather would decide to do next.

No sooner had we sat down that the valley entrance to the west had cleared, so we decided to go for it. The only remaining challenge was that the winds dictated that we take off to the east, and in that direction it was still raining, and it would also require that we make a 180-degree turn in a very tight valley in order to get out of there.

Take a deep breath, strap on your harness and give it a shot.

People are milling all about, taking pictures of our biplanes and asking questions and pointing. They are quite used to seeing the private jets of the rich skiers who come here, but I'm sure they haven't seen the likes of these biplanes in here before! I was sitting in the cockpit of my plane, with my head down doing pilot stuff when I was startled by a flash and looked up to see a man only a few feet from my face taking a picture. Hey, guy, are you thinking that you wanted to get a shot of the fool who flew his biplane in here in the rain, and is now going to fly it out of here in the rain. Did you want a photo of the nut that thought he could turn around in this valley?

Matthias and I take off side by side down the wide jet runway, heading into the gathering gray mass at the end of the runway. I'm on the right, closest to the mountain. As I clear the departure end of the runway and fly more to the right, closer to the mountain, I look down to see the power lines pass beneath my wheels, by a lot less of a margin than I would have liked.

I've got full throttle, of course, but at this altitude my engine is gasping for air. The wings are scratching and clawing in the thin air, desperately trying to get a better hold. I'm doing everything I can to help, keeping airspeed at the critical 76 mph, right rudder, ball centered, but it isn't easy because the biplane is getting buffeted around with the rainstorm. The reduced visibility and the rain are not making this any fun. Matthias is on my left, and I need to make a left turn. I don't want to turn into him, so I call him on the radio and coordinate our turns.

That was one of the toughest turns I have ever made. Getting bounced around with the weather, the rain, the altitude, the narrow valley, it all added up to a real nail biting situation... if I had the time for it. The other side of the valley is fast approaching and I've still got to climb and turn, but when you are turning, you lose lift, and with this density altitude, there is not much lift to begin with. And with the turbulence, it's just not possible to keep a climb going. Get UP, dammit! No, better than UP, what I really want now is to TURN. That mountain is getting too close for comfort. If I turn too tight, I will lose altitude, and if I lose altitude I will not clear the terrain.

These are the times when I get to thinking that maybe I should have taken up checkers for a hobby.

You already know how it turned out, of course. I did make the turn, I did clear the terrain, and so did Matthias. We probably had a lot more clearance than we needed.

Maybe I worry too much. I like to fly when conditions are PERFECT. Anything less and my imagination goes to work.

The rest of the flight back to Birrfeld Flugplatz was relatively uneventful, except for the final approach to landing. Matthias was ahead and on the right downwind for runway 26, and I could see a motor glider, low and slow close below him. I radioed a warning and he went around. So did I. This airport is really busy! How busy? The people here say that it is in fact the busiest airport in all of Europe without a controller.

Total flight time for today was only three hours, but it felt like 30. I was really glad to be down again. On the way home, right in front of Matthias' driveway, a black cat ran across our path. Too late, cat, I'm already home!

Day 43: A Bit of a Dip in the Strip

Geneva, Switzerland

This is officially Nici's first day of vacation, so she drove her toddler son, Hendrik, to her sister's home in Geneva, about three hours by car from Zurich. Her sister, Ulricka, will take care of Hendrik for the next week or so that Nici will be flying along with Matthias and me.

Our plan for today was to fly our biplanes to Geneva International airport and pick up Nici and then fly somewhere over into Germany. It almost went that way.

Geneva International is a major league airport, possibly the largest airport I have flown into so far this tour. It requires a pre-filed flight plan, a lot of radio communications and navigating to published checkpoints. It is all very regimented. Everything must be done exactly just so. I hate this kind of flying.

My plan was to let Matthias handle all the radio and navigation and I would just stick like glue to his wing until he turned base, then I would throttle back and land close behind him. I had all the charts and radio frequencies just in case we got separated and I had to deal with the controllers myself, but I truly dreaded that possibility.

The hour and a half flight went flawlessly. Matthias handled the radio and navigation beautifully through the Bern control zone as well as Geneva. The air was relatively calm, and the temperature was so warm that we both flew with only light shirts. The view was, again, spectacular. There are some Alps we didn't yet get the chance to explore south of Lake Geneva, and the air was clear enough to see them all lined up for our inspection. Above them all stood Mount Blanc, the highest peak in Europe.

Geneva International airport has got to be the most enlightened major city airport I have yet visited. They have a grass strip just for General Aviation aircraft! And it is so very well taken care of; it may well be the best grass strip so far.

The grass strip is very close to, and parallels the long main runway. This sets up the possibility of wake turbulence from the big jets spilling over onto the grass strip, and I was concerned about getting flipped over on my back at low altitude by some "heavy" coming in before me. Actually, there was nothing to worry about because there was no big iron landing while we were in the pattern.

My landing was good, from the standpoint that the biplane suffered no major structural damage and will probably be flyable again tomorrow. Other than that, it was not one of my best landings. The wind was only about 5 knots down the runway, so it should have been a really nice landing. Unfortunately, there is a dip in the runway right past the approach end. I thought I had this landing really nailed and put the Waco down smartly in three point position right beyond the numbers... right at the dip. That left me in full stall for a perfect landing, if the runway had been up at the level it should have been. Instead, the Waco fell out of the air, dropping about two feet into some very forgiving grass that saved the day. If I ever again land at Geneva International, I'll know just what to do.

It was almost 4 pm when we landed and we hadn't had lunch yet, so we decided to stay in Geneva for the night and make the flight to Germany in the morning. Our taxi driver directed us to a very nice hotel right on the lakefront at the extreme southeast shore. Here's the view from the window of my room.

The little I've seen of Geneva, I enjoyed. Lots of sidewalk cafes, very clean, lots of shops and historical buildings. We had a fine meal this evening at a sidewalk cafe in the oldest section of town, made even better because of the great weather. The temperature stayed in the 70's all evening. We walked back to the hotel for desert and cappuccino, and talked of our fantasy vacation plans.

Where would we go? Nici wanted to see some coastlines, and we all agreed that was the best plan of all. The Alps are magnificent, and I have thoroughly enjoyed my time among them, but I'm getting a little burned out on big lumps of rock, dirt and snow. I need some oceans! We decided we would fly north through Germany until we reach the north coast of Europe, then fly west along the coast through Denmark, Netherlands, Belgium, and then France. And skip across the English Channel to England, Scotland then Ireland. LOTS of coastline.

All of the foregoing is, as you know so well by now, completely dependent on the weather.

Day 44: Wake Turbulence Monster

Donaueschingen, Germany

We checked out of our hotel, the Beau Rivage in Geneva, early in the morning to get a good start on the weather that was moving in from the west. But no matter how fast you try to move in aviation, it seems like there is always something else to be done that slows you down.

This time it was an endless phone call from Matthias' credit card company who wanted to be sure that it was really him who was spending all that money on his plastic. He seldom uses his credit card and all of this recent activity tripped their computer program.

Speaking of spending money, the cost for a liter of aviation fuel in Switzerland is 1.77 Swiss francs, or about $8 a gallon. It's about half that if you are a Swiss citizen, and you are flying only within the country.

The goal today was to reach Ansbach-Petersdorf airport in Germany to meet Hermann Betschler, a good friend of someone I have never met, but with whom I have traded a few e-mails during this trip (Bill O'Dwyer). It's a long story, and I'll try to clarify it later. Anyway, Hermann Betschler and Bill O'Dwyer have started a museum of interest to pilots, and I've been invited to stop by for a tour "when I'm in the area." And since we'll be passing right by on our way to the sea...

The takeoff from the grass runway at Geneva International was really a lot of fun. Matthias was taking his bride Nici and some of her luggage so he was heavily loaded and only added enough fuel to make it to our first stop at Donaueschingen Germany. This jawbreaker-named town is about halfway to Ansbach-Petersdorf and is also where Matthias keeps his biplane when he's not touring around Europe. It is also where the beautiful blue Danube River is formed by the confluence of the Brigach and the Breg rivers. People around here spell Danube as "Donau," hence the name of the town. So much for the geography lessons.

Now back to the takeoff from the grass at Geneva. Heavily loaded, Matthias goes first and is finally off the ground so far down the runway I figured he'd never get off. The culprit was not so much the weight of his biplane, but the tailwind that picked up just as we taxied into position. It was only about 4 or 5 knots, but enough to make it interesting.

My turn wasn't so bad because I wasn't as heavily loaded, even though I was serving as the mule, carrying an extra bag or two from their plane, and I did top off the tanks. I was more concerned about the tailwind, which can be no fun at all for tail draggers like the Waco. I stood on the brakes, gave it full throttle, released the brakes and started down the grass; everything is going fine. A little, just a very little, forward stick to lighten the tail wheel, gaining speed all the time, and pretty soon the Waco is getting around to the idea that it's time to fly. Right about this time, the runway falls away into a dip, the plane tries to fly, but it's not ready yet, falls back down, hits a bump, launches itself a foot or two in the air, and is still not ready to fly, so it lets down again just in time to hit the other end of the dip and launches itself again, this time just barely hanging on to the air and sure enough, we are flying! It reminded me of the great film clip you have probably seen of Lindbergh's takeoff on the grass, heavily loaded with fuel, for his trans-Atlantic solo flight.

On my takeoff I had one other factor to contend with. Here I am, climbing out at about 50 feet off the grass when something catches my eye, off to the left, and I turn to see one of those monster steel tubes carrying several hundred people taking off right beside me on the main concrete runway. Now, this big guy is way faster than me and within seconds he is up, up and away while I'm still working on getting to 100 feet altitude.

Then, something I read in the Jeppesen airport data sheet for Geneva comes flashing back to mind: "Wake turbulence from traffic on parallel runway has to be expected." And this is the exact situation they had in mind. Wake turbulence from these heavy commercial aircraft is the kind of stuff that can trash a slow little toy like my biplane. You can't see it, but it's very real. It can flip a plane like mine over on its back, and at this low altitude there would be no possibility of recovery.

All these thoughts are bouncing around in my mind while I'm hanging on for dear life, waiting for the inevitable. I figure that the only thing I can do to avoid it is to head right and away from the source of the turbulence, but Matthias is climbing out to the right ahead of me and if I go too far to the right I'll cut him off in the pattern. But there is no real choice here, I'm fighting an unseen enemy, and this is not a time to be playing by the rules. I want out of here, NOW!

Of course, you already know that the wake turbulence monster did not get me today. And I was never any real concern to Matthias because I turned way inside of his turn. I never felt even a ripple from that big plane. I was lucky.

The rest of the flight was a breeze. The conditions were very hazy with a high overcast, so the air was very still and the flying was silky smooth. We flew over several lakes, along the foothills of some mountains. We hit some light rain for a few minutes, and then out again into the clear for an easy straight-in approach to Donaueschingen. (It's pronounced the way it looks!)

I gave my camera to Nici for this flight and she took a shot of her favorite Waco pilot (Matthias), looking back at him from her separate cockpit up front.

And here's another one Nici took of my favorite Waco, flying in the haze over Lake Geneva:

There's a really good restaurant and hotel at this airport. We had an excellent lunch, but we all ate way too much, and even the cappuccino I had didn't do much to get me awake again. The weather report for the next leg into Ansbach-Petersdorf (a lot easier to pronounce) was calling for thunderstorms in the late afternoon, and that just made it easier for us to take refuge in the hotel for the night.

We refueled the planes and discovered that they don't take credit cards for fuel here, and we didn't have any Marks! Right, we are in Germany now, so we need a whole different kind of money. It will be a good thing when they get the Euro currency in circulation, but many people think it will never happen. The only way to get money for gas is to go take a taxi into town and raid an ATM machine. In the meantime, to cover some other expenses, I convert some other small-denomination, folded money that was building up in my pockets, remnants of my earlier travels to Sardinia (lire), France (Fr. francs), Switzerland (Sw. francs), into a few marks. What a mess!

Before the ATM raid, we decide to put the biplanes in the hangar and out of the rain that is just now spitting the first few drops, warning of a lot more to come soon. Matthias keeps his biplane hangared here, and there is room for his and mine in a large communal hangar at the end of the taxiway. This hangar has a most unusual feature, a turntable! You push your plane onto the turntable, push a button to rotate your plane into an empty slot on the perimeter of the table, and then push it off. This is such a cool thing I want one for my own hangar, except that I want one that will fit just the Waco, and I want it to turn around all day long so I can see my lovely biplane from all different angles all the time! The only problem is that I'd have to dig up the floor of the Fun House in order to get it installed. Well, maybe in the next Fun House. But it sure was fun to play with this turntable!

After we returned from town with the money and paid for the fuel, we decided to clean the biplanes. Actually, Matthias decided to clean his, and I just could not bear to see his cleaner than mine, which was getting extremely grungy with all the bugs from the grass runway playing. I usually delegate this kind of work, but today there were no delegatees around, so I knuckled down and did the job myself. And now I have one superfine looking ride, yes sir! I am also one super-tired dude. So by the time you read this, I'll be dreaming of flying the Baltic Sea coastline.

I lost a batch of e-mail I was downloading, due to lightning strike here in Donaueschingen.

Day 45: To Go or Not To Go

<u>Stuttgart, Germany</u>

I woke up early after a night of good sleep, fully rested and ready to fly. The weather outside the window was sunny, but with puffy rain clouds in the vicinity. The ceiling looked low, but high enough to fly. Soon the phone rang with Matthias' call. He had already looked up the aviation weather forecast and mapped out a route to our next stop. The forecast was for ceilings no less than 500 feet above the ground, with rain throughout the day, but getting worse around 11 am. The long-term forecast was for more of the same, and worse, for the next two days. His feeling was that if we left before 9 am we could make it. We agreed to meet for breakfast after showering and go for it.

By the time we finished breakfast and checked out of the hotel, the weather was looking a lot different. The ceiling was still flyable, but the sky was a lot darker. I was not feeling comfortable. There was additional pressure to go flying because Nici's vacation would end next Wednesday and she wanted to see the north coast of Europe as soon as possible.

Matthias felt okay with going flying because he knows the territory. I reviewed the proposed route on the chart, looking for radio towers and power lines, obstructions that would be a nasty end to the flight if visibility and ceilings forced me into harm's way. There were none. Matthias and I discussed the details. He said he felt we could fly around rainstorms, but if we got separated, like we did in the Alps, I would probably be on my own to find an alternate destination, or to make it through. That really didn't bother me. I had all the right avionics to find my way.

What I didn't like was the way the sky looked. Big dark gray cumulus clouds hanging low and moving fast from the northwest. It had already rained this morning, and the sky in the direction we had to go was not looking good.

Go or No-Go? That's the big question in aviation. Sometimes there is just no clear answer. According to the numbers (forward visibility, ceiling, wind speed, forecasts, etc.), it was flyable, but just barely. The final decision came down to unquantifiable gut feelings.

My philosophy on the Go or No-Go question is based on the premise that I am flying for pleasure, not business. There is just no reason that would force me to go flying the way an airline pilot is required to. I have no schedule to meet or paying passengers counting on reaching their destination. I have the great luxury of looking up in the sky and deciding if it will be fun. And this morning, it didn't look like fun. The final straw came when we considered that even if we did reach our destination for today, the next couple of days would be even worse weather, so why push it?

We decided to keep our biplanes snug in the hangar. So then what? Jump on a commercial airliner and head for sunshine? How about Madrid? Guaranteed to have sunshine. No, because it would take a day to get there, and a day to get back, and we would only have a day to play before the sun was due back in Germany. We decided to rent a car and drive to Stuttgart, about 100 kilometers from Donaueschingen for a first class hotel, some shopping, entertainment and good food. Nici really brightened up at the thought of shopping, and had never been to Stuttgart before. Things were looking more like fun.

About five minutes after we absolutely decided not to fly, the sky opened up with a huge torrential downpour, and lasted for the next hour. If we had just gone flying, without all the decision making, we would have been taking off, or sitting on the ramp in all this rain and we would have been totally soaked.

Matthias rented a big Mercedes Benz, and soon we were on the main highway to Stuttgart. Matthias drove, Nici was stretched out in the back seat, and I was riding shotgun. Out of my peripheral vision I saw a car riding our bumper, and Matthias was doing well over 80 mph. He pulled over to let the other guy go by, and a couple more cars passed us like we were standing still. Then the thought came to me: This is Germany. Autobahn. No speed limits! And I turned to Matthias and said: "Hey Matthias, let's go driving on the Autobahn, where is that?" His reply was simply "This is it!"

It was incredible. Ever since I was a kid dreaming about fast cars, the Autobahn has always had an irresistible pull. No speed limit at all. What a fantasy. Here you could drive as fast as you wanted, and never have to look in the rear view mirror for police. No radar. Wow!

We were still in a driving rain (pun intended), and since this was the first time I've been on the Autobahn, I figured I would take a pass at driving this big Mercedes for now, and take it for a spin when the road was dry, maybe on the weekend when the big truck traffic is less, it isn't raining and I know more about the road. I can't wait!

Matthias did a great job of driving, and in some stretches we were doing over 110 mph. It was an eerie feeling to blast along without looking over my shoulder for police. I am thinking how great it would be to drive my Ferrari over here.

After checking in at the Hotel Inter-Continental with the assistance of the fun-loving and spirited Daniella at the front desk, we all went shopping on Konigstrasse. This is a two km long shopping mall, with loads of good stuff. Nici loved it. I keep looking for a PCMCIA card for my laptop that I can use to download video from the JVC digital video recorder. Nobody over here seems to know anything about it. I want to upload some video to the website, maybe some action shots of landing on a grass field, or what it looks like at 150 mph on the Autobahn, or flying low over the English Channel.

I love this stuff. This morning, I didn't even know where Stuttgart was. Now I'm here, and really enjoying it. What an adventure! I wonder what will happen next?

Day 46: Magical Mercedes

Stuttgart, Germany

Last night, we took in the movie "Con Air," tantalized by the theater's outdoor posters featuring flying machines and big explosions. It looked like it was in English, but it was in German, so I had an interesting 90 minutes of trying to decipher the plot without understanding a word. I wouldn't recommend the movie for any reason, and neither would my friends, Nici and Matthias, who understand German perfectly.

The only change in the weather for today is that it got worse. There was no break at all in the low clouds, and it rained continuously. It was a perfect day for visiting the museums. The Porsche factory and museum are here, and they give tours, but not on Saturday. But the Mercedes Benz museum is also in Stuttgart, and they are more accommodating, so we spend a most delightful afternoon tracing the history of automobiles from the very first Daimler all the way to the modern retractable hardtop SLK sports car. They had the cars of emperors, popes and movie stars, and world champion racecars as well as the ordinary touring sedans, limos and sports cars through the past 100 years. It was very well done, as you would expect from Mercedes.

My favorite Mercedes of all time is the 1936 Type 500 K Special Roadster, which achieved 160 kph on a supercharged engine of 160 hp. To me, it is a fabulous example of the extraordinary automotive designs produced in the mid-'30s.

It is very reminiscent of the US-made Auburn boat-tailed speedster of the same era. Both of these cars drove the rich and famous in luxury touring at the same time as my Waco first took to the air.

The favorite of Matthias and Nici was the 1954 Mercedes Benz 300 SL Coupe with those famous "gull-wing" doors. I finally got them to pose for a picture:

Just to show that the museum isn't limited to automobiles, here's a shot of the 1987 Mercedes C-9 race car (720 hp and 402 kph!) with a Mercedes-engined monoplane called the Komrade.

Mercedes racecars used to be all painted white, until one year the newly designed car showed up for the first race of the season weighing exactly one pound over the limit. The night before the race the car was completely sanded down to bare metal to get rid of the extra pound. It went on to win the race, and henceforth, all Mercedes racecars have been silver.

The gift shop at the museum was too much to resist. I bought a model 300 SL Coupe model for Matthias and a Mercedes pen set for Nici, in appreciation for their hospitality during my stay at their home in Zurich. And I got a model of the 500K in red, for my toy car collection at Mikie's Fun House.

On the way back to the hotel, we had the opportunity to try out the GPS system in our rental Mercedes. Simply enter your desired destination in the dashboard mounted computer and a voice guides you every step of the way with directions such as: "Bear to the right 200 meters ahead," or "Turn left 500 meters." It even knew, and advised us, about a very subtle right jog in the road, preventing us from following the train tracks into a train-only tunnel. It is incredibly accurate, knows every road, hotel, restaurant, airport, gas station and place of interest in Germany, but unfortunately for me, speaks only

German. I'm wondering when the day will arrive when it will be smart enough to know that the car ahead of you is planning on making a right turn in 500 meters, but he is in the left lane, so be careful. Or when it could recognize that you spent the night at the hotel InterContinental on Willy Brandt Strasse and would you like directions to, and reservations at the InterContinental in Cannes, the next destination in your itinerary. It could easily bring to your attention various places of interest before you get to them, and give you more information about them if you wanted with the touch of a button, could recognize that you haven't stopped for lunch yet, and suggest a place to stop which offers your favorite cuisine, and even... well, you get the idea. I have the feeling that the future is coming at us so fast that by the time we get around to dealing with each new wonderful advance, it is already obsolete and replaced with something even more miraculous.

Throughout Germany it is raining, and has been for so long that they are calling it "The Flood of the Century." Above the thick cloud layer, the sun is shining. Someday soon the clouds will move away to the east, the sun will again shine on the grass runways and my beautiful Waco biplane will again take to the air flying north to the Baltic Sea.

Stay tuned.

Day 47: First To Fly

"On August 14, 1901, almost two and one half years before the Wright Brothers flew at Kitty Hawk, Gustave Whitehead lifted his acetylene-powered monoplane into the air at Fairfield, Connecticut, for his first flight."

So reads one of the documents in the Gustave Whitehead (Weisskopf) museum in Leutershausen. But every pilot, every schoolboy knows that the Wright Brothers were the first to fly, so what is going on here in this little town in Bavaria?

Fascinated with flight as a young man, he tinkered with many different aspects of flight, including balloons, kites and parachutes. He watched birds in flight, built and patented a hang glider, built engines, experimented with fuels and was an inventor of an incredible variety of innovations that ultimately led to the first powered flight by man.

The machine that took him into the air for the first time, his No. 21, included advanced features such as powered landing gear, folding wings and adjustable pitch propellers. He was also the first to land a plane on water. His early flights are documented in several respected publications. So with all of this fact supporting his rightful place as the Father of Aviation, how can it be that he is virtually unknown?

A clue can be found in this modest little museum. Enclosed in a glass case is a copy of an agreement between the Smithsonian Institution and the estate of the Wright Brothers, which gives over to the Smithsonian various artifacts, and binds the Smithsonian from doing anything which would cast any shadow of a doubt that the Wrights were the first to fly, thus protecting the estate of the Wrights. It's a very suspiciously self-serving contract.

You may be as incredulous about all of this as I was, but if you had the opportunity to visit this little museum, and take the time to consider the evidence, you might very well come away questioning the history lessons you learned as a child.

I would never have come to Leutershausen, a small walled city of 3,000 people, built in the 14th century, in the middle of nowhere in Bavaria, if it were not for the urging of a fellow named Bill O'Dwyer. I have never met Bill, except that we have swapped numerous e-mails over the last month or so. He was turned on to my tour by a mutual friend/pilot/writer Budd Davisson. Bill O'Dwyer is a retired Air Force Major, lives in Fairfield CT (site of the first flight) and was highly instrumental in the founding of this museum after discovering and researching evidence of this historical event. I consider it to be one of the highlights of my tour to have met Bill on the Internet, and to have found my way to the birthplace of the true First Flyer.

Here's a photograph of the monument erected just outside the ancient walls of Leutershausen, honoring their most famous citizen. What you see here is a replica of Weisskopf's flying machine No. 21, perched atop the monument.

Below is a photo of the two men who took the time to show us around the museum and explain all of the fascinating details. On the left is Matthias Lechner, Vice Chairman, and on the right, Hermann Betscher, Chairman of the Historical Flight Research Committee, pictured here at the base of the monument.

Here's the museum itself, housed in a relatively modern building for Leutershausen, built in 1624.

There's a lot more to this great story than I have been able to mention in this brief e-mail, but maybe you will take the time to find out more by reading the Bill O'Dwyer book, *History by Contract*.

The weather pattern of the last few days seems to be breaking up and we are still trying to get to the north coast of Europe, so we had to head back to our planes hangared in Donaueschingen. It was finally my turn to drive the Autobahn in our big, bad Mercedes Benz! Maybe it's just a "guy thing," but I have always liked to drive fast, and part of the price you pay for driving fast is the risk of getting caught by the police. This is true just about everywhere in the world except on the Autobahns of Germany where there is no speed limit whatsoever.

What a fantasy: to be able to drive a very good car, built for high speed touring, flat out along excellent roads, blasting past every car on the road, without ever once looking in the rear view mirror for police, without ever once worrying about a radar trap. The last time I was able to come close to this was when I was doing some SCCA sports car racing on the racetracks on the east coast of the US, in the mid-60's. Driving today on the Autobahn was like being a kid again, like coming home.

There was never a time when I felt unsafe. The big Mercedes was built like a tank and highly stable on the road. The people who drive these roads are used to very high-speed drivers coming up behind them, and they melt out of your way as you approach them; very courteous and respectful. I was able to sustain speeds at well over 100 mph, occasionally exceeding 120 mph for some stretches for about one and a half hours before being slowed down in the traffic around Stuttgart, where I turned the wheel over to Matthias and dozed in the right seat. What a great ride!

What a great day!

Day 48: Luxem-bored

<u>Luxembourg</u>

It was a beautiful morning in Donaueschingen, Germany. The sky was clear blue, with high clouds far out on the horizon. The air was crisp and a light fog hung close to the ground. We knew it would burn off quickly and would be a great day to fly. But the weather forecast did not agree with our plans to fly to the north coast of Europe. The central part of Germany was blocked with heavy rain and low ceilings.

So we did the next best thing. We went around the bad weather, to the northeast, over France and into Luxembourg. Now that's what I call adventure. When I woke up this morning, the last place I would have thought I would spend the night was Luxembourg. Actually, I may not even have thought of Luxembourg three times in my life, for any reason. (Have you?)

We took off in formation, down runway 36 out of Donaueschingen Germany, and turned left to 312 degrees for a direct shot to our destination. We followed the Autobahn for part of the way as it passed through the Black Forest, then into France and into Luxembourg. The sky was overcast the whole way, and it was cold, but the air was relatively smooth. The cloud bases became too low for us to get over the mountains at one point and we had to go around them. Other than that, it was an easy flight.

This place is really small (only 400,000 people in the country), old (over 1,000 years), and really boring; a good place to go to read a book. Maybe it's just because it's a Monday night, but all the shops closed around 6 pm, and that left the streets empty.

Except for Abi. I met Abi as Matthias and I were walking down one of the deserted streets of Luxembourg. She was dressed in a tutu, ballet slippers and leg warmers, and was juggling a few colored balls... in the middle of the intersection! There was a crowd of exactly *nobody* gathered around to watch her act. But it wasn't because she didn't try. This girl is completely zany. She even ran up to a bald-headed man walking down the street and kissed him smack on the top of his head, leaving a perfect set of lip-tracks for all the world, except him, to see. She danced all around, juggled and did all kinds of tricks and talked to passers-by in several languages. I was entranced, but it seemed as if the Luxoids were comatose.

I wanted to take a photo of her juggling a torch, but she couldn't get it lit, even with the help of two different lighters offered by tourists. Some days it just doesn't pay to get out of bed, but you don't know that until after you get up! Poor Abi couldn't buy a crowd in Luxembourg. But she has a great heart, you can just tell. Here's a photo. Note the complete lack of audience in the background.

Taking a walk around the city, I was struck with the beauty of this particular bridge and the park below it. I just can't look at a bridge like this without wanting to fly under it. This one would be challenging.

Luxembourg prides itself on its bridges and parks.

Tomorrow, the weather should be good enough to fly to the coast. We haven't yet decided which way we will go, left toward the English Channel, or right toward Belgium, Netherlands and Denmark. Maybe the weather will decide for us. I am hatching a scheme to invite the Prince and Princess of Luxembourg to come for rides in our biplanes tomorrow morning. I think they need it. It might add a little zest to things around here.

Day 49: The North Sea

Luxembourg tower denied our request for a formation takeoff; it would probably have been too much excitement for them. So Matthias went first and I caught up to him easily. There was no wind at ground level, and the skies were sunny between the scattered cumulus clouds. It was a lovely day to fly.

There was considerable low fog over the Forest of the Ardennes, so we kept to the west at first and then headed straight north on our way to the sea. The clouds became lower, and thicker as we approached the coastline, and when we reached the North Sea, the clouds dissipated and there was nothing left except an absolutely clear sky.

After an easy flight, the first order of business was to get into town for lunch. It was already 3 pm and we hadn't eaten since breakfast at 9 am. We took a taxi and were given a tour of the more interesting spots, including the previous king's vacation home on the beach, the racetrack where Michael Jackson will have a concert this summer, the casino and various 4-star hotels. Oostende is a rather large resort town of 60,000 and with today's excellent weather, it seemed as if everyone was out enjoying it.

After lunch, I found my way to the beach and walked at the surprisingly warm water's edge for a while, collecting a few shells, then came upon a long jetty of smooth sun-warmed stones which proved irresistible for laying down and taking a nap. What a great treat it was to bask in the sun at last. It must be several weeks since I have seen a cloudless sky, and at least that long since I have been thoroughly warmed by the sun. Here's the first sunset over water I have seen in two months:

I have looked forward to this moment since the beginning of this tour. There is something extraordinarily refreshing and at the same time relaxing about the sea. The sound of the surf, the fresh air, the great variety of wildlife (including the people!) all provides stimulation, while the vast expanse of water and sky offer an indescribable peace.

And while the coastline is a great place to be while on the ground, it is even better in the air. Flying along the beaches is one of my favorite things to do, for many reasons. First and foremost, you can fly low. There are no restrictions about how low you can fly over water, as long as you stay away from persons, property, vehicles and vessels. Flying low heightens the sensation of speed and gives the pilot a much greater feeling of actually FLYING! There is just nothing which can compare to charging low over a deserted beach, banking wings in and out of an irregular coastline, diving and climbing with the rise and fall of the cliffs and rocks, dodging birds and boats and lighthouses.

Another reason I like flying the coast is that it requires virtually no navigation, which is work, therefore leaving only FUN. Navigation over the land is a constant chore to be sure you are avoiding restricted airspaces, staying away from towers, checking distances to the next checkpoint, staying on a compass heading, checking the effect of winds and so on. When you are simply following the coastline there is virtually nothing left to do except watch out for traffic, and even that is substantially less work. Along the coast the traffic is almost always taking the same route as you are, but when you are over land, the traffic can come at you from any direction.

So here I am at the North Sea, the northern coast of continental Europe, with coastline extending east and west as far as I could ever want to fly. I am really looking forward to getting in the air tomorrow. And as usual, I have no idea which way we will go, or where we will wind up. The adventure continues...

Nici left our tour yesterday morning and traveled by train to Geneva to pick up her son, Hendrik. The previous three days of bad weather, the prospect of more of the same, and a growing case of homesickness (this was the first time she had been away from her son for more than a day since he was born) finally overcame her. Her great smile and fun loving disposition were wonderful gifts for the past several days. Thanks for coming along, Nici!

One thing that wasn't boring about Luxembourg was my landing. Runway 24 was in use, and the wind was from 360 degrees, giving a quartering tailwind. In Europe, the custom is for the controller to radio the wind direction and speed only when you are established on final, and for my landing he called it at 6 knots, which is about all the quartering tailwind I want for my tail dragger. If it was any more, I would have asked for the opposite runway, and maybe I should have requested it anyway. My landing was really quite good considering the circumstances. As I was touching down, the controller advised the plane landing behind me that the winds were 8 knots! I put the Waco down on the right main wheel, keeping the right wing low into the wind, with lots of left rudder to keep the plane straight. As soon as the tail settled on the runway, it popped back up again with a gust of wind from behind. It had all the ingredients for a ground loop, but it just didn't happen, this time. There's an old saying about pilots and ground loops: "There are those who have, and those who will." I haven't yet, and I'm sure not looking forward to it.

Day 50: An Absolutely Perfect Grass Runway

As I walked to my biplane this morning, I noticed a car speed across the ramp and stop in front of the prettier of our two biplanes (mine, of course!), and some very businesslike people got out, along with a cameraman who started videotaping. There is an air show here at Oostende this coming weekend, and they were doing a segment to announce the show on the TV news. They were using my biplane as a background for the announcer.

After I refueled, performed the preflight inspection and jumped in the cockpit, the cameraman and the on-screen personality came over to the cockpit and said, "Will you stay?" (referring to the air show). I gave him my best biplane pilot answer "I love this place where you live and I would like to stay, but no, I cannot, the sun is shining and the wind is calling me. I must fly away." If you have a satellite TV antenna that gets 500 channels, tune in to the Brussels channel and you may catch it on the 5 o'clock news.

The prince of Luxembourg married the princess of Belgium (or maybe it's the other way around), and since their countries are right next to each other, there are some similarities in these two different lands. So I wasn't too surprised when the controller at Oostende airport (Belgium) refused to let Matthias and I take off in formation, even though the runway was enormous. I think these people are fun-deprived. Even when they stand in awe admiring our two airplanes, they don't smile. They are a very serious people.

The weather was clear to the north, so Matthias figured he would like to go northeast, and since it sure didn't matter much to me, we turned right when we hit the coastline and followed the beach for two hours until we got to the island of Texel, The Netherlands.

The visibility was very hazy for the entire trip, but when we approached Texel, there appeared low, almost-but-not-quite transparent little gray puffball cumulus clouds hanging lower and lower until we were forced down to 500 feet above the ground. If it got any worse, we would have had to turn around, but Texel was only a few more miles.

My GPS could not find Texel in its database, so I was following Matthias. His GPS was more knowledgeable. This grass strip airport is situated somewhere in the middle of the island, surrounded by rectangular farms, all of which are growing something green. What I am trying to describe is an airport that is impossible to find visually. I was sticking like glue to Matthias' rudder, and I thought he said it was right hand traffic for runway 22, and when he started doing some left turns, I was looking in all the wrong places, and completely disoriented. But when he finally announced he was on final, it all snapped into focus.

When it was my turn to land, there was a strong crosswind all the way down to about 50 feet above the ground. I had a difficult time maintaining my position in the air along the extended centerline of the runway. As I approached ground level, everything smoothed out, the biplane kept straight without any special controls, and it touched down.

Or did it? Did it really touch down? At first I thought it did, and then I thought it couldn't have. It must be floating above the grass, just an inch or so above, because I know my biplane is very close to the ground, but I can feel nothing. It will touch any second now... What was that, a little bump? Yes, it must have been a pebble under the wheel, almost a microscopic pebble because it was so slight, but it proved to me that the biplane must in fact be on the ground, and yet I never knew the exact second when it first touched.

What was even more mysterious was the fact that my biplane is rolling along this grass runway for some several hundred feet and I am feeling almost nothing in my feet, or with my hands, or the seat of my pants. I have had only one other landing in my four years of flying that was this good, but it was on asphalt. I have never experienced a grass runway that was as perfectly maintained as this one.

We taxied off the runway and parked right in front of the outdoor restaurant, which was filled with spectators pointing at us and taking pictures. There was a big crowd farther down the line, beyond the parking area. They were skydivers, and there must have been a competition going on. What a great sight, the sky alive with colorful parachutes popping through the low clouds, and landing with precision in the circle around the big red X. I love to watch these jumpers, but you'll never catch me bailing out of a perfectly good airplane!

And speaking of a perfectly good airplane, here's the photo of the day, good old November Two Five Zero Yankee Mike, on the grass on the island of Texel, in the North Sea, The Netherlands:

The airport manager here has his hands in just about everything. When we asked about getting rooms for the night, he said everything on the island was fully booked. Pause. But he could find us something. He made one phone call, and a bed and breakfast became ours. "How about a taxi to town?" He suggested that he could arrange that, but how about going the Dutch way, on bicycles? Pause. I can rent them to you!

It seemed like a very Dutch thing to do, so we went for it. I use a backpack to get my daily needs into town, and Matthias picked up this trick after he spent the first week hauling his huge duffel bag of clothes for the entire trip back and forth to the biplane. With just a backpack, it was easy to choose the bikes. So here we are, bicycling three miles to town, down a country road on the island of Texel, a place we never even heard of until early this morning, when we looked at our charts.

We arrived at our bed and breakfast lodging, and found that there was only one room, but with two beds. I asked the landlady if I could call back to the airport for another room. The airport manager said it would be virtually impossible to find another room. Pause. But he would make a call, can you hang on the phone for a minute. Pause. Pause. Yes, I have another room, right across the street from where you are, it is all arranged.

After checking in, we headed for the beach, just a couple of blocks away. The North Sea (it's called Nordsee hereabouts) was delightful, almost 70 degrees! The cloud layer had evaporated and the sun was warm. The lunch I had at the airport was making me groggy, so I lay down on the beach to relax and soon I was sleeping like a baby. About an hour later, the flapping sounds of a child's kite nearby woke me, and I immediately noticed that the lowering sun was returning the island to its natural state of cold and wet. Time to get off the beach and get a cappuccino to warm up and wake up.

The town we are in is called De Koog, which is just a little bit north of Den Hoorn and west of De Waal. We are staying on Duinroostraat. I mention this in illustration of the curious Dutch habit of sticking in an extra vowel everywhere they can. If one vowel is good, then two of the same is even better.

It's tough to figure out what to eat around here. This is not the kind of place you find Americans going on their vacation, so the menus are not translated into English. What would you choose from this list: Rolmops, Zure Bom, Garnalen, or Gerookte Paling? See what I mean?

The bed and breakfast place where I'm staying is quite minimalist. No phone or TV, share the bathroom with other boarders (who are in there most of the time), the bed is really a cot, you must provide your own soap, etc. I give it a 1-star rating, but only because it was available. This is the top of the season here in Texel, and people from nearby Amsterdam and Rotterdam flood (oops, shouldn't use that word here in Netherlands) here to get away. I looked in the Guest Book and I'm the only American to stay here since the book was started in '94.

Day 51: McCafferty's First Law of Meteorology

<u>Den Burg, The Netherlands</u>

I awoke at 3 am and couldn't get back to a sound sleep for the rest of the night, so it was easy for me to beat the other boarders to the community shower. I really do not enjoy getting into a community shower while the floors are still wet from a previous use, and I figured that I would find a fresh dry shower and give the displeasure to my neighbors. I was wrong. It was still wet from their use of it the previous day. Things do not dry out easily by the North Sea. Yuk.

Breakfast was in the minimalist style of this establishment and I figured that I would augment my morning nutrition with a cappuccino at the airport restaurant. So it was back on the bikes for the three-mile morning ride. My bike performed flawlessly along the slight downhill sections, but slowed dramatically when we came upon a hill. I discovered that if I would make the pedals go around using my feet the machine would continue to move forward, a condition somewhat reminiscent of *work*, a dull and dreary activity I remember from my pre-retirement days. When I mentioned this to the airport manager/bicycle rental agent, he admitted that this particular model of cycle did indeed operate in accordance with its manufacturer's intentions. Pause. However, he had other models that would operate fully automatically. It was a bit late for all that right now, having already reached my destination, so I declined the opportunity to evaluate one.

So began a day of on and off flying. Upon arriving at the airport, the weather looked "iffy" to say the least, but the forecast for Borkum, Germany, our goal, was better than here. So we would go. And then it started to rain, and we decided not to go. But after a while, it was not a heavy rain, so we decided to fuel the planes (in the light rain), and at least be ready to go if it seemed better later. It did indeed get better, so we decided to go, but by then we needed some lunch first. After a very quick lunch, the weather had gone nasty again, and we decided not to go. Then, some people arrived from the direction we wanted to go, told us it was not so bad and so we decided to go and went back to the tower to re-file the flight plan. The manager immediately replied that we were going nowhere right now, that there was a line of thunderstorms right in our path, having just appeared on his computer screen. So we decided not to go. Finally. Period. We called for a taxi to get out of there, being finished with Dutch-style transportation.

Matthias asked for the manager's assistance in finding lodgings in a different town on the island and was advised that none were available. The island is fully booked. Pause. But he could make a call, and on the first try secured two rooms at a first class hotel. Kinda makes you wonder.

After we loaded the bags into the taxi, we noticed that the sky had gone from bad to really quite flyable, and within an hour the skies were clear! All of which proves conclusively McCafferty's first law of aviation meteorology: "At the moment one is fully committed to a no-go decision, the weather will improve dramatically."

During one of the several periods of waiting for the weather to improve, we were given a private tour of the museum of Texel aviation history by Nico, the assistant manager of the airport ("I am his left hand"), extending all the way back to the first water landings here in 1913. Some of the highlights included scale models of the Dornier DO-X, a gigantic 12-engine seaplane built by a man who actually saw the plane fly more than 60 years ago. The only real plane in the museum was the first homebuilt airplane made in The Netherlands. Until that time, it was actually forbidden to build a plane in this country, so it was done without the approval of the law, and when it flew the law was changed! There was also a Rolls Royce Merlin 12-cylinder engine that was salvaged from an aircraft wrecked on the beaches of Texel during the war. Parts of old warplanes are still being found along the coast! All in all, it was an entertaining and educational experience, and a real treat to find it all in such an out of the way place.

Tomorrow we plan to stay at the airport until the weather clears, no matter how long it takes, then fly to Borkum. If it doesn't clear, we'll take the ferry to the mainland and drive to Amsterdam, where we can get in a lot more trouble than on Texel.

* Ed de Bruijn's business card lists his title as "Director Airport-manager" but his duties include bicycle rental, arrangements for lodging, and many etceteras. When I asked him what else he did, he simply said, "I am everything," and although there may not have been much humility in the statement, I got the feeling that there was much truth to it, at least as far as the island of Texel is concerned.

Day 52: Foot, Bicycle, Taxi, Rental Car, Ferry, Bus, Train, but No Biplane

<u>Amsterdam, The Netherlands</u>

The morning began with a continuous light-to-medium rain shower. After breakfast it looked like it had quit for a while, so we went into town for some shopping and got completely soaked in a raging downpour on the way back, despite the umbrellas we just bought. It looked like a day that would never let us fly. And the airport manager agreed, saying that even if the weather would allow it, the runway conditions were just too soggy. Pause. However, he could guarantee that tomorrow would be better, saying that this was the worst weather for this time of year around here, ever.

This is the weekend; the hotels on this North Sea resort island are fully booked. If we are to be forced off the island, then the nearest large city is Amsterdam. We took a taxi to the rental car place and secured the last rental car on the island, an aging Peugeot station wagon with 147 thousand kilometers on the odometer, and no reverse gear. We drove this gem to the ferry and floated across the North Sea to the mainland, took a bus, then a train to the center of Amsterdam, then a taxi to the hotel on the "Dam," the center square of Amsterdam.

Amsterdam is the seedy underbelly of Europe. Activities that are illegal elsewhere are openly solicited in Amsterdam. Of course, there is the red light district, with shows both public and private. There are also all sorts of shops, bars and coffee houses where the sale and smoking of marijuana is legal. There is a certain section of the city that is reserved for the pursuit of these activities.

Where there is smoke, there is fire, so you can imagine what else is available without looking too hard. It didn't take me too long to find it: Guinness! And even better: Murphy's Irish Stout!

We stumbled on a place called Dirty Nelly's Irish Pub, just about a block to the right of The Grand Hotel Krasnapolsky, a 3-star (down from 4-star) shelter smack dab on the square (the "Dam"). Here I introduced Matthias to the smooth taste of Murphy's Stout, and he agreed it had some magical properties, capable of cooling one off and warming one up, as well as letting things go and putting them into perspective. And this is just with one pint! And we moved on...

Further exploration led us to Rick's Cafe (named after the bar in the movie Casablanca with Humphrey Bogart). This is my second time at Rick's Cafe, the first visit was almost 10 years ago, and nothing much has changed. It is the core of Amsterdam. Here a cappuccino with a shot of Jameson's Irish whiskey was the perfect protection from a cool North Sea breeze that freshened the early evening.

Here's a photo of Rick's Cafe, looking at it from a sidewalk table, across the cobblestone walkway, by the side of the canal.

And looking to the right is the Chinese restaurant where I almost died when I was last in Amsterdam. I piece of fowl got lodged in my input plumbing and I thought for the longest time what a comedy life is to choke to death on Peking Duck in a Chinese restaurant in Amsterdam. Did I struggle so hard, so long, for it to end this way? No way!

I learned more about Texel today. This great grass runway was the site of an American Airlines first. The first touch and go on grass by an American Airlines jet (Fokker F 100). The runway is over 5,000 feet long!

Tomorrow we'll walk to the taxi, then train, bus, ferry and rental car to the biplane, and maybe go fly. What an incredible thing is happening!

Day 53: Party Capital of the North Sea Islands

Borkum, Germany

The morning came prematurely, as all mornings-after do. My excesses of the night before were minor league compared to what most people in Amsterdam did, but for me a pint of Murphy's Irish Stout and a splash of Irish whiskey are about all I can handle if I want to fly the next day. I was restored to functional status by a couple of cups of coffee, a shower and a look out the window. It was a brilliant blue sky, just perfect for flying. All we had to do was retrace our steps from yesterday, using just about every mode of transportation known to modern man, except ski lift and space shuttle, and we would be back to our biplanes on Texel.

On the ferry back to Texel Island, I was fascinated with the gulls flying close to the ship, playing in the air currents and probably showing off and begging for scraps. I watched one of them for a long time, envying his consummate skill as an aviator, amazed at the incredible ways he would reconfigure his wings to suit the needs of the moment. It's easy to see how humans have looked at these birds for millions of years and longed to do the same thing. And it's only been for the last 90-some years that we have been able to do it. For me, only four years. Four of the most interesting, challenging and fulfilling years of my life. What a fantasy come true!

A light lunch at the restaurant, and a quick good-bye to the very friendly people (and a special thanks to the lovely and always smiling Janeke) at this world-class grass strip, and we were airborne. At 1,500 feet, looking down on Texel between some scattered mini cumulus, it was easy to see why this place is such a favorite of the Dutch. It's absolutely beautiful from the air.

Today's flight was one of those I'll remember for a long time. It was too brief, only 1.1 hours, but it was silky smooth air and we were following a chain of islands strung out before us like colorful beads on a necklace floating in the dark blue/gray North Sea. Over each island gathered a short line of cumulus clouds at around 3,000 feet, just perfect to go up and play among them.

Borkum Island is, like Texel, a favorite vacation spot for the people in the country. And like Texel, all rooms were booked. Only this time, we didn't have the good fortune to have the friendly services of Ed ("I am everything") de Bruijn to help find us the only room left on the island. We had to do it the old-fashioned way. We took a taxi to every hotel on Borkum, and one by one, got out to beg for a room. We were turned away each time, until one beach-front hotel finally had two rooms which they hardly ever rent, up in the attic of the hotel, with single beds under the very low sloping roof where the WC is across the hall from my room and the shower is down the hall. The ceiling slopes so low and so far into the room that only children's furniture can fit! I am hoping that I don't dream anything that would wake me up with a start because the ceiling is only a few inches away from my head when I'm sleeping. I suppose if I woke up quickly, I'd knock myself unconscious and never know it happened.

The beach here on Borkum is very wide, and filled with probably a thousand or more colorful little rental lounges, each of which is surrounded by a little wall of sand to mark off your private territory.

When we arrived at the beach at around 6 pm, there was already a major party going on, and they looked like they had been at it for a good while before we got there. There were various vendors selling all kinds of German beers, as well as sangria, vodka and tequila based drinks, and just about every kind of *wurst* you could ever imagine. The band that was playing then is still playing, five hours later, and they haven't taken a break yet. The only recognizable instrument in the band is the accordion, and every song sounds like the last one. These Germans are real party animals!

There is a lot of synchronized hand clapping while yelling "Hey, hey, hey, hey," singing along, beer swilling and wurst munching. The men rub their enormous bellies and give lecherous red-faced smiles to the not quite so ingenuous *frauleins* who encourage even more boisterous behavior.

Okay, guys, this isn't fun anymore. I'm going to need some sleep soon, or else I'm just going to have to get back out there again and show them how Irish people party. Yo! What's this? They just started yodeling! I'm going to do something I never thought I would do on this trip: I'm praying for rain!

The accordion is one of those instruments that need a lot of alcohol to appreciate; otherwise, it can drive you nuts. The beachfront here in Borkum has several large sanatoriums mixed in with the hotels. I'm wondering if this endless accordion music hasn't inspired some miraculous cures of people who devised their own recovery just to get away from these mind-numbing sounds. The ones who stay for more than a week are surely lobotomized without the need for all the messy surgery. One way or the other, there would be few complaints. I gotta get outta here!

If we can stay ahead of the weather front which is moving in from the west, we might be able to make it to Denmark and then Sweden, and who knows, maybe even the Arctic Circle and the land of the Midnight Sun. I wonder how many open-cockpit biplanes have flown north of the Arctic Circle. I have a friend in Umea, in the north of Sweden, and he says the weather is fine.

Day 54: A Walk On The Beach With Jessica

My request for rain, as a cure for excessive yodeling and accordion noise, was promptly fulfilled last evening. Unfortunately, it stuck around the entire evening, and most of today. I'm considering requesting just enough yodeling so we can take off and fly out of listening range.

I woke at 5:30 am to the sounds of high winds and rain slapping against the skylight/window in my slant-roofed cell in the attic of this 4-star hotel on the North Sea. I wasn't so much concerned about the rain as I was the high winds because unfortunately we did not tie the biplanes down yesterday. We thought we would go for an evening fly around the island, but it took so long to find a room, we didn't have the energy.

The winds continued to pick up, and when I was getting in the taxi to go to the airport, the wind slammed the door right out of my hands. We were dealing with winds of at least 35 knots, and we were wondering if we would find our planes where we left them, or if we would find them at all! But everything turned out just fine, they were still firmly planted on the grass parking area, looking as if nothing was the matter. We tied them down and retrieved a change of clothes for the day.

The rain stopped and the visibility was good enough to fly, but the winds continued at high levels and it would have been no fun at all to beat ourselves senseless in the air just to get someplace else. Since this was Sunday and some vacationers would be going home, freeing up some nice rooms, we could move out of our little half-rooms.

In search of the Internet, I was sent down to the hotel's conference room so I could send my e-mails through the hotel's only phone plug adaptable to a computer. Upon opening the door I was met with the loveliest sounds I have ever heard issue forth from a human being. And she was only warming up! Jessica Brinkmann was playing the piano in this large conference room, and practicing vocal scales. She had her back to the door, fully engrossed in her work, and never noticed my presence until my computer's speaker barked some very un-musical sounds to announce that I had e-mail. She stopped, and turned and acknowledged her audience with a smile, and I was surprised to notice that she was as lovely as her voice. I apologized for my computer's bad manners, and complimented her virtuosity, and she came over to check out the computer. After she had finished her practice for the day, I was stunned when she invited me to go for a walk on the beach.

Stunned, I say, because this wonderful child of only 20 years had pried out of me the fact that I am 2.7 times her age and yet would feel comfortable with that. And stunned also because the weather outside was definitely not what I would have chosen for a walk on the beach. It was a raging North Sea gale going on out there! But I'm a sucker for a pretty face, which I will share with you below. Here's Jessica, with her million-dollar throat swathed in several scarves:

Jessica will be a famous opera singer someday, I am sure of it, and you can say you heard about her here first. She has come to this remote island for two weeks vacation, alone, for the peace and quiet, and to practice. In real life, she also studies Economics at the university, works in food retailing, loves to ride horses and speaks English well. She also took me for a walk on the beach that assured me that the only thing on my mind would be sleep! A "walk" against a 35 knot wind, in wet soggy sand that sucks your feet down with fresh air forced down your lungs, sweating from the effort on the inside and chilled from the wet sea air on the outside, to me was more like the Bataan death march. And yet, strangely, it was fun. Young girls have a way of doing that!

Lunch after the walk was even more memorable, and considerably more civilized.

Some unfortunate news came our way today. Yesterday, at the air show in Oostende, Belgium, our stop of just a few days ago, a biplane didn't make it all the way through a low-level loop and found its way into a crowd of spectators, accelerating the ultimate adventure for eight spectators plus the pilot.

Day 55: Leap of Faith

<u>Copenhagen, Denmark</u>

Jessica Brinkmann joined Matthias and I for breakfast, then came to my room to see the photo I took of her (the one you have already seen in the e-mail). And then I showed her some of the other photos from the previous two months on the road. Soon it was her time to practice, and Matthias and I had to get in the air again, so it was time to say goodbye, but not after I stopped in to her practice session one more time to listen to this angel sing. She warmed up with a rendition of Die Pilgrimen auf Mecca by von Gluck and then just blew me away with Ah Spiegarti, Oh Dio by Mozart. At the end of her performance, a tear of joy squeezed itself past my defenses. She has an awesome gift.

We said goodbye again, traded addresses, promised to write and hugged. As the taxi pulled away, I could still hear her golden voice trailing off in the distance.

It wasn't until later that I finally realized what it is about Jessica that seems so familiar. She reminds me a lot of my youngest sister, Eileen.

At the airport in Borkum, there was no fuel. The truck hadn't made it across from the mainland yesterday, so we had to figure a destination within range of what we had left in our tanks. And speaking of fuel tanks, a minor miracle has happened. For the first time since the biplane was reassembled in Paris over 45 days ago, the left fuel tank gauge has decided to start working again. It is a float type device, and had been stuck solid. No amount of hammering would free it, and it has always been a minor pain to see it not working, even though any pilot in his right mind knows to never trust any fuel gauge. In any case, it is nice to see it working again.

What has decided to stop working is the radio. It hasn't quit altogether, but there is an awful lot of noise that seems to be caused by interference from the engine. When I turn off the right magneto, the noise stops. I'd rather have the magneto working and put up with the noise, but I'm going to be looking for some repairs soon.

With the limited fuel on board we decided to head for St. Michaelisdonn, Germany, a 90-mile jaunt skipping over a series of 10 islands in the North Sea along the north coast of Germany. We took off from the grass runway at Borkum and took a non-standard right turn to the coastline to avoid a large, dark and very active rain cloud passing nearby on our left. There were a lot of cumulus formations along the island chain, but the air was relatively smooth. What was surprising was the tailwind that pushed us along at over 120 knots.

When the last of the islands slipped past my wing, there was still about 30 miles to go across water with no landfall possible. This is the great leap of faith. If the engine stops, the biplane will be a total loss. And I will get very wet and cold, at best. There is something about crossing large bodies of water that spooks me. I know it shouldn't, it isn't rational. The engine has never quit on me, yet. The weather is clear and not likely to change during the crossing. So what's the problem? It's all in my head, of course, just like any problem. So I focus on the instruments, checking everything to be sure it's set right. Mixture leaned just right. Throttle set at 2,000 rpm. Artificial horizon set in harmony with the vertical speed indicator, just in case that gray/blue mass in front of me is a fat cloud instead of haze obscuring the other shoreline. Check that the life preserver is still stowed by my right shoulder. Alternator still working. Radio check. Compass heading and HSI in agreement. Nothing much to do except relax. I just let it go and enjoy the scenery: That big freighter pulling into the North Sea from the Elbe River, those whitecaps breaking on a sandbar, that buoy marking the channel. The other shoreline. And then it's all over. The engine never even coughed. The plane never knew the difference between over water and over land, it only knows it's in the air. It just kept on doing its job.

The tailwind delivered us to St. Michaelisdonn with such efficiency that we had enough fuel to keep on going. We decided to go straight north, for Flensburg, the northernmost airport on the mainland of Germany, just a stone's throw from the Denmark boarder. The decision to continue flying was made in the air, on the fly, so to speak. It always adds a bit more interest to a flight to land someplace other than where you planned when you started.

Matthias was in the lead going into Flensburg, but he got screwed up somehow and wound up across the border into Denmark, heading for an abandoned airfield. He discovered his mistake and found his way back to the real Flensburg. This was the first time Matthias has shown any flaw, no matter how slight, so it was good to see he is human after all. The winds were really howling by now, and the controller assigned us to runway 29, but the winds were coming from 250 degrees at 22 knots, gusting to 29. I noticed that there was a runway 22 and asked for that instead, thereby giving us 10 degrees less crosswind to deal with.

Matthias was still in the lead, and flew the right hand pattern for runway 22, which was grass, and a lot shorter than the other main runway. Matthias calls his turn to base, then final, and then "Hotel Bravo Uniform Papa Zulu, I can't see runway 22, and I'm going around to land on 29." That's the first time Matthias has gone around! What could be wrong? I could have sworn that I saw a runway aligned with 22 as I was turning downwind, how come he couldn't see it?

I soon found out as I turned toward final. Runway 22 starts out as a grass strip, then an asphalt taxiway cuts into it and becomes an integral part of it for a few hundred feet, then leaves the runway in another direction, and then the runway becomes all grass again. It is the weirdest looking runway I have ever seen from the air, and I'm really not sure I want to land on it, but the wind feels real strong, and I know I'm going to have more trouble on 29 than on this one, so I go for it, drop the biplane right on the approach end and roll out to a stop in no time at all, helped by the strong headwind. I'm on the ground and stopped while Matthias is still coming down final on 29, so I watch him come in for a very nice landing. Piece of cake! I guess it didn't make any difference which runway we used, but I think I had more fun on the weird runway.

We got a lift into town from another pilot, had some lunch, and walked back to the airport to refuel and file a flight plan for Copenhagen, Denmark. There were lots of billowy cumulus rain clouds in the sky, and the wind was really strong, but it was a shame to miss out on this strong of a tailwind going our way, so we decided to go for it.

The flight to Copenhagen was similar to the last leg, smooth and fast, but we had plenty of rain showers to keep us company this time. The big visual treat of this trip was looking down on the huge new suspension bridge being built between Nyborg and Korsor that will finally connect the major landmasses of Denmark for rail and auto traffic.

As we neared our destination airport of Roskilde, we were racing a long line of rain showers. I felt we would get around in front of the rain and be able to land, but thought we would quickly get drenched while tying the planes down and dealing with baggage. We were lucky, and never caught a drop of rain.

On final approach at Roskilde, there was a major crosswind and I had to keep almost all the right rudder I could manage just to stay straight. But what is this? It looks like there are some papers blowing across the runway, from right to left. But that doesn't make sense because the wind is blowing from the left. My visual clues and my physical senses are not agreeing with each other. And then, bingo! That's not paper; they are birds! Birds can do what they want, paper goes with the wind. Problem solved. The landing went smoothly, at first, but when I got on the ground the crosswind pushed me all the way to the right of the runway before I could get it stopped. Good practice.

We arrived at Roskilde a bit early. The town is having its 1,000th (one thousandth!) birthday next year. This town was a favorite place for Danish kings and queens to be buried, there being 38 of them lying in various places in town. It looks like a really nice place to visit and I would like to spend some time here someday, but right after we landed all I wanted to do was get a taxi to Copenhagen and get a shower and a good meal.

The best dinner in Copenhagen wound up on my plate tonight, I'm sure. The Danish have something in common with the French: great sauces! I highly recommend the restaurant named Leonore Christine at #9 Nyhavn.

And what's going on with the spelling of these city names anyway? These people spell their city "København" not Copenhagen. So why do we spell it the way we do? Of course, they also put a funny little slant through the "o" in København, and I'm not so sure why they feel the need for that. Oh, well, new country, new money, new Internet access number, new customs, new language, etc.

And speaking of customs: As I was building my breakfast at the buffet table this morning in Borkum, a lady was giggling and laughing and having a grand old time, all the while talking German to me and pointing to the toaster I was using. I told her I didn't speak German, only English, and since she didn't, she just went away laughing. When I got back to the table, new friend Jessica started laughing too. It seems that I was stupid enough to toast brown bread. It just isn't done in Germany!

Day 56: Aliens!

Roskilde, Denmark

A knock on my door woke me up early this morning. It was Matthias, looking grim. He had received news that his mother, who has been very sick for a couple of months, has taken a turn for the worse. He has decided he will fly his biplane home to Zurich today. I shower quickly and join him for a somber breakfast downstairs. There's just not much to say at a time like this. It's a call he's got to make on his own. I sure would like to keep flying along with him, but he plans to make the flight to Zurich in one day, and at the speeds we fly, and the headwinds, it would be more than six hours in the air, a real grind in an open-cockpit biplane. So it looks like we will be parting company here in Copenhagen. I take a taxi back to the airport at Roskilde with him to see him off. My plan is to hang out in Copenhagen for a day or so, and then continue into Sweden.

In the taxi, his cell phone rings. It's Nici, his wife, who tells him not to try to get back right away, that being there by the weekend will be best. So the pressure to hammer out the miles is off, and we work out a plan to fly together for another couple of days.

We wanted to fly into Sweden, but there are no airport directory books available for Sweden in English available at the pilot shop here. We could make photocopies of some airports, but it wouldn't be the right approach. Another bug in the plan is Customs. It is available only with 24-hour notice at the smaller airports, so it's not an option for today. The bigger airports are not interesting to us. So that leaves us nowhere; at least, not in Sweden for today. Unless...

We have noticed that when we get to an airport without filing a flight plan they just ask us where we are from, we tell them, and that's all there is to it. We figure that if we didn't file the obligatory flight plan (needed for inter-country flights), and just landed at an airport that wasn't expecting us to be coming in from another country, then we could easily tell them that we were coming from another airport within the country. Foolproof! So we could fly out of Roskilde, tell them we are going for a local flight, or to another uncontrolled airport, and then fly over to Sweden, land at some little grass strip, like Hoganas for example, and simply tell them we are coming in from, say Eslov, or wherever. How could they possibly know the difference, and why would they even care? This is all starting to make very good sense, and the idea of being an international fugitive, and an illegal alien in a biplane... well it's kind of exciting!

We map out a local flight which will take us in a circular path, northeast from Roskilde along the west shore of the Isefjord, then northeast along the coast of the Nyrup Bugt, the local bay of the much larger Kattegat (you do have an atlas for all this, right?), all the way to the northernmost tip at Gilleleje, then southeast along the coast of the Oresund until we get to the Copenhagen airport Traffic Control Zone, then head back to Roskilde via the VFR corridor.

The essential element in our plan is that we do not miss our turn southeast at Gilleleje, because if we do, then we will continue across the water just a few miles to

Sweden, and the beautiful little grass strip airport at Hoganas. And of course that would be illegal without filing a flight plan, and requesting Customs clearance 24 hours in advance. We couldn't do this no matter how bad we wanted to land in Sweden, and even though we would be heading south of Germany tomorrow, and not back this way for a long time, we just shouldn't, mustn't, fly over the line between Denmark and Sweden, which is just a little more than a mile from this lovely little green grass strip of perfection sitting on a point of land jutting out into the sea. No, it would just be the wrong thing to do...

I gave Matthias my camera, so he could take a few photos of my favorite biplane in the air, just in case anything interesting happened.

We took off in formation, into a gusting 11 knot headwind and turned northwest to the shoreline, where we met up with some lower scattered-to-broken cumulus that looked just right to play with, so I radioed to Matthias to let's go upstairs where the air was smoother and the sights were better. Here's what it looked like:

We played up on top for a while, keeping our bearings from time to time by looking at the shoreline between the broken clouds. When we had enough we dropped down through another hole and popped out over... well, I'll be darned, it was Sweden! We must have stayed up on top just a little too long! Gosh, this means that we are here illegally, and we better get out of here and back into Denmark airspace right away. But wait a minute, look down there; it's that perfect little grass strip at Hoganas! And there isn't a plane anywhere in sight. Why it's just begging for a couple of neat old biplanes to come and tickle the grass. It would be downright unfriendly to refuse. But it would also be illegal. Unless a guy had some engine trouble, then he could land there in an emergency. And if the engine trouble cleared up right away, then it would be okay to take off again! Some aviation laws leave gray areas and loopholes. Hmm. The engine does seem to be running a bit rough...

Can you see the two intersecting grass runways in the photo above? Can you see the shadow of a Waco on one of them? It would be difficult to prove that it is *my* shadow.

It was a great flight!

Day 57: Future Aviators

<u>Gromitz, Germany</u>

The sky was so blue and clear this morning, I just couldn't wait to get to the airport and fly. However, nothing in aviation happens very quickly, so it took more than three hours to go through the morning shower/shave ritual, eat breakfast, pack, taxi to the airport, remove the tie downs, load the baggage, refuel, add oil, pay for the landing fees, get the weather, file a flight plan, select the charts, preflight, and then sit at the end of the runway and wait while half a dozen other planes take off and land ahead of us.

I am dragging you through all of this drudgery so that you will more fully enjoy the bright spot in the middle of it all. While we were refueling, two young boys stood watching us from about 100 feet away. It was obvious that they were fascinated with our biplanes, possibly never having seen such flying machines before. But while they were very attracted by the planes, they seemed very timid about coming much closer. So after a few minutes of watching them watch the biplanes, and us, I waved hello to them, and they half-waved back, still very shy.

I waved again, this time with a "Come on over and see the planes" kind of wave. They stepped closer, still wary, and whispered between themselves, walking around the biplanes and pointing. "Do you speak English?" I asked. The redheaded boy shakes his head no. "Do you like airplanes?" I asked. "Oh yes" he says. (It seems like he does understand and speak English after all!)

I was pouring cans of oil into my biplane, so I asked Matthias to help them get into my cockpit, one at a time, so they could see what it's like in there. First to get in was Mikkel, and it sure seemed that he enjoyed it. Then I said to the redheaded kid, "Okay, you're next!" and he shakes his head NO WAY! Now I have seen enough young boys hanging around this biplane to know that when they say NO it really means OH BOY! So Matthias helps Christian up on the wing, then into the cockpit, but instead of putting his first leg on the seat, he puts it on the floor, and falls way down in, leaving only his trailing leg sticking up out of the cockpit! We all got a great laugh out it. What a great picture that would have been, but I didn't have my camera ready. Here's a photo of Christian, aviator of the future, loving every minute of it:

I think we made a couple of Danish kids happy this morning because after Matthias and I came back from the airport office where we paid for the fuel, they came up to us and gave us each a set of decals, four different sizes, with the logo of the local flying club. What a great present! We thanked them profusely, making a big deal of it, and asked them to be sure to watch our formation takeoff.

And so it was that when Matthias and I charged down the runway, side by side in our magnificent open-cockpit biplanes at Roskilde airport in Denmark, there were two little boys sitting by the side of the runway watching our every move. And you just know, that when our wheels lifted up off the asphalt and our planes climbed into the air, that those two little hearts were beating faster and their spirits went flying with us, and stayed with us until we turned south and disappeared into the distance.

Matthias and I figured we would head back into Germany, a town called Lubeck, northeast of Hamburg. The weather today was perfect, but a storm front was moving in from the west and it was forecast that we would not be flying tomorrow, so we wanted to be in a big city for our day on the ground. But for today at least, we are on the beach here in Gromitz, a sleepy little seaside community where we drove in our rented BMW Z-3 roadster, red of course, with the top down.

We did a lot of over-water flying today, and I made a wrong turn, but discovered my error before too long. Everyone has made a wrong turn in a car and thinks nothing of it, but when it's done in an airplane, it seems a lot more unacceptable for some reason. Maybe it was because I was focused on taking some pictures, or just rubbernecking at all the great scenery and just forgot to navigate, or I lost track of which island I was overflying.

There was no harm done, I had plenty of fuel and there was almost zero traffic in the sky. In fact, we saw only one other airplane in two hours of flying.

Today was a day for play. We cruised a lot of coastline today, getting down low on the water, buzzing deserted beaches and uninhabited islands, and then pulling up in sharp climbing turns before we got too close to signs of civilization. I just love the look and feel of my biplane in a hard climbing turn. The angle of the wings against the horizon, the feel of the G-forces as I pull back on the stick, the way the surf and sand slip away below me, the rush of the air, the pull of the big, round engine as I give it full throttle. Best of all, I know what effect this has on people who see it from the ground. It is pure poetry in motion, a startling maneuver, yet gentle and sweet as a whisper in the breeze.

It was just this sort of maneuver that stole my breath away when I first saw it done by a biplane, over the beach, in front of my window, almost 15 years ago. And when my breath returned, and I realized that I had just experienced a moment of Destiny, I whispered a promise to myself: "Someday. Someday I will do that!" I wonder if young Christian said something like that today.

Day 58: The GPS Of The Future

<u>Hamburg, Germany</u>

The weather didn't look too bad this morning in Gromitz, even though the forecast from yesterday called for unflyable conditions. So we kept our options open, planning to drive back south to Lubeck and check on our biplanes, and if the weather still looked good, we would take to the air.

Today was my turn to drive our rental Beemer Z-3, and I had the opportunity to get it up to speed on the Autobahn. A fine piece of machinery it is, but underpowered, and way too much wind noise with the top up. Other than that it's hard to find fault with it. It's red, the top goes down, and it's reliable and good looking, in a Teutonic way. What's not to like?

The weather in Hamburg was as forecast. It was the kind of low ceiling that turns the day dark. It rained on and off the entire day, so we didn't get a chance to do much walking around except for a short tour of the high-rent district stores. It was a perfect afternoon for a nap.

We found our way around yesterday and today with the help of Matthias' brand new handheld Garmin 195 GPS, the same one he uses in his plane. It's an incredible piece of equipment. The most amazing thing about it is that its moving map shows, in amazing detail, all of the land features such as rivers and lakes and cities as well as main highways and railroads. It cost about one fifth of what I paid four years ago for my then state-of-the-art panel-mounted GPS/Moving Map system that shows no topographical features at all.

Technology is really moving fast in this area. While dozing off for my nap, I fantasized about what the GPS of the future would do for aviators. Of course, it will have voice output capabilities, just like the GPS in our rental Mercedes from a couple of weeks ago, so it will be able to give you hints as you are flying along allowing you to keep your eyes outside the cockpit where they belong. Here's a sample conversation with the GPS of the future:

"Hello, (pilot name), sorry to interrupt your concentration on the scenery, but we are (user-selectable) miles from your destination, and you should throttle back now to achieve a decent rate of XXX feet per minute to arrive at pattern altitude before turning downwind. I can load your radios with ATIS and Tower frequencies if you like. (Click the joystick button once for Yes, twice for No)."

"According to my information the wind speed is XX knots from XXX degrees (calculated from the airspeed and heading of the airplane) so the runway in use should be XX, please click once to okay this selection.

"Thank you, (pilot name). Please notice the displaced threshold on this runway.

On final approach, the GPS could take the pilot through his own checklist for gear down (in a biplane?), mixture setting, etc. Even this:

"I'm picking up some gusting crosswind conditions, (pilot name), so you might want to add XX knots airspeed to compensate."

"Stick back, oops too much, lower the nose a bit. Nice job, now some more stick-back. You're a bit slow here, give it some throttle, trim, okay fine, just let it settle down. Keep your (right/left) wing down into the wind and keep it straight with (left/right) rudder. Touchdown! I rate that landing X (on a scale of 0 to 10), and your average is X, so you are doing a bit (better/worse) than usual. Shall I add this rating to your log when I update your logbook?"

"You have never been to this airport before, so I would suggest that you refuel at (FBO name) which has the brand of fuel you prefer and takes your credit cards. The X-star (user selectable) hotel closest to the airport is (hotel name); shall I make a reservation? I arranged for your rental car while you were busy on downwind, and it is waiting for you.

"Very nice job, (pilot name). It has been a real pleasure flying with you today. Be sure to unplug me and take me with you so I can guide you to your hotel."

Later, in the rental car:

"Hello again, (pilot name), good to be with you again. Thanks for plugging me in to this 2001 Ferrari F50; it's one of my favorite cars. This one has a tendency to pull left under heavy braking (information taken from the on-board computer in the car), but otherwise, everything else is working fine. Turn right out of the parking lot and then left at the stop sign. Would you like to stop and pick up some flowers for (girlfriend name, depending upon current city)?"

And then I woke up!

Day 59: Unplanned Landing in Communist Territory

<u>Nordhausen, East Germany</u>

I had more fun behind the wheel of the Z-3 this morning on the Autobahn from Hamburg to Lubeck. What a great idea: No speed limit! Actually there are speed limits on the Autobahns, but only in congested areas around larger cities. The rest of the time it's just a free for all!

It was raining in Hamburg this morning, so we took our time getting out of the hotel (Hotel Steinenberger, really excellent). We did our typical formation takeoff from Lubeck in the early afternoon, and the sky was already showing major sections of blue, so we figured it was going to be an easy flight south to Leipzig. NOT!

It was clear and smooth for a while and I had a chance to get real low over some farmlands, and see and smell the countryside up close. But it didn't last very long. Here's a photo of Matthias' plane, with lake, farmlands and some low clouds, before the sky fell even more.

We didn't get far before a large, dark rain cloud formed on our right, so we deviated left from our course for several more miles. Then we came upon an even larger and darker rain cloud to our left. Both of these masses were raining very hard, and visibility was zero all the way down to the ground. There was no way we could get over them. The only solution was to turn around, or go for the lighter slim alley between them. We went for the light. Even then we were hit with considerable rain, and I kept looking over my shoulder to make sure that we could turn around if the way ahead was blocked.

We kept flying like this for another hour and a half, dodging around or between angry looking local storms, but all the time we were being forced to deviate to the west. Soon, Leipzig was no longer an option. The storms were pushing us up over the mountains to the west of Leipzig, so we started looking for an alternate. Matthias' GPS showed an airport 20-plus miles more to the west, but I was concerned we might head into another storm since the weather was coming from that direction. I opted to land at the nearest opportunity, a little grass strip only eight miles ahead, where it was clear at the moment. Our info showed that no fuel was available at this strip, so we agreed that we would just land and wait out the storms, continuing when (if) it cleared up later in the day.

We were fortunate to find this grass strip. The runway was perfectly aligned with the wind, which was really kicking up at the time we landed. It was even a good bit uphill so the wind helped us roll to a stop quickly. And that was a good thing too because the runway was pretty bumpy.

We pulled off to the side of the runway and waited. On the other side of the field were half a dozen people and two gliders, taking turns launching their gliders with the rope winch. Soon a couple of them came over to inspect our biplanes.

One of our hosts was an attractive young lady named Katrin Breitrueck, an aeronautical engineering student at the University of Stuttgart who holds licenses in gliders and motor gliders. Last summer, she flew with a friend from Canada to Florida. She was here on break from school, for a week of gliding fun with some friends who were members of the local flying club. She speaks English well and was very enthusiastic about the biplanes, mentioning that it reminded her of Richard Bach's book, "Biplane."

Today was a big occasion for one of the members of the local flying club. It was his day to do his three solo flights, after which he gets his solo glider license. We watched all three and he made flawless landings each time. Good show. Afterwards, there was a party in his honor, and Matthias and I were invited to attend. It's the custom around these parts that when someone achieves their solo privileges, they must be paddled on the butt while holding a large handful of sticker-weeds!

I like our customs better. When I soloed in gliders, they only dumped water on my head, which I really appreciated because it was such a hot day.

It didn't look to me like the weather was going to get much better, so we decided to stay over in Nordhausen. One of the members of the flying club offered us a ride into town (of about 50,000 inhabitants), and to the "good" hotel.

It wasn't until we were in the car and driving through town that I noticed that something seemed different about this place. I couldn't put my finger on it right away, but it finally dawned on me that this town was in the former East Germany, only 12 kilometers from the border. Until only 10 years ago, this was Communist territory, and these people had none of the freedoms that we take for granted.

There was still some evidence of the old ways. I saw my first Trabant automobile, if you can call it that. It is one of the worst cars ever made, and went out of business soon after quality cars became available when the Berlin wall came down. Somehow, it was still clunking along, but just barely, and it was the only one I saw on the road.

The hotel was a pleasant surprise. I was expecting some real dingy digs, but this place had been completely gutted and totally refurbished. Everything about it was new and first class, a complete turnaround from the days of Communist rule.

If we are lucky, the weather tomorrow morning will be good and we may make it as far as Matthias' home airport in Donaueschingen, Germany, just north of Zurich Switzerland.

Day 60: Runway Snake!

<u>Zurich, Switzerland</u>

While waiting for the weather to clear so we could take off, we took a taxi tour of Nordhausen (Germany) to learn more about the place. We found out that Nordhausen was a separate nation/state from 1220 to 1802, and then became part of Germany. It was the third largest city in East Germany, behind Berlin and Dresden. We talked with several people in town about how their lives were affected by the end of the Cold War and the reunification of Germany. The general consensus is that people are having a hard time adjusting to the new scheme of things. There are lots more choices in the stores, but they don't have the money to buy the stuff. Under the old system, the government had everyone working, and earning a wage they could (barely) live on. They could depend on the government, but they didn't like it because they had no freedom. Now, they have the freedom, but not the money to go with it and they have to depend on themselves, not the government. Although it is challenging, they prefer the new way.

We arrived at the airport at Nordhausen as it was clearing to the south. We needed fuel (there is none at Nordhausen) so we planned to go just a short distance to Erfurt. The sky conditions were marginal, flyable but not great. We figured that we would make it to Erfurt, a meteorological service, and we could get a better idea of the weather en-route to Donaueschingen, about 200 miles to the south.

The flight was an easy one, and after landing, we took on fuel, lunch and the latest weather information. The lady at the weather info desk, after learning of our hoped-for destination, suggested that we would enjoy staying in right where we were! The flying conditions were classified as "Difficult" and indicated that we would have a probability of rain, drizzle and ceilings as low as 500 feet. Not a pretty picture.

Matthias has flown this territory before and he is familiar with the accuracy of these weather forecasts, and his suggestion was that we go fly and have a look. The conditions at Erfurt were good, even considering the towering cumulus in the area. We could see at least six miles in the direction we wanted to go, so we went for it.

It turned out to be one of those dream flights where everything went amazingly well. As we crossed over each new range of hills, it looked as if we might hit a wall of clouds and have to divert. The closer we got the more the clouds parted and let us through. Only once did we hit rain, and it was negligible. When we hit ceilings that were too low over the mountains we were crossing, we simply sidestepped into a valley running in the direction we needed to go. It seemed just too simple and I was waiting for things to go wrong at any moment, but for some strange reason, they didn't.

I never thought we would make it 30 miles on this trip, but we completed the entire 200-plus miles without much more than a few bumps. In fact, because of the solid overcast, it was quite smooth.

Here's a photo I snapped showing a rare patch of sunshine far out on the horizon off my right wing, and the very low overcast that we flew just below, so as to have enough ground clearance to avoid any surprises by radio towers lurking in the reduced visibility.

When we got within a few miles of our destination and I could see that we weren't going to get hit with some last minute rain shower, I had to keep myself from getting too excited about our good luck. "It ain't over, till it's over," I kept telling myself. In fact, all my troubles came at the end.

My landing was disgusting. For some reason, I got myself so completely out of shape that I actually started laughing at my predicament at the same time I was struggling to regain control. There was never a moment when it was dangerous, just very strange and awkward, a ridiculous landing for someone who has performed this delicate maneuver over 1,600 times. You would think I would have it down by now. And I really can't say why it was so bad. The wind wasn't that bad, but there is always the chance of a rogue gust that comes out of nowhere and humiliates even the best of pilots.

When the driver of a car winds up in the weeds or hits a parked car, he usually claims that he swerved to avoid an animal (long gone by the time the police show up). And so, when a pilot's landing is less than adequate, it is sometimes blamed on a "runway snake." Yeah, that's the ticket! It was a runway snake, and a big sucker, he was!

Donaueschingen, Germany is where Matthias hangars his Waco. It's about 90 minutes by car from his home in Zurich, Switzerland. Tonight, both of our biplanes are safe and snug in his big hangar. Matthias' wife, Nici, drove out to pick us up and drive us back to their home outside Zurich. We weren't 10 minutes away from the airport when the sky went dark, the clouds reached the ground and it rained like mad. How lucky can you get?

Day 61: Rest and Reflection

Zurich, Switzerland

Today is a day of rest — a welcome break from life on the road, living out of a suitcase, eating hotel and restaurant food, flight planning, flying, making decisions. Today, I can do my laundry, organize my navigation charts, update my airport info books and make lists of all the stuff I need.

Matthias is back home with his wife and son, and it's good to see them together again. He is great with little Hendrik, very loving, gentle and patient. They have just returned from a visit with Matthias' mother, who is very sick, and the reason why Matthias has cut short his flying vacation. Hendrik is asleep now, Nici has gone swimming, and Matthias is tending to some things around the house. The sun is shining through broken cumulus clouds and big jets are passing low overhead on final approach to Zurich airport just a couple of miles away. Except for the occasional jet, it's quiet around here right now. Tonight, Nici and Matthias will have another couple over for dinner (so I'll eat well again).

All in all, I am in the middle of a typical picture of a typical home lived in by a typical family doing all of the typical things they do on a typical Sunday. When I am flying above the cities and farms and looking down on all of the homes below me, this is the way it is with them, living their lives in quiet anonymity and relative peace, loving and sharing, and yet not without their daily challenges of hardship, illness and death. All of these experiences are happening below my wings, and I know it, but I do not know of it. The great tapestry of life is unfolding below me, and to the participants in this great play it is the totality of life, their life, but to me it is just another passing town, just another rooftop, or the shape of a car in some long line on a highway waiting for a light to change.

From their perspective, my biplane is possibly just a vague noise overhead, or a shadow that crosses their lawn, just another airplane going somewhere. There is no thought of the pilot, the human being at the controls. I am as anonymous to them as they are to me. We are lost in each other's lives of the moment. We mean nothing to each other. It is as if we never existed at all.

Only rarely is there any connection between us. Sometimes, I will look down on an ancient castle perched on top of a hill, or a sailboat running with the wind, or a family cooking on a fire in their back yard, and I will think about their lives and wonder how it is with them. Just as, sometimes, I know they see my biplane and wonder what it must be like to fly such a wondrous machine, or to fly at all! Such connections are for the most part fleeting, and the real world quickly returns. The father in his backyard must turn the meat on his barbecue, the sailor must tighten a line, the lord in his castle must order his drink, and I must turn back to my original heading. And we are again alone in our worlds. And so it goes.

Once in a great while, there are the exceptions to this humdrum noise of life. Once in a great while, I will meet some special person whose eyes light up with an inner beauty and it seems to me that we have known each other from another lifetime, or how else could there be such a strong recognition between us. It is for these moments that we all live, it seems to me. It is for these rare connections, a smile or touch or glance or brief word of knowing, a spark or chemical reaction, a remembrance of long ago. I wish I could collect these rare people and keep them for later, to get to know them better, to find out more about why we have made such a connection, regardless how brief it is. But all too soon, I am gone again — a brief encounter, a bittersweet meeting and then separation.

I have thoughts that all of Europe has been preparing itself for my brief visit, the Alps have been growing for millions of years, the people have been building their castles and bridges and towns, having their wars and babies. And now I am here, and now I am gone. I'm a solitary bee, visiting a few flowers in the field, impossible to sample them all, too little time, too many flowers.

But for today, I rest.

Day 62: Preparations

Donaueschingen, Germany

I woke up late, still in the spirit of rest from yesterday. The weather just begged to for me to go flying, but it was not to be. Today was reserved for repairs to the biplane. The radios have been giving me a lot of trouble with noise. It's not the sort of thing that would cause me to cancel a flight until they are repaired, but it is a nuisance.

Matthias has a mechanic at his home field. He is one of those special people who just cannot say "No" to a request for help. And since Matthias asked him to look at my radios, I have the services of a first-class mechanic who is also familiar with the Waco YMF-5. He is probably the only one with experience with this airplane on this continent, so I should take advantage of his availability while I can get him.

I drove the 90 minutes to Donaueschingen in Nici's Toyota, only getting slightly lost once. Mike, the mechanic, got down to business quickly and found a ground wire that was "kaput," and fixed it. While he was working on it, I asked him if he could help me with an oil change, and of course he said yes. I have flown more than 50 hours since the last oil change, so it is in serious need of some new oil. And when Mike had everything buttoned up, I pushed my luck a bit and asked him if he knew anyone who could wash my plane, which was revoltingly filthy. True to his reputation, Mike just couldn't say "No," and jumped right in with the help of his daughter, Trina.

Now my biplane is looking good and running good. Further preparations included scoping out the charts needed for the next trip and getting together all of the information needed, such as which airports have Customs, when they are open, on what frequencies, if there are any active military areas along the way, is fuel and food available, what is the distance to the next stop and the weather, etc., etc.

I have gone through this ritual of preparations many times before, and I know that any one of a thousand different things can occur, usually at the last moment, which will change the most carefully detailed plan. It has been suggested that a pilot should expect to not fly right up to the moment when his plane lifts into the air, and then to be pleasantly surprised when it actually happens, but only momentarily, because from that moment on he should then be expecting his airplane to quit running at any moment and have to execute an emergency landing.

This seems to be a painfully negative view of flying, but the pilot who thinks this way will sooner or later be right, and therefore, prepared for the situation. My approach is to prepare as fully as possible for each flight, and see it through to completion before I fly, actually visualizing the entire flight including the landing. This way, I am usually right compared with the pessimist's approach of being usually wrong. Therefore, we will only know who is right when things go wrong, but if things don't go wrong, who is right?

Day 63: Tribute To Lowell Williams

<u>Donaueschingen, Germany</u>

All of the previous day's preparations came to naught today. While every step in the process leading up the flight was carefully executed, my timing and the weather conspired to keep me on the ground.

For a variety of reasons, we got a late start on the 90-minute drive from Zurich Switzerland, where I have been staying at the home of Matthias and Nici, to Donaueschingen, Germany, where my biplane is hangared.

While we were driving north to the airport, we could see the sky change from a calm, clear blue to an ever-darker mass of cumulo-nimbus clouds. Some hope still remained that I could make it into the air because the clouds were mainly to the north, and I wanted to go west, but when I got the meteorological reports from the control tower, I decided not to go.

I remember very clearly the look on the face of my flight instructor, Lowell Williams, when we discussed weather. Lowell is a WWII P-51 Mustang fighter pilot, an ace, and even at the age of 75 still teaches aerobatics every day, and in my opinion is one of the best pilots alive. And when he talks about weather, he is very clear on the subject. It's one thing you don't play around with.

I'm a very conservative pilot when it comes to weather. When I make a "No-Go" decision, I feel very good about it. I consider it to be an opportunity to do the right thing, not as a lost flight. To me, it's a tribute to Lowell Williams. I would much rather be on the ground than in the air, if being in the air means dealing with deadly thunderstorms, gusting high winds, reduced visibility and low ceilings. That kind of stuff is just not fun, and if it's not fun then why fly?

I'll stay in a hotel here in Germany tonight, and get an early start tomorrow, before the heat of the day brings more trouble in the sky.

Day 64: Stress Test

Rheims, France

Late yesterday afternoon, I helped Matthias wash his plane, then shook his hand and said "Thank You!" for being such a great wingman for the past several weeks. He is extremely knowledgeable about the various customs and procedures regarding flying in Europe, and he can speak several languages. He has been a terrific help, and I'm going to miss his companionship as well. Now I'm on my own. Here's the man and his machine:

Today, I was up at 7 am for an early start, the necessary ingredient to go flying before the heat of the day spawned unwelcomed thunderstorms. Everything went according to plan this time. I took off from Donaueschingen, Germany into a light wind with a high ceiling at more than 10,000 feet, more than enough to allow me to cross the mountains to the west at only 4,500 feet. The first part of the flight went very well.

However, things got plenty stressful when I crossed the border into France at Colmar. This part of France is crisscrossed with lots of restricted military areas which should not be entered without first contacting the controlling authority on the radio. And that was the problem. My radios. They have developed an increasingly bad noise problem that is intermittent. I had a mechanic check them out, and he found a loose ground, but it hasn't cured the problem. I can still transmit perfectly well, but hearing clearly is sometimes difficult. When you add to this the already difficult time I have with foreign languages and accents, and my lack of familiarity with the convoluted airspace and the general topology, you get a scenario which is just about as nasty as I have had to deal with.

For the entire duration of the flight from Colmar to Rheims, about 90 minutes, I was switched back and forth between various controllers, both military and civilian, close to two dozen times. Each time I had to get used to a different accent, some of which were just plain unintelligible, and more than once, I just told them where I was and where I was going, period. I got tired of saying "Say Again?" I left it up to them to deal with it. I figured that if I was committing some horrible violation of their airspace they would scream at me, so without hearing anyone screaming, I just kept on going while keeping an eye out for hot-rod fighter jets.

Several times in the flight, I had to change course around some clouds that were building up into thunderstorms, or climb up over them, and I'm sure that gave the controllers fits trying to keep track of me. I probably had every controller in western France rerouting traffic around "that crazy American biplane pilot."

Within 60 miles of Rheims, the clouds started to form below my altitude, going from just a few clouds when I started out, to a scattered base in the middle of the flight, to a thick broken layer close to my destination. When I got within 20 miles of Rheims, I figured I had to get under the clouds right away, or I wouldn't be able to get down further on. I chose a hole and dived into it, losing 4,000 feet in little over a minute. What a rush! The visibility was excellent and the air was cool on top of the clouds, but when I popped out underneath, it was a shock to see how poor the visibility had become, and the air was hot and humid.

For the next 20 miles, I was bumping along at only 1,200 feet above the ground, looking out for towers in the murky unstable air, while trying to stay on course and keep in communication on the Rheims information frequency. At the very last possible moment, the runway appeared right off my left wing, and I was in perfect position for a short, left base entry. Although I had already been cleared for landing (I was the only one in the pattern), I was probably a little too greedy to get down fast so I pulled the power and put the Waco into a radical slip to lose altitude, but it wasn't going to happen fast enough, so I fire-walled the throttle and went around, this time doing it right, and touched down gently for a sweet ending to a stressed-out flight.

Rheims is a great city. My first stop was the cathedral to say thanks for my safe arrival. This awesome, yet unfinished, cathedral was built in 1211 and has been the site of the coronation of every French king, except two, since they started having kings in the 10th century.

The photo above is the center city carousel (unusual for its double-decker architecture) that kept me company during lunch.

The area surrounding Rheims is Champagne territory, so I had the chance to tour the Taittinger Champagne cellars. Here they have three million bottles stored in limestone caves that were originally built by the monks who first developed "champagne." The highlight of the tour, of course, was the complimentary glass of Taittinger bubbly. Yummy stuff!

There are more than enough champagne bottlers here in Rheims to keep me busy with tours and free samples for a week. So this is one time I won't be too disappointed to see rain in the forecast. And the food is absolutely superb. Tonight's dinner was the best meal in weeks.

The forecast, by the way, is for rain tomorrow, but clear and sunny on Friday. If things go as planned, I'll be crossing the English Channel soon.

Day 65: Why Am I Here?

<u>Rheims, France</u>

Yesterday's forecast of a rainy Rheims didn't come true. It was a great day here, but the forecast of rain on the north coast of France, my destination, was accurate, so I wouldn't have been flying anyway. It would have been a perfect day to sleep late, and then go sightseeing and champagne tasting, but I felt that I should spend some time with my flight manuals and charts. I didn't feel comfortable with my last flight, and I thought I could use some more preparation and review of the airspace.

If things work out with the weather tomorrow, I may go for the English Channel crossing, and since it's another international border, it will require just that much more planning. So while the rest of the visitors to Rheims were enjoying a spectacular summer day, I was stuck in my room with lots of charts, papers and books, making phone calls, and figuring out how to deal with the various governmental aviation agencies involved.

Here's an example of tomorrow's flight notes:

Get last minute weather information for current conditions and forecast for destination airport and en-route reporting locations.

File flight plan.
Refuel plane.
Complete preflight inspection.

Set altimeter to Rheims (Prunay) field elevation of 312 feet.
Set Radio 1 to 118.05 Rheims (Prunay) Information.
Set Radio 1 (standby) to 129.12 Le Touquet ATIS.
Set Radio 2 to 119.80 Rheims (Champagne) Approach.
Set Radio 2 (standby) to 120.37 Lille Approach.

Set GPS destination to Rheims (Champagne) VOR.

Take off Rheims (Prunay) runway 25 or 7, depending on winds.
Runway 25, turn right immediately to 269 degrees to avoid noise sensitive area.
Then turn right to heading of 070 degrees.
Take Runway 7 for straight out departure.
Climb to 1,300 feet.
Intercept 305 degree radial of Rheims (Champagne) VOR and turn left along radial.

Call Rheims (Champagne) Approach on radio frequency 119.80; announce intention to overfly their airport at 1,000 feet AGL.
Set transponder code assigned by Approach.
Call Rheims (Champagne) Approach again on 119.80 when at reporting point "Sierra One," 7 miles from airport on 305 degree radial.

Navigate between two tall radio towers (925' and 1083'... I'm at 1,300') on the way from "Sierra One" and "Sierra Two."

Call Rheims (Champagne) Approach again on 119.80 when at reporting point "Sierra Two," 2.3 miles from airport on 305 degree radial.

Follow instructions from Rheims Approach until out of the area.

Reset GPS for Le Touquet airport, turn to new heading.
Contact Lille Approach on 120.37; advise them of my destination, altitude, and request info on any active military areas.

Climb to 4,400 feet to fly over or under various restricted airspace along the way, but moving to the left or right of other airspace that may be active, depending on advice of Lille Approach. At the same time, alter course as needed to stay clear of any clouds along the way, and then try to get back on course.

Call Le Touquet ATIS for weather, runway, and wind info on 129.12.
At about 10 miles from Le Touquet, intercept 296 degree radial and report position to Le Touquet Tower on 118.45.
Reset altimeter to values given by Le Touquet Tower.
Descend to 1,000 feet.

Report again to Le Touquet Tower when over reporting point "Echo," five miles from airport, on 296 radial.

Land on assigned runway.

Do all of the above while keeping my head on a swivel looking out for other air traffic, and while also looking down at my navigation charts to confirm actual location according to landmarks (rivers/lakes/cities/towers, etc) on the ground, and turning knobs, pushing buttons, talking on the radio, controlling the plane, monitoring instruments and engine status, while still trying to have FUN!

Are you kidding? How can anyone have fun when they are doing all this work? What ever happened to just jumping in the airplane and going flying? That's what I do when I'm flying in the desert around the Fun House. I just look outside, and if there's daylight, then I look at the windsock. If it's still attached to the pole, then I go flying! No METAR/TAF weather reports to get and decode, no flight plans, no ground control to ask if I can start up my plane, no control tower to call to request permission to take off and land, no restricted air spaces (okay, not as many) and no noise sensitive areas. I can fly a lot lower, there are no landing fees, gas is a lot cheaper and they talk English!

So why am I here?

Day 66: Happy To Be Alive!

Rye, England

The plan was perfectly set out from yesterday's full day of preparation. All the radio frequencies were known and written down, all the altitudes were decided upon and the course lines drawn on the charts. I had visualized every last detail and I had done it several times. There was nothing left but to do it.

It is incredible how things can go wrong no matter how well we plan!

The takeoff from Rheims (Prunay) was flawless. There was no wind, the sky was clear and the weather was good enough at Le Touquet, my destination on the north coast of France. However, there is one rather important note on the airport chart for Le Touquet that mentions the unpredictability of the weather in that spot. The note mentions that fog can roll in from the English Channel very quickly and unexpectedly, and that pilots should be prepared to go to an alternate airport. I had therefore identified my alternate and was fully prepared.

The flight to Le Touquet was really easy. There was a very high thin overcast that kept the air still and smooth. As the 90-minute flight wore on, the visibility grew progressively worse, even though I was flying at 4,500 feet. At one point, a broken layer of cumulus clouds developed under me, and I considered going down under them, but I decided to stay on top as long as I could still see the ground. When I got within radio distance of Le Touquet, I dialed in the ATIS weather broadcast and discovered that the ceiling was down to 700 feet! The conditions had worsened instead of getting better! It is a good thing that I didn't go down under the cloud layer. If I did, I would have run into lowering ceilings, and the visibility was down to minimums. It would have been a trap.

I had plenty of gas, and I could have gone to the alternate airport at Abbeville, but I decided to fly around on top for a while and see if things got any better. Sure enough, the ceiling went from 700' and overcast to broken and then to 1,400' scattered, and then I radioed to the tower that I was coming in. On left downwind for runway 24, I had to stay real close to the runway because visibility was so bad I thought I might lose sight of it. And then there were the scattered clouds in the pattern to deal with: I stayed up over them, but with my wheels dragging in the clouds just to keep low enough for a landing as well as to keep the runway in sight. I turned base and final, and dove between two clouds, and got on the ground with a great sigh of relief.

I refueled, had a quick lunch, checked the weather on the other side of the Channel (looked good), and jumped in for my first, and eagerly anticipated, crossing of the English Channel. I really wanted to land in a place where they talk English. It would be the first time in two-plus months that I would hear everyone speaking something I could understand. I may have been overly enthusiastic about "getting there" because of what happened next.

As I was taxiing out to runway 24, the same one I used on landing, the wind kicked up a good bit, and changed direction, and the controller asked if I would prefer to use runway 14, more aligned with the wind. All of my preflight planning was based on using 24, and I had noticed a newly forming layer of scattered clouds blowing in from the south, but they seemed to be dissipating before they got to the airport, so I figured it would be okay. But the change in runways at the last minute threw off my plans.

The forward visibility from the holding point of runway 14 looked okay, but not great. There was a lot of haze and it was difficult to tell where it was haze and where it was cloud, if any. It was easy to tell when looking in the other directions, so I figured it was all the same, and I gave it full throttle. As my biplane lifted off and approached the end of the short runway, I was completely engulfed in a thick fog that was lurking behind the haze. I was less than 200 feet in the air and I could see *nothing* except gray. Gray in all directions: up, down and sideways. I was flying completely blind.

I have trained for, and received, my instrument pilot rating, but it is not current. I took the training solely for the purpose of knowing what to do if I ever got into a situation like this. And I have been in this kind of situation only once before, very briefly, about a year ago. It's not something I want to practice!

So here I am, doing an unexpected IFR (Instrument Flight Rules) takeoff, illegally because I am not a current Instrument pilot, but I'm not thinking about the illegality of it right now, I'm thinking about staying alive. There is only one thing to do and that is climb. My eyes are riveted on the airspeed, artificial horizon, heading indicator. Keep the wings level, keep the airspeed at climb speed, full throttle. Sooner or later I have got to climb out on top of this stuff and then maybe I can figure out my next move.

And sure enough, what seems like an entire lifetime later, I finally break out on top. What now? I consider going back and landing, because I have just had the living daylights scared out of me and I would like to relax for a while, but that would gain nothing. I'm already on my way for a Channel crossing, the weather is better on the other side, so I keep on climbing and head north along the coast of France until I get to the point where the Channel is narrowest, between Calais France and Dover England. The only problem is that the air is steadily getting more and more hazy, to the point where it is almost impossible to tell how much visibility there really is. I can see straight down, but only barely. I can see nothing of the coast of England. When I turn in that direction all I see is gray/white.

I keep climbing, all the way to 6,500 feet, and there is no improvement. It just makes it harder to see the ground. Do I continue, or go back? With the way the clouds were coming in at Le Touquet, it's probably socked in by now. I could go land somewhere else, but that would be going backwards. It's only 25 miles of open water to Dover England. I'm not worried about the engine quitting, strangely, but I am thinking about the visibility. What I have here is IFR in VMC, a condition where measurable visibility is (barely) good enough to be VFR, but since there are no reference points within the visual range, you are really in a virtual IFR situation. So technically I am legal to do the crossing under these conditions, but am I skilled enough? Concerns nag at me. What will happen if I get disoriented (vertigo) because of no visual cues? Will I get sick? I have never gotten sick in an airplane. Will I go unconscious? I haven't before, but just the thought of getting dizzy makes me kind of woozy! Hey, calm down! All I have to do is watch the instruments. Keep my altitude (plenty of that), keep the wings level, and I should be able to make out the other coast in about 10 minutes. A very long 10 minutes.

I'm not just thinking about me up here in the soup. There are other airplanes crossing both ways under these same conditions! So what really concerns me is meeting up with one of them abruptly, as in a mid-air collision.

Soon there is something taking shape in the continuous gray, a shape like a row of clouds, down low and in front of my left wing, far away. But it's too well defined to be clouds. It's... ... ... the "White Cliffs of Dover"! It's England. I'm saved. I did it!

I have wanted to take this photo for some time now; I just never realized that it would have been so hair-raising to get it:

Now I can get down from this ridiculously high altitude, follow the coast southwest until Lydd airport shows up. Piece of cake! And it was.

I parked on the ramp next to another biplane, a 450 Stearman, obviously set up for air show work. I went into the restaurant and had a pint of Bitters, which I sorely needed to slake my thirst. I must have sweated off 10 pounds in that last flight! Having lunch were two characters that were undoubtedly the ones attached to the Stearman, but they were engaged in deep conversation and lunch, so I didn't interrupt them. As I was making hotel arrangements and clearing customs, they came up to me and introduced themselves (they saw my Waco biplane t-shirt). Meet Barry Tempest, the pilot, and Rachel Huxford, the wing walker! Here they are trying to get into their life jackets before they fly across the Channel on their way to Belgium for an air show:

Barry Tempest has been flying for a long time, doing air shows since the Sixties. Now, he is the Head of Sporting & Recreational Aviation Section of the Civil Aviation Authority in England. He wears a hard hat when he is flying, just like I do, which is very uncommon in open-cockpit biplanes. When I mentioned it to him, he presented me with an autographed photo of the instant when the plane he was flying was hit mid-air totally destroying both planes on impact. He fell 150 feet to the ground wearing a hard hat. The helmet was shattered, but he's still around telling the story.

Rachel Huxford is a wing walker because she loves to be in the air and found it too expensive to be a pilot, so now she's very much in the air and gets paid for it. Here she is climbing up on the wing:

I walked around the center of Rye for a little bit, found an old book store and was lucky to find a couple of rare first editions about some WWII aces, one German and one English. I also stumbled on a very old (12th century) church, and was drawn inside by an overpowering need to say "Thank You, God" for coming out of today's flight alive. At dinner, I sat behind an old woman who was dining alone. On my way out, I had the cashier put her bill on mine, and asked that she be told only that "a friend" took care of her bill. A random act of kindness. What's getting into me? I must be happy to be alive!

Day 67: Great Hotels, Great Memories

London, England

Rye was interesting and I might have chosen to stay another day, but last night's lodging (The Olde Vicarage on High Street) was booked for tonight, and after trying at several other places which were also full, I decided to move onto London. I was looking forward to getting into a different hotel anyway, as the Olde Vicarage had not lived up to its "4-Crown" (Highly Recommended) rating. The plumbing was quite medieval: the toilet didn't work, there was no shower, only a bath, and there were separate faucets (not just handles) for hot and cold water, which means that you get scalding hot out of one and freezing cold out of the other, with no way to compromise the two except by filling the basin. As my luck would have it, there did occur another method. The place ran out of hot water completely in the middle of my bath, leaving room temperature water for the rest of the morning. My complaints were not limited to the plumbing however. There was no air conditioning to ward off the very hot and muggy Channel air, and the very noisy children in the building across the narrow street seemed to be right at the foot of my bed.

Needless to say, I was looking forward to an authentic first-class hotel, and London has lots of them. But first, I had to get there. The local Rye taxi took me into Lydd to fetch my large duffel bag out of the airplane, and then I took the taxi back to Rye to catch the train to Ashford. I would then catch a different train to London's Charring Cross station, the very center of town.

I had no trouble booking a room at The Savoy, a 5-star Art-Deco landmark hotel in the business district. I am told that the short street leading up to the front door of The Savoy is the only place in all of the United Kingdom where traffic stays to the right. No one seems to know why, just part of the very quirky charm of the place.

Yes, it is expensive. However, when I consider the fact that I have suffered through some of the most awful lodgings in all of Europe on this trip, I feel the need to pamper myself every once in a while.

I really enjoy staying at world-class hotels, not just for the luxury of it all, but because I like to see how they have planned the details. I owe some great measure of my success in business to my commitment to creating effective systems. A system is a documented, consistent way of doing things that produces the desired result. McDonald's (hamburgers) is one of the more effective systems-based businesses in the world. So partly, my stay here is research.

One of the hallmarks of a first class hotel is that the staff treats you with highly personalized attention. They all address you by your name, and sometimes, it seems as if they must be clairvoyant when they do that, because you cannot imagine how they could know your name. You can be sure they do it easily because they have a system for it. When I got to my room and turned the TV on, it immediately welcomed me with my name on the screen. My bags were already in the room, and the person who checked me in guided me to my room. There were fresh flowers in the room when I arrived, and within half an hour, a complimentary bottle of Champagne was delivered, with mixed nuts.

There are three phones, (each of which has three lines!) one in the bathroom, one on the desk and one by the bed. Near the desk, in plain view and within easy access, are labeled the outlets for electric, fax and modem (UK and US adapters, and a third for ISDN). It is clear that these people cater to the business traveler.

By the bed, there is a control box that will summon the three most commonly needed assistants: Maid, Valet, and Waiter. These buttons turn on the appropriately marked light outside the room door, alerting the floor assistant, as well as automatically ringing the required assistant, who phones back immediately.

There is a CD player and stereo tuner by the bedside, providing whatever music you could want, and a fully stocked mini-bar/refrigerator has more than you could want for refreshment or snacks.

But the area where these hotels really go whole hog is the bathroom. Here at The Savoy there is a heated (adjustable) towel rack, and the bathroom is separately heated (adjustable). There is a full-on shower and bath of course, but this shower is extraordinary: the shower head is very high overhead and is at least 12 inches in diameter, so you can stand directly under it like a gentle waterfall. There is also a separate hand-held showerhead. The entire ceiling is mirrored. Of course, there is marble and granite throughout the room, and as a nice touch, there was a nice terry cloth mat placed in front of the sink, a comfortable place to stand while you consider your reflection in the mirrors. And the best mirror of all is the one that can be extended from the wall, has an internal light, and magnifies the reflection so that it is the world's best mirror for shaving.

When I get to a place like this, the first thing I want to do is get a shower to get me equal to my surroundings, getting rid of the sweat and grime of a long day of travel. Good hotel people know this, and they provide several towels of absolutely magnificent texture and size. Huge, thick terry cloth towels already heated to perfection on the heated towel rack. Now the place is a mess, but no problem, just push the button and the maid will have it put together in a jiffy!

When I'm out for dinner, somehow they know that and send a maid to perform the "turndown service" which includes removing and storing the bed cover, and turning down (hence the name) the upper near corner of the blanket and sheet, a gesture which is designed to welcome you to a good night's rest. Of course, you can order your breakfast for the morning by filling in a card and hanging it on your doorknob, so that it will be delivered whenever you want, with the newspaper of your choice. The best hotels put a note on the paper with the day's weather forecast. The great hotel in Hamburg had an umbrella in the closet for guest use, but not The Savoy, which is strange considering the weather here in London. I'm sure you could get one from the valet or bellman. And speaking of bellmen, here at The Savoy they wear black morning coats, top hats and white gloves.

And while we are on the subject of staff, let me mention a standout here at The Savoy. Her name is Letitia, in London for only a year; she seems lonely when she says she's gong back to visit her parents in South Africa. She makes an absolutely perfect cappuccino and smiles sweetly while she engages you in conversation in such a skillful manner that you can get lost in the feeling that she may even have more than a professional interest in you. This is the way of the truly gifted in the hospitality industry, but it is also a skill which can be taught as part of a system of success in business, and I'm making notes of her technique whenever I break free of the reverie and daydreams of what might be if she were not going to South Africa tomorrow, and I were not three times her age!

An essential ingredient for any great hotel is location, and The Savoy doesn't disappoint. I took a walk around the block before dinner and discovered the legendary river Thames, and the spot where the great 3,500-year-old Egyptian obelisk is displayed. A discreet brass plate explains the many irregular holes in the base of the obelisk: a German bomb during WWII exploded in the roadway nearby.

Some cultural differences are just too great to overcome by even the most inspired hotel management. And here I am referring to the food. Unfortunately, the English have just never caught on to the fact that eating can be a very pleasant experience if the food is tasty. More of their chefs should take a short hop across the Channel and have a meal or two in France.

So after a mediocre dinner at a world class hotel, and one last smile and cappuccino from Letitia, I am ready for a great night's sleep on the most comfortable bed and pillows I have yet experienced. A brochure in the room explains that they are each custom made by craftsmen in the same firm that has been doing this for over a hundred years (the Savoy is 110 years old). I have put out the "Do NOT disturb" sign on my doorknob, and will be going to sleep knowing that I will not be greeted in the morning by the sounds of the street urchins of Rye.

These great hotels produce great memories, so if I live long enough, the cost per remembrance of staying here gets downright reasonable!

Day 68: The Conservative Club

<u>London, England</u>

Today was one of the highlights of this tour. I had the opportunity to visit with a good friend from my TeleMagic software days. Tricia Gregory is a person of extraordinary wit as well as exceptional talent in business. She was the distributor for TeleMagic software in the United Kingdom until The Sage Group purchased my company in 1992. We have continued to keep in touch by phone and e-mail, but I haven't seen her since before the sale.

Here's a photo of Tricia with her Jack Russell terrier "Dog," a name which gives you some indication of the nature of her good humor.

Getting to her place in the north of London was an adventure in itself. The London Underground ("The Tube") was crowded, hot, humid and dirty. I admit I was a bit apprehensive about it, thinking it was a lot like New York City subways, but somehow I survived the experience.

Tricia picked me up at the end of the Piccadilly Line, and we drove to the home she shares with Keith, her significant other. There I met Keith and his business associate, Arthur, and the four of us drove on to their favorite private pub "The Conservative Club." This is indeed a very private club, and in order for me to be there I had to sign a document that specifically prohibited me from buying anything while there. What a great place! I can drink all the Guinness Stout I want, and they won't let me pay for it!

Have you ever played Snooker? Well, I hadn't either until today. In fact, I had never even seen a snooker table. They are huge compared to a standard pool table, and the pockets are smaller, which means that it is a much more difficult game. In college, I was a fair pool player, but I was humbled today. And with the increasing effects of the Guinness, you could say that I was humiliated. I need some practice.

Let me introduce you to James, a young lad who took over Tricia's place on the opposing team in the game we played. He has a most confident manner about himself, which I found to be amazing. He is destined for greatness.

Another future great is Victoria Punt, a young lady of uncommon beauty, who proceeded to dazzle me with card tricks while getting me to lose a few quid and feel wonderful about it!

I had a great time at The Conservative Club, and after a few pints of Guinness, it was time to leave while we were still behaving somewhat conservatively. It was a fine taste of English culture. We returned to Tricia and Keith's place, and continued to talk, drink and eat until it was almost tomorrow. I'm sure we solved all of the really important issues facing the world, but I know I'm not going to remember the solutions tomorrow. Pity.

The best part was to see and spend some time with a good friend I haven't seen for too long. The day before I visited Tricia, this little poem came to me via e-mail. It got me to thinking about how really important it is to keep in contact with good friends, and so I'm sharing it with you:

(Around The Corner By Henson Town)

Around the corner I have a friend,
In this great city that has no end,
Yet the days go by and weeks rush on,
And before I know it, a year is gone.
And I never see my old friends face,
For life is a swift and terrible race,

He knows I like him just as well,
As in the days when I rang his bell.
And he rang mine
if, we were younger then,
And now we are busy, tired men.
Tired of playing a foolish game,
Tired of trying to make a name.
"Tomorrow" I say "I will call on Jim"
"Just to show that I'm thinking of him."

But tomorrow comes and tomorrow goes,
And distance between us grows and grows.
Around the corner! - yet miles away,
"Here's a telegram sir"
"Jim died today."
And that's what we get and deserve in the end.
Around the corner, a vanished friend.

Day 69: Down and Out, and Just Around the Corner

<u>London, England</u>

The morning does not come easily to me today. Despite the peace and quiet of the ultra-serene Savoy Hotel, there is a nuisance in my head, which can only be punishment for the prior evening's excesses. There will be no flying today, of course. Although the sky is clear, the pilot is fogbound.

This is one of those circumstances where a superior hotel becomes worth more than the price of admission: juice from the in-room mini-bar, workout, swim, massage, shower, breakfast in the room, and a nap in a freshly made bed, then a walk around Covent Garden. It's amazing the recuperative powers of the human body when the right resources are applied to the task!

Feeling better than new, I wandered into the "Upstairs," a tiny corner of the hotel serving as a casual bar/snacks/restaurant, and situated just one floor above the ground, with a great view looking down on the front entrance of this legendary hotel. From my table by the window, sipping cappuccino, I can look down, secure and anonymous, on the comings and goings of everyone. It's the perfect place to do some serious people watching:

A gaggle of ladies in print summer dresses,
a school of executives on the trail of a deal,
a honeymoon couple, here, but not really,
an Indian princess, with forehead red-dotted,
North Carolinians who have saved for a year,
an old man and his pretty grand-daughter
(really? I doubt it!),
a Filipino family with squabbling kids,
Arabs and Texans, Orientals and Brits,
Movers and Shakers and wanna-be fakers.

Patrick the doorman greets them all smiling,
assisting them into and out of their Rolls-Royces,
Bentleys, Jaguars, and Mercedes-Benzes,
but mostly it's black London taxis that slip 'round the corner
where down on their luck and out on the street,
the other end of the spectrum of life in the city,
they arrange their flat cardboard pieces in doorways,
settling in for an evening of drinking and begging,
and eventual sleep.
Open air double-deck buses of tourists glide by and admire.
From every corner of the Kingdom, and places beyond,
they come for a stay in an island of fantasy.
Few can maintain it, for most it's just a taste
of what life could be like, if only...

We need places like The Savoy to inspire and reward. Tomorrow I'll go back to the south coast of England, to plan my next flight.

Day 70: Back at the Beach Again

<u>New Romney, England</u>

It was with mixed feelings that I packed up and left The Savoy in London. The hotel, of course, was excellent, even if it was outrageously expensive. And London is a place that could be explored for years, but it is also a big city, and I can only survive in these cement mausoleums for a couple of days before I need to breathe fresh air and feel real earth under my feet, and see a horizon un-blighted by civilization.

Taxi, train, taxi, and within a couple of hours I was back at the Lydd airport to stow my large bag back in the biplane, and continue to the hotel selected by Zoë at the airport. Unfortunately, Zoë thought that a four-poster bed in the room would more than offset my absolute requirement for a shower, and I did ask her to find the best hotel in the area of Lydd, but what I got was clearly substandard, so I decided to take my chances and keep looking.

I couldn't believe my luck when I found the Romney Bay House, a delightful small hotel fronting on the English Channel (more precisely the Romney Bay part of the English Channel). Not only did it have a shower, but the room looked out over the Channel and I could watch airplanes from France appear out of the mist and make a left hand turn into the airport at Lydd. The visibility for them, today, was much better than it was for my crossing.

The hotel is situated off by itself, away from everything else in town. It looks almost lonely. I have heard that it was originally Hedda Hopper's home. At first, I was wondering how I would entertain myself at this out of the way place, but was made to feel at home by Helmut, the Austrian-born owner, who has a great sense of humor. It wasn't too long before I was enjoying the company of the other guests, and in particular Jim and Claire, who were here for dinner, on vacation from their two young children and their apple and pear farm about 40 miles away.

I really enjoyed being by the beach again, and walk along the water's edge. It isn't a great beach, there isn't much sand, only lots of small rocks, but the natural open space and the sound of the waves is very relaxing.

On the train from London to Ashford, I had the very enjoyable experience of meeting the lovely and charming Anna Peterson, a medical student who is on vacation and going home for the obligatory visit with her parents for a week before she is off again to spend the holidays with her friends. She has toured Spain, Peru and Chile.

My biplane is resting comfortably in a large hangar at Lydd. I visited it today, and it is looking well. The weather is supposed to be marginal for tomorrow (thunderstorms, etc), but much better for Thursday and the weekend. I should be flying again soon.

For now, it's time for some sleep, and the window is open to the sounds of the surf just a few dozen yards away.

Here's the Romney Bay House. I have the upper left room.

Day 71: Hangar Flying

<u>New Romney, England</u>

My sleep was rudely interrupted by a thunderstorm that passed directly over this little hotel. It was a phenomenal show. I sat at the window watching the lightning out across the entire 180-degree view of the English Channel. When I thought it was all over, I went back to bed and was almost asleep when the fire alarm in the hotel went off. I lay there considering the options: 1. It was probably set off by a lightning strike; so there was probably nothing to worry about, so go back to bed, or 2. The place is really on fire, in which case there would be lots of other people shouting and acting like it was a real fire, but there wasn't any other commotion at all. I figured it was just a false alarm, so I went back to sleep. It wasn't until the morning that I realized that there was another option, that everyone else in the hotel thought it was a false alarm and went back to sleep, and if it had been a real fire, we all would have burnt up, a just reward for our indolence.

The storm cleared the air nicely, and today was a lot cooler and sunny. Unfortunately, there were still plenty of storms in the area, and along my route to Duxford, so today was not a flying day.

I have been away from my biplane too long, so I took a taxi over to the airport and hung out with the guys in the tower, Frank and John, and we swapped stories for a couple of hours. One thing I learned was that the Lydd airport was used in the filming of several movies and TV shows, most notably the James Bond movie *Goldfinger*. It was great to just relax and talk about flying in general — no rush, nothing specific, just pure random "hangar-flying" stuff, all done in a proper English fashion, over a cup of tea.

The day was just too nice to spend it all inside the control tower, so I headed back to the Romney Bay House where the big decision of the day was whether to take a nap outside by the ocean or in my room where the bed was more comfortable. I know, it's a tough life, but somebody's got to do it. All of Europe is on vacation in August and I'm just getting into the spirit of it.

If the weather forecasters are right (when was the last time that happened?), tomorrow will be spectacularly nice, and I'll fly to Duxford to see the greatest collection of WWII aircraft in all of Europe. The Queen herself came here August 1st to dedicate the new building that houses this amazing collection.

The guys in the tower at Lydd did give me some tips on dealing with the airspace around London, so it should be a relatively easy trip. Remember what happens when you start thinking that way.

Day 72: Mustangs Forever!

Duxford, England

One last walk on the beach at New Romney, then a quick taxi ride to the airport at Lydd, and before too long, I was rolling down runway 22 in calm wind and into a clear sky. The weather was completely un-English: it was perfect!

It was an easy flight to Duxford, only about an hour, including a little bit of time to fly over the coastline and do some exploring. There is grass and a hard surface at Duxford, so you know I took the grass. What a great feeling it is to land on grass!

Duxford is a historical landmark, a national treasure. This airfield was established in the *first* World War and has been active ever since. Many pilots had told me over the last few months that if I only visited one airfield in England, then it should be Duxford, but I really had no idea what to expect. In fact, this place is mind-boggling.

I had just parked the Waco when a fellow came up to me and mentioned that there was going to be an air show here at Duxford on the 7th of September, featuring American aircraft, and would I like to participate in a fly-by? Oh boy would I! What a wonderful way to spend my birthday! He said he would check out if it were possible under UK Civil Air regulations for me to participate without having a special air show license. Hopefully my new friend Barry Tempest, who is the head of the Sport Aviation Safety department for the UK Civil Air authority, can help with this. I'm not on the ground more than 10 minutes, and already I'm really getting to like this place.

The first thing I did on landing was to make the obligatory visit to the control tower and pay my landing fee of 6 pounds sterling, about $10, which was cut in half for me, presumably because I'm flying a good-looking biplane.

Walking back to the biplane, another fellow, Klaus, asked me if this was the Waco from Germany. I figured he was talking about my first Waco, the one that my flight instructor had flipped on the runway in Carlsbad, California, when he landed with the parking brake on. The plane was completely destroyed, and I turned in the parts and the insurance payoff and took delivery of a new one that looks identical to the original. The Waco factory rebuilt my old pile of parts and sold it to a fellow in Germany. So this guy Klaus, who comes up to me in Duxford, asking if this is the German Waco is actually the instructor who taught the German how to fly his (my) Waco! Is this a small world, or what? Better yet, Klaus is just about to leave on a low-level film mission in one of two P-51 Mustangs. So I drop a few Mustang names, which he happens to know, and then I let it slip that I have a few hours in a Mustang. Who knows, maybe I'll get a ride! I can dream, can't I?

Next priority was to get a hotel for a couple of days. I wanted to find a place as early as possible because the rooms around here could fill up fast with the weekend coming. I found a 3-star place, just a couple of miles away, the Duxford Lodge. A quick shower, and then I headed back to the airfield.

Duxford has a Concorde on display! And a B-52! There are Mustangs, Spitfires, and all manner of war birds. There are five monster hangars full of perfectly restored aircraft, and the jewel of the airfield is the new American Air Museum which opened just two weeks ago, and the Queen herself came to dedicate the place. The American Air Museum houses the B-52, an F-111, a B-29, B-25, Mustang, Stearman, T-6, Spad and a dozen other aircraft, all under one roof! It was too hot inside for me to stay around. I think they need to sort out their air conditioning. I'll go back in the morning when it's cooler.

The highlight of the day was when two P-51 Mustangs rolled down the runway in sequence then formed up on the downwind leg and made a low pass before going out for a low-level film mission.

What a sight! An hour later, they are back overhead, circling the field to get everyone's attention, and then proceed to do formation loops, rolls, and wingovers! It was a great impromptu air show, with the best airplane ever made! I was right with them every step of the way. I was inside those planes, at the controls, flying every inch of the way. I can say that because I have actually done these aerobatics, and more, in a P-51 Mustang and it was one of the greatest thrills of my life. That machine is so smooth, yet so very powerful, that it does everything effortlessly. The fact that it looks so beautiful and sounds so awesome (a V-12 engine!) just adds to the mystique. It is incredible that this perfect airplane was built in just 117 days from the first pencil sketch, and it turned the tide of the war in Europe. It is a legend, and an inspiration.

Later in the day, I was buying a cold drink at the restaurant, showing up at the cashier at the same moment as a lady who was buying the same thing. Just on a lark, I told the cashier I would pay for both. The lady was pleasantly surprised, thanked me and we both left in opposite directions. About 10 minutes later, she found me and offered me a baseball cap with the Royal Air Force Association logo. Well, sure! I'm thinking I got the better end of this trade (which I hadn't intended to be a trade), so I started talking with her and we found our way back to the table where she was sitting with her husband and some friends. Jerry, Elbert, Joyce and Jean are all retired, now involved in fundraising to help British war veterans, but for today they are just taking the day off and enjoying Duxford. And by the way, would I like to attend the air show next weekend at their local airfield at Clacton-on-Sea, just an hour away?

We are sitting there having a good chat when a Spitfire rolls down the runway, lifts off just slightly, raises the wheels, keeps low to build up speed, then pulls straight up revealing the most beautiful set of wings ever put on an airplane. It then proceeds to roll out at the top and continue to play right over the runway for the next 15 minutes, doing all manner of aerobatic maneuvers and we are all just loving it.

The shows put on by the Mustangs and the Spitfire are completely unplanned, not for any other purpose except for the pure fun of it. People are not here expecting this sort of thing, but it sure is happening. What an extraordinary place this is! I have booked a room for several days; I really want to inspect this legendary airfield in detail.

Day 73: The American Air Museum

Duxford, England

Before I went to sleep last night, I had the thought that I would go flying in the morning, probably just a trip to the coast and back, or maybe some "circuits and bumps" as the British call touch and go's. I wanted to get there early, before there was a lot of traffic in the pattern. Unfortunately, my morning's ambition was not as strong as my vacation spirit, and I slept late. There is always tomorrow...

The main priority for today was the full investigation of the "Imperial War Museum" (not a very pleasant name, is it?) at Duxford airfield. It is difficult to come up with enough of the right superlatives to describe this place. Today, I visited the new American Air Museum, which is just one (very large) building on the grounds. There are seven large hangars and many smaller buildings that comprise the entire Imperial War Museum at Duxford. A thorough visit could take a week!

The American Air Museum houses an awesome collection of some of the finest aircraft ever assembled under one roof: The huge B-52D Stratofortress with eight jet engines is the center of the collection, and everything else is grouped around, or suspended over, it. Just to name a few: F-111, C-47, A10, P-47 Thunderbolt, U-2 spy plane, B-17 Flying Fortress, T-6 Texan, PT-17 Stearman, P-51 Mustang, the monster B-29A Superfortress, T-33 jet trainer, B-25 Mitchell, TBM-3 Avenger, F-86, Huey helicopter, a collection of mobile missile launch vehicles including the SAM and Cruise, a section of the Berlin Wall, a collection of aircraft engines, various video exhibits, a collection of uniforms and other memorabilia, and lots more.... all under one roof. It was sensory overload.

One of the displays featured the life of a fighter pilot. Here are the words: "The public image of the fighter pilot is that of a dashing aerial knight whose prowess was assessed by his score of enemy victories. In reality, the majority of US fighter pilots flying over Europe never had the opportunity to engage in Air combat! The fighter pilot experience of war was one of lonely fatigue, strapped in a small noisy cockpit for three to seven hours at a time. To survive it was necessary never to neglect monitoring instruments and to scan the sky constantly for the enemy. The task that took the lives of most fighter pilots lost in combat was ground strafing of heavily defended enemy installations. Overall, with enemy action and accident, the fighter pilot's chance of surviving a 300-hour operational tour was no greater than that of a bomber crewman."

I continue to meet extraordinary people. Today I had the good fortune to get to know Les Batt and his brother Keith, who flew to Duxford in a very old De Havilland DH82B Queen Bee, which looks almost identical to a Tiger Moth, but was built originally to be a radio-controlled target!

It is the only one still flying in the world. Les is quite the character. He gave me his card, and it reads "Dragons Slain, Maidens Rescued, All Round Good Egg, Never Fails To Buy His Round, Les Batt." Les and Keith flew in from about 20 miles south, on a shakedown cruise in preparation for an air show tomorrow. I sat in the cockpit for a few minutes to get the "feel" of the plane. It has an extremely short travel for the rudder pedals, and Keith admits that it is very "twitchy" in the air, requiring constant attention. The plane has no tail wheel, only a skid, and no brakes, so they must land on grass.

I didn't get to fly my biplane today. I had to make do with getting a ride in one. Not just any biplane, but one of the prettiest twin-engine biplanes ever to take to the air, the 1934 De Havilland Dragon Rapide:

Unfortunately, it allows only one pilot, there is no co-pilot seat, or I would have begged some stick time to bolster my meager multi-engine time. However, I was fortunate enough to get the seat directly behind and to the right of the pilot so I could see everything he was doing. I had a good view forward during takeoff and landing, as well as excellent views to the sides. Taking off on the hard surface and climbing out, I distinctly got the impression this was a solid and capable aircraft. We went for a tour of the local area for about 10 minutes and came back to make an excellent smooth landing on the grass. It's a delightful machine in every respect; a twin engine biplane! That's a first for me!

I spent the entire day at the airfield and haven't begun to see everything on display. I can't wait to go back for more…

Day 74: Punting and Picnicking

Cambridge, England

This was the morning I was supposed to go flying at Duxford. Last night, I had no alcoholic beverages at dinner and got to bed early, fully preparing myself to have a good bit of flying in the early morning. NOT!

When I arrived at the airfield at 8 am sharp, expecting to be one of the first to fly when the place opened, I was the only one there! It was like a ghost town. That's when I consulted my airport directory to find that the airfield opens at 10:30 am. What a bummer! I was sorely tempted to just jump in and go flying. The grass strip looked great, the pattern was empty, the sky was blue and there was a challenging 90-degree wind kicking up which made me want to practice some crosswind landings on grass. Very tempting.

And then I thought better of it. This is a private airfield, not public, and I suspect that one is not allowed to use it when it is closed, but there's nobody around to ask. That old saying is rattling around in my head: "It's better to ask forgiveness than it is to ask permission," and maybe I'm just being conservative, but it doesn't seem applicable in this instance. I figure that if I do something stupid here/now it might hurt my chances of flying in their air show in September. As disappointing as it is, I walk away.

Yes, I could have waited until they opened, and then gone flying, but I had already made plans to go to Cambridge, just to the north of Duxford, with some friends I met while touring the Taittinger Champagne caves in Rheims, France, just a couple of weeks ago. Sandra and Keith Stillton live just outside London and had invited me to join them and their friends Mike and Sue, for a very British afternoon of punting and picnicking in Cambridge.

Punting, for those of you who haven't (and I certainly hadn't until today), is a peculiar mode of transportation whereby the method of propulsion is a long pole poked into the river bottom whilst standing on a small slippery deck at the back of the flat-bottomed boat. The boat is called a punt, I believe, but it just may be the pole, which goes to show you how much I know about punting. However, I can tell you this: I spent at least two hours in the boat, and watched carefully the many other punters on the river, and I can say without reservation that this is a most ridiculous method of getting from A to B.

First of all, nobody I saw in the punter position (actually sticking the pole in the water and shoving off the bottom) seemed to have the hang of it. It must be incredibly difficult to steer one of these things because it has no rudder, just that damn 15-foot long wooden pole. I *know* it must be difficult to steer because we rammed into half of the boats on the river. The other half of the boats rammed into us! And during all of this, we rammed into the shoreline more often than not. I was beginning to think that this was some form of aquatic bumper-cars, but these people were very serious about trying to steer straight, and seemed quite embarrassed with all their banging about.

I should say right off that Keith, our primary punter (pole man) did an admirable job, keeping us from ramming the other half of the boats, but the river is so narrow, and it was so crowded, that we just had no room for evasive maneuvering.

After punting up-river for an hour, we off-loaded the picnic baskets and Sandra spread out the blankets and the nice lunch of cheeses, fruit, ham, wine and desert. It was simply marvelous sitting in the grass, under the shade of a tree, sipping some wine and talking very British, you know. Every once in a while one of us would pop our head up to look over some bushes just to be sure that our pole was still around. It must be jolly good sport to steal someone's pole while they are not looking.

Actually, the boat comes with a backup system in the event of a lost pole: a paddle. It seems that a lost pole can also occur from natural causes, such as when it gets stuck in the mud at the bottom, the boat continues to move forward while the punter tries in vain to pull it free and it finally slips out of their wet grasp. This leaves the punter without a pole, and the paddle is the only way to get back to the pole.

Another way you can lose your pole is much more traumatic. There are several low bridges along the Cam River (hence the name Cam-bridge, get it?) that are so low that the punter must duck down to get under them. If his timing is not just right, the pole may be stuck in the bottom on one end, and the other may be sticking up higher than the low part of the bridge. The boat continues forward, and, as in the previous scenario, boat and pole are rudely separated. If his timing is completely wrong, it is just possible that the punter will be separated from the boat as well and left hanging on the pole.

It is difficult for me to imagine how this punting thing has survived. Surely, it must have been one of Early Man's first modes of water travel, and just as surely he must have quickly invented the paddle, which could be used while sitting down (eliminating another danger of the punting experience: slipping off the wet deck). So when we got into the paddle thing, why keep punting about? Maybe because the English are just so into tradition. Maybe that's why they cling to separate faucets for hot and cold water. And when the outboard motor came along, you would think they would have reconsidered the pole concept. But noooo...

There was one more aspect of this punting experience that I didn't expect. On the way back down river, we came round a bend where lots of pre-pubescent children were swimming and playing in the water. Lots more were playing on the banks of the river. A few were swinging on a rope, starting on the bank and lofting themselves out into the water. And some were even in the trees, jumping into the river. What a lovely scene of young children frolicking in the water on a hot weekend afternoon. Then it all turned very grim...

These little buggers started dive-bombing us with their bodies! Out of the trees they dropped and hit with great splashes that covered us with water. Then more came running from the shore, taking long leaps in our direction and cannon-balling us with sheets of water. And just another 50 feet or so and we had to run the gauntlet again. We had no choice but to pass under one of those low bridges, and above us they were standing at the edge like buzzards waiting for their turn at us. We got drenched! Of course, they thought it was great fun, and secretly so did I, knowing that I would have done the same thing if I had the chance.

I'd like to come back here with a proper punting machine, with a hidden motor and rudder for fast, evasive action, and a crew of pirates hidden under a tarp who would leap up at the last minute and shoot high-powered water guns filled with permanent ink which would turn these little demons pink! Now, that would be a great sight! I'd love to see the looks on their faces when the tables were turned.

And then, being the entrepreneur that I am, I reconsidered the revenge motive and thought like a capitalist. It would be much better to stage a punt before the dive bombing area, and sell "flood insurance" to punters heading into the danger zone. Purchasers of the insurance would be assured safe passage by displaying some sort of sign on their boat. The proceeds would be split with the kids, God bless them, and everyone would be immensely happy.

Punting is one of those things that you really should do. Once.

Day 75: A Most Incredible Day

<u>Duxford, England</u>

Today was probably the most incredible day in the last 75 days of this tour. I will try to relate the story as closely as I remember it:

It began with my arrival at the Duxford airfield at 10 am sharp with the firm intention of going flying in my biplane. All I really wanted to do was a few takeoffs and landings on the grass before the pattern got too busy, and then spend the day investigating the contents of the some of the big hangars.

I went directly to the tower and discussed my plans with the controller, and asked him if he was expecting any heavy traffic (today being Sunday, I thought an airfield such as Duxford might get a lot of weekend visitor traffic). He advised me that if I wanted to do any pattern work, I should do it right away because he was expecting about 20 ultralights to show up sometime soon. That didn't make me too happy to think about flying around in the pattern with 20 ultralights, some of which probably didn't have radios! So I got right out to my biplane.

There was a nice breeze, 9 knots directly across the runway, so it was going to be fun getting some crosswind practice. I was conscious of the eyes and cameras of plenty of spectators gathering by the fence — watching me prepare my biplane for flight. My biplane was right next to the control tower, the only airplane in the grassy parking area for transient aircraft. Across the taxiway, ground crews were preparing a P-63 Kingcobra and a P-51A Mustang and a PBY Catalina amphibian. It looked like I was going to be sharing the pattern with some awesome iron!

I strapped in, fired up and the tower cleared me to taxi. Soon I was rolling down the grass on runway 24, keeping the left wing low into the crosswind with lots of left aileron. Pushing the stick a shade forward to lift the tail wheel and then a little backpressure to lift off, I climbed to about 300 feet and started my left turn into the wind. At about that time, I heard the controller advise a "Cessna" to turn left downwind and I looked up and saw a jet in front of me, about a mile away, turning into a wide downwind. I knew I could easily beat him around the pattern so I asked the controller if it was okay to go first, but he told me to follow the Cessna Citation-Jet. Bummer. The real reason I wanted to go first was that if I had to follow him in, I would have to fly so far downwind that I might lose sight of the runway, it was that hazy!

So I just throttled way back, stayed high, and waited my turn. The landing was just so sweet; I wish you could have been there. On final approach, the crosswind was a lot more than 9 knots and I had to do some serious crabbing to keep aligned with the runway, but the wind slacked off the closer I got to the ground, and I touched down with the left main wheel first, rolling for a while before the right wheel came down and then the tail wheel.   It was so smooth I don't think there was any sensation of actually touching, just the sensation of rolling along the grass. I was so very impressed with me!

I had intended to do a touch and go, but I was having so much fun rolling out along the runway, I decided to pull off to the side and taxi back for another full takeoff. As I was taxiing back past the Kingcobra and the Mustang and the Catalina, the ground crews all took a break from their work and turned to watch me go past. Many of them waved or gave me the thumbs-up.

The next takeoff was a little less perfect. The crosswind was variable, and at times was even a bit of a tailwind, which probably caught me just as I was lifting off because the biplane settled back down on the runway from about a foot in the air. It wasn't bad at all, but I shouldn't have let it happen. I think I should have kept more speed on the ground before liftoff, considering the variable wind.

This time, as I am on downwind, the controller gets a call from the first of the expected 20 ultralights, so I immediately decide that this will be my last landing for the day. It was another lovely piece of work, if I do say so myself, which I have to, because I was there! There is something about grass that is just so right for this biplane. It is as if it *wants* to be on grass, and when it gets to play on grass, it rewards me with nice landings. I have never treated my biplane as if it was a living thing with emotions of its own. I am a very logical person, so anthropomorphosis is not something I get into. But I have been flying this machine for about 800 hours and I'm starting to think seriously about the concept. More on that later. Back to why this was such an incredible day:

I taxi off the runway, and park next to a T-6 Harvard, idle the engine for two minutes, as always, while filling out my logbook, then shut down and jump out. I walk directly over to the control tower to pay my landing fees, but on the way I notice a lady in a flight suit coming toward me, carrying a parachute bag, and being followed by about eight people: two ground crew types, the rest non-flying civilian types. The lady in the flight suit sees me coming toward their group and brightens with a big smile and says, "I really love your airplane!" She catches me completely off guard because I never saw her before, and I'm sufficiently far away from my biplane by now that I can't figure out how she knows I'm the guy who owns the biplane, but I stumble out my typical response to that kind of statement, something like "Yes, I know what you mean. I really love it too!" She and her entourage, keep on moving, out across the grass to a Spitfire, which wasn't there when I first took off. I never gave it another thought and continued up to the tower to pay my fees.

While I was in the tower, I stayed around to watch the Kingcobra take off and do all kinds of great low level loops and rolls and all-around play right in front of the tower. Right in front of me! This Duxford sure is a great place to hang out!

The show is over now, so I go back downstairs, and I notice that this lady in the flight suit is acting remarkably like a pilot who is about to go flying in that Spitfire, and I am also now noticing that this particular Spitfire has *two* cockpit canopies, and it is looking for all the world like she is about to take somebody for a ride in it because most of the other people are taking videos and photos of this guy with a big grin on his face!

I should stop here for a minute to let you know that the Spitfire is right up there with the Mustang as the best fighter plane of all time. I have flown a Mustang, and I burn red hot inside to fly the Spitfire. A major incentive in coming on this tour has been the million to one shot that, somehow, I could get a ride in a Spitfire. When I first came to Duxford, I asked about getting a ride, and was advised that it was impossible; there is a 3-year waiting list. There are only two Spitfires in existence that are equipped to take a second pilot, and here is one of them, right in front of me. Now. He who hesitates is lost...

I walk directly over to this lady in the flight suit and wait until she is apart from her entourage and plane, for just the briefest of moments, and appear before her and say something like: "Excuse me, I know already what the answer is, but I feel I just have to ask. You like my airplane and I like yours, so how about if I give you a ride in mine for a ride in yours?" Her reply, after she stopped laughing, was the typical "I'm sorry but the plane is booked for three years in advance, so it's impossible."

I don't remember what I said next. It was kind of like a great athlete going into "The Zone" where there is no perceptible effort in performing, no remembrance of the details, and yet somehow everything just clicks. I'm sure there was some element of me acting like a hurt puppy dog, some slight mention that I had some time in the front seat of a Mustang (just to reassure her that I was not just some guy with a nice biplane, I really *love* these fighters), and she may have even noticed that I was wearing my P-51 Mustang t-shirt. In situations like this I go on auto-pilot. I learned long ago, selling used cars, that "when you stop talking, they start walking," so I just kept on talking. I think that's the way it went, but I can't be sure. I was mesmerized and salivating heavily. Things started to come into focus again when I heard her say "You know, I do have a flight next Saturday. I have to go to an air show in the south of England, and it just came up so it wasn't on the schedule to put anyone else in, and you would have to find your own way back from there, do you think you could make it on Saturday, would you still be in the area, and oh, by the way, it costs a thousand pounds?"

Now I think I know how Neil Armstrong felt when he was selected to be the first man to walk on the moon.

The rest of the day passed in a blur. I stood around and watched as this lucky guy gets strapped into his parachute, briefed about bailout procedures, controls, etc. I am standing with the small group of his well-wishers who are taking videos and soon we are talking. I learn from his wife Liz that this incredibly lucky guy is Adrian Troy, and this is a belated birthday/Father's Day gift, and that these other four people are his children, and they have just flown in here from the island of Jersey where they live. And by the way, they flew in here in that Citation-Jet that I followed in for my first landing today. And they were all watching my lovely biplane from their jet! (Hold on, it gets better!)

Liz Troy starts telling me about this very special Spitfire, and this very special lady in the flight suit. This lady pilot is none other than Carolyn Grace, the only female Spitfire owner/pilot in the world. She has been flying it for many years. Her husband, Nick, restored it, from two truckloads of bits and pieces, over a five-year period and they flew it together for some time before he died in a car crash in 1988. She then mastered flying it solo and has kept it flying in his memory ever since. She is also the mother of two teenagers. (Do you think her kids like to brag about their Mom being a Spitfire pilot, or what?)

Carolyn Grace is a very special person, undeniably. And her airplane is too. It served in active duty during WWII, naturally enough, but amazingly it is credited with the destruction of the first enemy aircraft during the D-Day offensive, among others! There is a very thoroughly researched and documented book about this great airplane, plus videos covering the restoration process and Carolyn's first solo in it. I bought all this stuff and am in the process of devouring it all.

Liz Troy tells me about her husband Adrian, and how as a very young boy he watched the Battle of Britain in the skies over his house, and how he watched huge formations of bombers, escorted by Spitfires, streak across London on their way to bomb the Germans. He has always wanted to fly in a Spitfire. And now he is.

Liz goes on: Adrian, as a boy of sixteen, got to fly with Douglas Bader, Britain's legendary legless Spitfire ace (20+ kills confirmed). A week ago I didn't know who Douglas Bader was, but I discovered a book about him in a little shop in Rye last week, and have been reading it every night since. Last night I finished the book. This morning I meet a man who flew with him.

This is obviously a very intense personal moment for Adrian, Liz and their family, and I am feeling that I should fade into the background and leave them alone to enjoy it together. Here's a photo of Carolyn and Adrian ready to taxi out in Supermarine Spitfire ML-407:

I watch the takeoff and then disappear, leaving the family to themselves. Half an hour later, the Spitfire roars down the runway for a low pass at 350 miles per hour, then pulls up, goes around, drops the wheels and comes in for the most perfect 3-point landing I have ever seen. Carolyn can fly!

There was much celebration and hoopla when Adrian finally climbed out of the Spitfire, and achieved the dream of a lifetime, happily surrounded by his loving family. I hung out in the shadow of the control tower and watched them all from a distance, green with envy, wondering how I am ever going to endure the wait until next Saturday.

I catch Carolyn briefly to reassure her, and myself, that we actually are going to do this, go flying in her Spitfire next Saturday, and she confirms yes, it is real, and she gives me her number to call Friday night for details, and I walk away in a daze. I wander around for a while, but none of the other airplanes seem to be interesting anymore. I go over to the restaurant for some lunch, but there is a long line, and it's hot and humid, so I decide to call a taxi and go back to the hotel for a good lunch with air conditioning, and sit down and read the book about Carolyn and her Spitfire.

I walk through the door of my hotel, and who's there but the entire Troy clan, plus the two Cessna Citation-Jet pilots who flew them in from Jersey, all celebrating Adrian's great day! I'm stunned to find them all here, in *my* hotel restaurant, but before I can pull my disappearing act, they invite me to join them for a drink, and lunch, and well it just can't get any better. We had a great meal, and they are obviously a very happy family, and they all love Adrian a bunch. It was great to be a part of it. Thanks guys! Thanks for a most incredible, day.

Life changing events hang on a slim thread of insignificant ones. If that ultralight pilot had a second cup of coffee before he left from home, I would have gone for a third landing, and missed Carolyn's smiling greeting. If I had spent another 15 seconds in filling out my logbook I would have missed her. Chance can present amazing opportunities, if we look for them. But action is essential to success.

If I had believed what I was told several times, that it was impossible to get a ride in a Spitfire, I never would have walked back up to her and asked again. And if I just walked away and gave up when she herself said it was impossible, I would now be writing a very different story about *almost* getting a Spitfire ride. Belief, coupled with Persistence, is omnipotent.

It was a beautiful experience to learn these important lessons in a positive way.

Day 76: Today Well Lived...

How does one face the day after such a great day as yesterday? One could easily remember it wistfully and hold on to it greedily while letting today slip through his fingers. Another option would be to apply yesterday's lessons to fully living today.

There is a quote that hangs on the wall of my home ("Mikie's Fun House"), and every home I have lived in for the last 20 years:

> Look to this day, for it is Life.
> The very life of Life.
> Yesterday is already a dream,
> And tomorrow only a vision.
> But today well lived
> Makes every yesterday a dream of happiness,
> And every tomorrow a vision of hope.

A Chinese poet wrote it more than 1,500 years ago, but the message is timeless. Intellectually, I know the truth of it, and I look for ways to practice it, to bring it into my being.

I have been fortunate to know two people in my 55 years who seemed to me to represent the perfect attitude in dealing with Life. They are both successful, a result of their manner and attitude, I am sure of it, but other than that they are quite different.

One of the most obvious traits of both of these people is that they make it a point to offer a smile and a pleasant greeting to virtually everyone they meet. And it happens automatically, seemingly as a natural, good-natured act, not a contrivance. As you can imagine, this sort of behavior, in many cases is the first step in a wondrous chain of events, which no man could possibly presume in advance.

As a proof of this theory, I offer to you the instance of yesterday's greeting by Carolyn Grace (which she initiated), begun with a smile and said simply "I love your airplane." How could such a greeting not charm anyone?

For most of my life, I have been a solitary and pragmatic being, living alone most of the time with my head in a computer and going out of my way to smile and greet others only as part of my work, or for some other self-serving purpose. I had never been interested in getting to know a person unless I had already judged that they would be worthwhile getting to know, either by reputation, or physical or chemical attraction, or some other external attribute. It has only been since I have met the first of my two special friends that I have even thought that there might be some better way of living. And when I met the second, I was sure of it.

The challenge I have been facing in adopting this open approach to life is a lifetime of habitually exercising the closed approach. But slowly, tentatively, I have been experimenting with this way of being, and it has been rewarding in ways I never would have imagined. First of all, it *feels good!* And not just for me, but it seems that other people enjoy receiving a smile and a pleasant greeting. Second of all, it starts a chain reaction that leads down a magical path.

I hear a distant roar, of what I have come to recognize as the sound of a V-12 Rolls Royce engine, and it has me scanning the sky for its source. Quickly enough I find it, or rather it finds me because it is diving straight at me! It's a SPITFIRE! He's coming in for a high-speed low pass. I have become rather used to high performance aircraft playing over Duxford airfield in the few days I have been here, but this particular airplane is coming in a *lot* lower than any I have seen before. In fact, I'm watching him diving toward the field and wondering when he is going to level off, but he doesn't, until the last possible second when his propeller tips are maybe only a foot or two above the ground. He roars down the runway like this, pulls sharply up into a downwind leg, drops the gear, and comes back in for a lovely landing on the grass, taxis back and parks directly across the taxiway from my plane, jumps out and walks away, like he has done this a thousand times before. Wow!

I turn back to reality, and busy myself with my charts, when down from the sky drops this vintage single wing airplane, slipping into the wind for a curving approach to a picturesque landing on the grass. The plane taxis back on the grass and parks in the open space next to my biplane. I take a break for a minute and watch this fellow until he shuts down the engine, unstraps his harness and pulls off his helmet. He's younger looking than I would have expected of someone flying such an old airplane.

In a typical situation such as this, I would never utter the first greeting. I would always hold back and let people identify themselves as friendly or not. But for some reason, maybe it was yesterday's lessons still bright in my being, maybe it was just his nice airplane, I smile and say something like "Looks like a lot of fun!" And the magical path leads on...

His name is Mark Hanna, (where have I heard that name before?) and we spend a few minutes talking about his plane, a rare French built Dewoitine D27 with a Pratt and Whitney 985 radial engine.

Then up walks another fellow, Ray, (Hey, this is the Spitfire pilot!) Hanna (Hey, this is Mark's father!) and we get to talking about my biplane and my tour and they suggest that if I would like a place to spread out my charts to do some flight planning, I can use their office in that little building over there, and there's some coffee or tea if I want some, and then they excuse themselves and walk over and disappear into that little building.

All of a sudden I'm thinking I really could use a table to spread out my charts, some place out of this hot sun, and I was probably magnetized by these two guys and wanted to find out more, so I mosey on over and, sure enough, there's Mark and he sets me up in a room with a great chart table and I'm looking around at all the neat airplane photos on the walls, and I'm getting the impression that there's more going on here than meets the eye. And there is, a lot more. Mark Hanna hands me their brochure...

Mark is the Managing Director of the Old Flying Machine Company (OFMC), which owns one of the world's foremost collections of rare vintage aircraft, most notably great piston engine fighters from WWII, as well as some classic and modern jet fighters. Ray and Mark do a lot of air show display flying as well as film work, having flown in most of the European based aviation productions in the last 10 years, including "Empire of the Sun," "Memphis Belle," "Air America" and many others.

Ray Hanna was a military pilot in 1951, flying FR9 Meteors and most of his missions were flown at or below 100 feet (he's gotten lower over the years but I don't imagine he can get much lower than he was today in that Spitfire). He was also the leader of the Red Arrows (like the Blue Angles in the US) from 1966-69, and then went on to a civil career with Boeing 707s and Lockheed L-1011s.

Mark Hanna was taught to fly at age 16 by his father and joined the Royal Air Force at 18. At 21, he was flying F4 Phantoms, and has since flown more than 60 different types of aircraft in 4,000 hours of flying, half in war birds.

I don't know about you, but when I get to meet people like this, I just want to breathe the same air they do —maybe I'll learn something.

Mark takes a minute to introduce me to Caroline who holds the OFMC together on the inside, dealing with the phones and paperwork and who knows what else because as soon as I meet her I'm on another planet because she is one of those rare people with a natural poise, grace and loveliness that leaves me either speechless or babbling. She would just as soon jump out of a plane (skydive) as she would fly, and she wears a necklace with a bone-colored Jonathan Livingston Seagull with outstretched wings. I'm smitten, and would like to know more, but I'm sure that's a common reaction with people who meet her.

Then there's Wayne Fuller who's working his way up the flying ladder at OFMC. Can you imagine learning to fly these great airplanes with Ray and Mark and getting *paid* to do it? Where do I apply? We get to talking and I find out he has an ultra-light (airplane) in his living room. He quietly demonstrates just how sharp he is by producing copies of some WWII airfield layouts he heard me mention to Mark that I was interested in checking out.

I'm talking with Wayne when in walks Peter Leggo (no, he didn't invent the toy), who is a geology researcher at Cambridge. He has built a lovely little biplane, a Pitts Special, from plans, and flies it, and that's an achievement that is completely beyond my imagination.

I have been extremely fortunate to meet some extraordinary people today, and it all started with a smile and a pleasant greeting. Try it yourself and see what happens.

P.S. For more about the OFMC check out: http://www.ofmc.co.uk

Day 77: They Saved the World

In a time long ago, throughout all of Europe, on the land, sea and in the air, a great war raged. An evil madman was destroying cities and killing millions of innocent people. It was a dark time for all civilized people, but the embers of hope continued to burn and young men with extraordinary courage carried this fire into battle.

One of the finest of these heroes, Lowell Williams, flew the legendary P-51 Mustang from an airfield in the land known as East Anglia, England. A quiet and unassuming gentleman, Lowell is now 75 years old, and five days a week teaches others to fly aerobatics in the friendlier skies over Southern California.

When I was just learning to fly, just four years ago, I had the good fortune and the privilege to meet Lowell, and he subsequently agreed to be my instructor. On one of our extended flying lessons, a six week tour from Michigan to the east coast and then back across the country, Lowell would occasionally talk to me of what it was like during those awesome times.

It was from these conversations that I learned about East Anglia, and the airfield called Leiston, and the 357th Fighter Group, and how pivotal the Mustang was at turning the tide of war in favor of the Allies, and about his personal experiences in aerial combat. From these conversations, I also learned from a master aviator and ace fighter pilot, other elements of safe flying: preflight preparation, weather, scanning for traffic, navigation, low level flight, formation flying, radio communications and more, which I would then put into practice in our subsequent flights, and which I still carry with me to this day.

The airfield at Duxford, where I have been staying for the last several days, is among the dozens of East Anglia airfields that were active during WWII. The field from which Lowell flew, Leiston, is just a little over 50 miles to the east of Duxford, so it seemed important for me to go there, and stand on the same ground where Lowell stood more than 50 years ago.

There are few traces left of the old air base. All the taxiways and two of the three runways are completely gone, and only a tenth of the other runway is left, but not usable. Most of the old buildings are gone without a trace, and there is no sign whatsoever that this place, now farmland, is where young gladiators of remarkable heroism lived, fought and died in the defense of freedom.

The local Leiston bookstore has no books whatsoever that deal with the topic of their local heroes, nor does the library. There is a museum in town, and when I went there expecting it to be a great resource of information, the very old lady at the admissions desk said that there was nothing inside about the airfield, or the Mustangs, or the war. It was an agricultural equipment museum, commemorating the machinery made on that spot by the former factory — another dead end. I was walking away dejectedly when a man came up to me and mentioned that there was a fellow I should meet, but that he was in a meeting and I should stop back in about an hour, and maybe he could help me. In the meantime, he suggested that I go out to the farm where the airfield once was, have a look around, and then come back.

It was as if the town had decided to forget it all as a bad memory. This is not an uncommon reaction for many of the people who lived and served during this period. Even Lowell will not speak of these times freely. It takes great patience and proper timing and the right company of a close friend before he will discuss it, and even then it does not come easily from him.

I was determined that I would not leave here without giving it a greater effort. The local gas station attendant directed me to the farm where the airfield once was. There are a few of structures, a long Quonset hut and a couple of small rectangular buildings which could have been of military design, which now house tractors and other farm implements. Mostly it was just farmland, and a couple of barns.

I wandered around and took a few photos, and soon I met the manager of the farm, Russell Thompkins, who was quite knowledgeable about the former life of this place. He confirmed that several of the buildings that I thought were of military origin were in fact from WWII, although their former usage is unknown. He drove with me to the middle of the fields and showed me the remnants of runway 13/31. He showed me how this narrow strip of runway was the center of the old runway, four times wider on each side of this center strip, and it was easy to see how the farmland on each side sloped down after the concrete was removed. He also showed me where the landing lights were embedded into the centerline. I reached down and lifted out a loose piece of concrete as a souvenir for Lowell, thinking of how the tail wheel on his Mustang probably touched down on this piece more than once in those perfect 3-point landings that he does so well even today.

Heading back into town, I met Tony Errington, who is the local liaison for the 357th Fighter Group reunions on the rare occasions when they come to England. The last time that happened was about five years ago. Tony told me that the museum did in fact have a small section of it dedicated to the Leiston airfield and the pilots who flew from there. He took us into the remotest corner of the top floor and there among the farm implements was a modest memorial. Some photos and some model Mustangs, and a twisted propeller blade dug out of the earth many years after the crash landing that killed the over-enthusiastic pilot who came in low on his last mission, and in the midst of his victory roll caught a wing tip in a tree.

From Tony, I learned about Gus Clutten. Gus was the groundskeeper on the airfield when it first opened in 1943 when it was used briefly for Thunderbolts. He fired up the ovens for the first meals on the base and cleaned the drains after rainstorms. He worked there every day the field was in operation. Gus now is still on the base, and at 82 years old, works every day as the manager of a caravan park called "Cakes and Ale" which is situated on a part of the old aerodrome. He was born in Leiston and has never left.

At the end of the road that leads into the caravan park, there is the only known memorial to the men of the 357th Fighter Group. It is small, but clean and well tended, with fresh flowers.

IN
MEMORY OF
357TH
FIGHTER GROUP
ESPECIALLY
THE 82 MEN
WHO LOST
THEIR LIVES
IN THE FIGHT
FOR FREEDOM

What it doesn't say is that the 357th Fighter Group was the first Mustang unit of the Eighth Air Force and destroyed the most enemy aircraft in a single day (55.5). They destroyed more enemy *jet* aircraft in air combat than any other group (18.5), and produced more aces than any other group (42). They were simply the best.

We drove back into town and had lunch in the bar at the White Horse Hotel, which today looks very much like it did when those great pilots gathered here to relax and enjoy some time off.

From there, I motored about 20 miles north to Seething, the site of another airfield where another good friend, Rusty Ruscetta, served in bombers. This field is still operational, but just barely. When I arrived, the office was closed and there were only two small airplanes on the parking area. It was deserted. There was a small monument by the entrance of the airfield, next to a building that could have been built in the 40's and used as a control room.

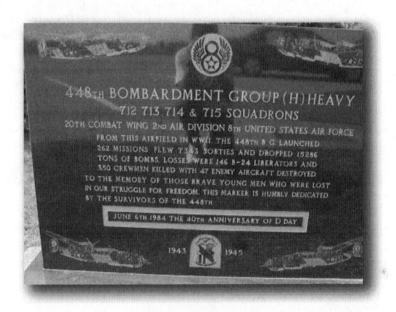

Only one of the original three runways is still in use, but it is now narrower, and the original concrete is now covered with asphalt. I found a large chunk of the original runway concrete and broke off a smaller piece for Rusty. I took a few photos and headed back to Duxford.

It seems to me that there could never be a memorial big enough to honor and thank all those men and women who served and suffered and died so that we can live free. Whether they served as pilots, like Lowell, or crew, like Rusty, or groundskeepers, like Gus, they united as a team against evil, and triumphed. These people saved the world for the rest of us. What will we do with it, knowing the great price that was paid?

Day 78: The Land Warfare Hall

Duxford, England

Tony Errington, the liaison for the 357th Fighter Group in England, who I met yesterday in Leiston, came over to visit Duxford today. His mission was to take some photos of the new American Air Museum, which had just opened August 2nd, and forward them to the members in the US.

First stop on Tony's visit was to check out my Waco biplane, which he seemed to like a lot, making all the right "ooh" and "ah" sounds and complimenting the workmanship of the builders. Of course, what he liked best of all was sitting in the cockpit.

Next, we visited the American Air Museum, and even though it was my second visit there this week, I still found plenty to keep me very interested. For lunch, we motored back to the Duxford Lodge where I'm staying, and ate in air-conditioned comfort. This was a really welcome break because there has been an unrelenting heat wave in England for a couple of weeks and the air is very humid and muggy.

In the afternoon, we visited the Land Warfare Hall, a part of the Imperial Warfare Museum, which I hadn't had the chance yet to investigate. There were many different Russian, US, and British tanks, motorized guns, Montgomery's Field Office vehicles, personnel carriers, amphibious vehicles and lots more. Tony really knows his stuff about these amazing machines. When he was only 16 years old, he volunteered for the Home Guard and soon found himself manning a 3.7-inch anti-aircraft gun. One of those guns is featured in the museum, and Tony was very informative in describing to me how it worked, and the routine for safe operation, and even the very risky procedure for removing a dud shell.

You can learn a lot about WWII in books, but you can't get the feel of it unless you talk with people like Tony. He lived through it, he fought the war on the ground in his own country, and he watched the dogfights in the air over his home. And more than 50 years later, he is still doing his part to show appreciation for the contribution the Americans have made in saving his country.

Day 79: Great Planes

The day started sunny, but by noon a solid layer of low clouds blocked the sun and lay over the airfield, creating a muffled quiet, and precluding any fun in my biplane.

I returned to the museums at Duxford and continued to explore several of the remaining hangars and attractions I haven't yet visited.

One of the better attractions was the Hughes 3-axis Simulator, which featured a five-minute ride called "Space Race." It left me sweating and exhausted, but enjoying every second of it. It's amazing how real a video can be when synchronized with full 3D motion. This is the future of home entertainment!

I have several friends who would like to see this next photo. The sign said it is a Chance Vought FG-1D Corsair, but I always thought they were F4U Corsairs. Anyway, it is one of the best airplanes ever built, and certainly one of the finest set of wings ever put on an airplane.

I have always liked the way the wings fold up on carrier-based aircraft, but I never saw a wing fold in two places, like this Fairey Gannet AS6. It was fitted with two Armstrong Siddeley "Double Mamba" turboprop engines mounted side-by-side driving two counter-rotating props, and with a crew of three was deployed for anti-submarine warfare.

From the bizarre to the good-looking, here's a shot of the Blenheim bomber that served the British during WWII:

Tomorrow is the day I make final arrangements for my Spitfire flight on Saturday. I hope the weather holds. I'm really looking forward to this.

Day 80: Playing On the Grass and in the Air

<u>Duxford, England</u>

Rain finally came to my part of England, but it had the good manners to occur overnight. Morning brought a thick cloud layer that started to break up before mid-day. By the time I strapped into my biplane, the day had cleared considerably, and the sun was shining brightly through scattered cumulus clouds.

I needed some time in the air. I have been on the ground too long, looking at other people's airplanes. I wanted to take an extended flight out to the east coast and fly along the water for a while, but the weather front that brought the rain last night was still between me and the coast, so it would only be some touch and go play for me today.

But that's plenty okay with me. After all, touch and go's at such an historical place as Duxford, on the grass, is a treat not likely to be matched for a long time.

As I fire up the big round Jacobs radial engine, and let it settle down to 700 rpm to warm up, I look down the line of airplanes parked on the grass next to me. To my right is a T-6 "Harvard," a B-17 Flying Fortress, a Grumman Goose (amphibian) and a Yak (Russian aerobatic). To my left is the Dewoitine D-27 flown by Mark Hanna a few days ago, two P-51D Mustangs (one of them "Big Beautiful Doll," is rigged up with 500 pound bombs for filming a new Tom Hanks movie), another P-51 Mustang (the early model A), a WWII twin-engine bomber and another T-6 Harvard. Most of these airplanes are being readied for use. It's going to be another great flying day at Duxford!

"Duxford Information, Waco biplane November Two Five Zero Yankee Mike, on the grass in front of the control tower."

"Zero Yankee Mike, taxi to holding point Two Four Bravo, wind is calm." I love that phrase "Wind is calm." It couldn't be a nicer way to go flying.

I push the throttle forward just a bit and taxi slowly to my left past the Mustangs with their crews working busily to prepare them for flight. This time, they barely take notice of my biplane as it passes them by. They have already seen it fly, and it has been here a week, so by now I'm just a part of the background, although this is the first Waco YMF-5 ever to visit England.

My biplane rolls smoothly along the grass, and I make S-turns to allow me to see forward past the big engine cowling. I'm in a very relaxed and almost euphoric mood as I drift slowly along this line of great aircraft, and on the same grass that has been graced by so many other historic airplanes, and a field that has hosted pilots of great fame over the last 80 years. This is the field where legendary legless British ace Douglas Bader flew sorties into the face of the invading enemy. This is also where many training accidents occurred, killing unlucky, or unskilled, or inattentive pilots. That thought gets me back to reality. Pay attention.

The run-up engine checks go smoothly. All instruments are okay. I visualize what I am about to do.

"Duxford, Waco Zero Yankee Mike, holding at Two Four Bravo, for the Grass."

"Zero Yankee Mike, takeoff at your discretion, wind calm, Left Hand pattern."

"Zero Yankee Mike is rolling, Two Four Grass."

Throttle full forward, the big engine growls and the biplane surges forward quickly, rolling along the grass with increasing speed until, with just the slightest bit of forward stick, the tail gets lighter and begins to lift almost imperceptibly, and I hold the stick back to build up speed enough to lift off in a three-point attitude. This is the prettiest takeoff to watch, as the plane seems to rise up into the air without any effort whatsoever.

As soon as we are airborne, I push the nose down and trim for level flight just a few feet above the runway, keeping the throttle full forward and building up speed until, right at the end of the runway, I pull stick back firm, climbing sharply to the left while the airspeed bleeds off rapidly, down to the normal climb speed of 75 mph. Then it's stick forward again to keep the airspeed in the climb-out.

The left turn to downwind is close in to the runway, and I'm hoping I'll be cleared for landing early, so I can make a short approach with power off, simulating a dead stick landing, but it won't happen this time around because the runway is obstructed with one airplane about to take off and another holding. I continue downwind, and notice the remainder of the weather front from last night still moving east about 20 miles away.

Keeping alert for traffic in the area, as well as watching the traffic departing from the runway, I turn left base and advise Duxford Information that I'm heading for final. "Zero Yankee Mike, cleared for the option, wind calm."

I turn left again, pull the throttle way back, gliding down from the pattern altitude of 1,000 feet AGL (Above Ground Level), keeping the runway numbers 24 in sight, just above the nose, continually adjusting pitch and power (but only by the very slightest amounts) to arrive at touchdown just a few feet beyond the numbers, in a perfect 3-point landing, and let it roll on without brakes, rumbling along the ground until, just before coming to a complete stop, I firewall the throttle, the engine comes to life and it's off we go again for more fun in the sky.

This is some of my favorite flying. Grass runways, calm wind, an open-cockpit biplane, hardly any traffic, spectators on the ground who appreciate (not complain about) the sights and sounds of aviation, the company of great airplanes, and great pilots from whom I can learn some of the finer points of flying.

I did about five circuits of the pattern today, some landings were perfect; one was a wheel landing (2-point), just for the practice.

One turn around the pattern was a low pass; just to practice what I imagined would be my "routine" at the September 7th Duxford Air Show. The low pass is the simplest of all display maneuvers and starts at pattern altitude just a bit past the numbers, diving down in a turn to the approach end of the runway, full throttle, pulling up maybe 10 feet above the runway for a level pass of the length of the field, and then pulling up hard for a climbing turn back downwind. That's it. Just a low pass so the crowd can see the biplane up close in flight. Simplicity itself. However, this will be my first air show as a display pilot. I have to start somewhere, and I can't think of a better thing to do on my birthday.

After my final landing, I taxi back to the parking area, unlock the tail wheel, hold right brake, and throttle forward to about 1,000 rpm, swiveling smartly 180 degrees to align my wings with the other planes on either side. Then, throttle back to idle for two minutes before shutting down. During this two minute period, I complete my logbook entries, and go through the process of removing flying gloves, turning off the avionics master switch, removing my helmet and kneeboard, stowing charts, etc. It's a quiet moment and I'm usually not looking outside the cockpit until I shut off the mixture control and the engine comes to a stop.

My ears take a few seconds to get used to the complete silence, and I'm sitting there reflecting on what a great time I have just had in the air, when I get the feeling that I'm being watched. Instinctively, I look left and there is a smiling face, standing about 10 feet away, waiting patiently for me to notice him.

Robert Hinton was watching my biplane in the pattern and wanted to stop over and say how much he likes it. He likes the idea of an open-cockpit biplane and may get one. Then he tells me about his airplane. It's a 1948 Swiss built Pilatus P2, with a 12-cylinder Daimler Benz Argus engine.

I made the hideous mistake of thinking it was a Chipmunk, which to me and from a distance looked similar, but on closer inspection it is much larger than a Chipmunk. It was like mistaking a Rolls Royce for a Checker Cab.

It is highly polished aluminum and shares the same running gear as German fighter ME 109. The air cooled V-12 is mounted inverted, and the finned spinner is of a very unusual design, probably something to do with the constant speed prop. Robert brought the airplane in for a complete engine overhaul at one of the restoration shops on the field. The TBO (Time Between Overhauls) is only 600 hours. Ouch! I'll bet that's expensive for a rare V-12!

We swapped stories about our airplanes, and Robert told me he took his tailwheel Pilatus off the first time without any tailwheel experience at all. Most of his time up till then was in his Beech Bonanza. It wasn't until a little later that he got to appreciate the demanding nature of a tailwheel airplane. I understand completely. I think it took me a couple of hundred attempts before the light of understanding and the learned reflexes finally started producing acceptable landings.

The more we talked, the more we had in common. He is in the computer graphics business, producing product-packaging designs, and has finished a database software program for the industry and is thinking about marketing options for it. He's also flown over to Ireland, my next big stop, and we talked about the various good places to visit. We swapped contact information and he gave me a lift back to my hotel on his way home. I have a feeling he may be flying a biplane in the not too distant future.

Duxford is feeling like home to me.

Day 81: Anticipation

Late yesterday afternoon, I learned that my Spitfire ride, scheduled for today, was going to be postponed for a couple of days. So instead of spending the day in a high euphoric state, I dragged my disappointed self over to the airport and generally moped around.

The weather was perfect for my mood — overcast with a strong gusting wind, over 20 knots most of the time. My weather senses tell me that the winds are bringing in another front, a big one this time. I'm getting the distinct feeling that the summer is drawing to a close. I don't want to dwell on that thought for very long.

The airport was very quiet today. The De Havilland Rapide that I flew in a few days ago blew a gasket and was grounded for repairs, disappointing others in their search for a memorable aviation experience.

I spent some time with my biplane, puttering about in the baggage compartment and rearranging some charts and equipment. Before I left, I turned it around on the grass facing into the increasing wind, and put some chocks under the wheels for the first time since I've been here.

I sat at a picnic table reading a flying novel for a couple of hours, the wind continually blowing cooler and wetter air, eventually forcing me to pack up and head back to the hotel.

As in Business, or Life, Flying has its Disappointments as well as its Joys. The only course is to look through the disappointments to the coming joy. I will fly a Spitfire, and it will be soon. As I write this, I am trying to find the way to look at this situation in a positive manner, and it finally comes to me: Anticipation of a pleasurable event is supposed to be half the fun of it. Therefore, by delaying the event a few more days, I have been given the great gift of even more anticipation! Meanwhile, it's a great day to do my laundry...

Day 82: Spitfire!

Duxford, England

The morning was a challenge. What would I do to while away the next 48 hours, waiting for my Spitfire ride? I have seen (almost) everything in the museums at the airfield. I enjoy waiting for things about as much I enjoy being boiled in oil while having my eyes jabbed with sharp sticks. There must be another way of "framing" this situation.

I'm sitting there in my hotel room thinking about my dilemma when through the open window I hear that awesome roaring sound of the magical Merlin-engined Spitfire! I leap to the window and stick my head out to get a better look. Sure enough, those lovely elliptical wings are impossible to mistake, as is the green-brown camouflage paint and the black and white "invasion stripes." It's on final approach to runway 24 at Duxford, but going much too fast to be landing, so it has to be going in for a low pass and probably a full aerobatic routine. I watch it until it disappears past the end of the building and then run to the other side of the hotel and watch through the window facing the airfield.

The pilot is definitely doing a full routine. I can't see it all because I am so far away, about two miles, and the airplane dips out of sight below some trees, but it's great to watch and try to predict exactly where it will reappear. At times, it comes very close to the hotel, which is at the edge of Duxford, the closest inhabited building to the airfield.

What was I complaining about? Did I need something to do for the next 48 hours? How could I be so blind? It's right here in my own back yard. I could watch these airplanes all day long. There is nowhere else in the world where I could enjoy watching Spitfires play in the sky, and take off and land on the grass. And it's free! And not just Spitfires; there are all kinds of toys that might be going up at any moment.

So, I will go back to the airport with a fresh attitude. I might not be able to fly one myself right now, but I can certainly watch, and imagine, and drool.

I'm downstairs and outside waiting for the taxi and another Spitfire is growling closer, then flashes overhead, straight and level, and keeps going to the northeast. It's the double-bubble canopy of Carolyn Grace's Spitfire, the one I'm supposed to fly on Monday. There can be only one explanation for this: Carolyn must be giving a ride to some lucky guy — it must be the "Yank" she mentioned, from Chicago. That means they'll probably be back within the hour. If I get over to the airfield quickly enough, I can catch their arrival and landing.

And besides, I've got to talk with Carolyn about my ride on Monday. She wanted me to meet her at an air show in York, which is a two and a half hour train ride north of here, and Monday is a Bank Holiday, so the train schedules are infrequent. I was thinking about going up there the night before, but she says the Spitfire has zero room for baggage. I'm not looking forward to waking up to my Spitfire ride without a shave and brushing my teeth and fresh clothes, so it looks like I'm going to have to get up real early on

Monday and take the only (very early) train that will get me to York in time to make my takeoff time slot at 1300 hours.

On the ride to the airfield, I watch Carolyn's Spitfire circling overhead, coming in for the low pass and aileron "victory" roll. We pull up to the front gate, I jump out, pay the driver and run a couple of hundred yards to where I can see them just coming in over the numbers for a perfect landing on the grass.

I ran over to my biplane, planning to be standing near it when they taxi past, so I can wave hello, to announce my presence on the field without being intrusive. I had in mind a discreet wave of my hand as I lean nonchalantly against my biplane, pretending to not even notice the Spitfire until the last moment. However, my natural enthusiasm overwhelmed me and I gave a huge sweeping wave of the entire arm, and even jumped up in the process. I did this twice; just to be sure it was not missed. I'm going to have to learn to get control of my emotions one of these days.

After Carolyn and her passenger dismount and take about 10 minutes to talk over the flight, I mosey on over and catch her eye. She smiles briefly, then walks over to me with a more serious look. She is concerned about the weather in York. It's raining there now, with ceilings down to 700 feet. If it continues that way for today, she won't be flying the Spitfire up there. And the weather is supposed to be even worse tomorrow, the day I'm supposed to fly. So she wants to wait a little bit and see what the weather is going to do today, and if it looks like it's going to continue to be bad in York, and if it's okay with me, then she'll takemeupformyflightthisafternoon.

Heavy emotional content received... Brain temporarily disengages during decoding of last transmission...

She'll takemeupformyflightthisafternoon?

She....will....take....me....up....for....my....flight....this....afternoon? What? I can fly the Spitfire today? In the air? Me? Spitfire? Today? Soon?

Hey, I'm not ready for this! It was supposed to be tomorrow, but actually it was supposed to be yesterday, and now it's today? Maybe. I just came over here today to *watch*. How is a person supposed to remain calm, normal and sane in the midst of all this uncertainty? I try to do an impression of a normal person, but I think my grunts and drooling and the leaping in the air gave it away. I am hopelessly unprofessional about it all.

I walk back to my biplane and hang out there for an hour or so. Carolyn said that if she was going to fly with me today, she would have me paged over the loudspeaker system. ("Michael McCafferty, alias The World's Luckiest Man for today, please report to the Spitfire for your lifetime supply of orgasms.")

For what seems like several eternities, I arrange and rearrange my baggage compartment as well as the front cockpit, then add some oil, update my logbook and read some of the flying novel I carry in my backpack for just such emergencies.

The wind picks up to about 15 knots, and a large dark cloud appears just to the north of the field. It is raining heavily nearby. We are definitely in for some unpleasant weather.

And then I look up and see Carolyn walking slowly across the grass, toward my biplane. The look on her face is not the look of someone about to go for a ride in a Spitfire.

She starts out the same way. The weather in York is awful, which is a pity because the organizers of the event won't have much of an event. The Red Arrows got within a few miles and had to turn back. She won't be going to York today. Soifyou'rereadywe'llgetyousuitedupforyourridenow.

I'm getting better at this decoding thing. This is it! The big moment. Gulp! I gotta pee! But there's no way I'm going to do anything that would delay this event. I know how things can change in an instant, and I wouldn't want to be telling my grandchildren the story about how I *almost* flew a Spitfire but I had to pee so it never happened because when I was peeing a big rain cloud dumped a hundred tons of water on the field, and then the rest of the day was shot with even worse weather.

This is where I discovered McCafferty's Second Law of Aviation: If you are going to fly a Spitfire, Fly now, pee later. Other than that, pee now, fly later.

Carolyn holds the seat-type parachute for me to climb into. I have done this before, so I am eager to show her that I don't need no stinking instructions, man. I back into the 'chute, put my right arm under the shoulder strap, then the left arm, then reach down to grab one of the leg straps, pull it up and start to thread it through... the D-ring! Duh! Hello? She catches me right away, of course, right about the same moment that I realize that I am doing a very stupid thing. Get hold of yourself, man. This is really embarrassing. You know very well where that strap goes. "Uh... just kidding Carolyn, I wanted to see if you were paying attention."

Next we walk over to the Spitfire, Carolyn stands on the wing root, and I'm on a step-stool contraption, and we are both hanging over the side of the rear cockpit, where I will fly, and she is giving me a briefing on the details of all the buttons and knobs and doodads and whatnots.

Most of it is about how I get out of the airplane in an emergency. Carolyn says simply: "If we have an emergency, I'll only say it once: 'Get out of the plane', then you pull this knobby thing, then punch out the canopy with your arm, and it *should* fly off, then unbuckle your harness, remove your helmet, and get out of the plane, keeping your hand on the D-ring of your 'chute, and pull it on your way down." Well, that sounds simple enough...

She continues: "However, if we *only* have an engine failure and have to make an emergency landing in a field or wherever, then you just want to pull the canopy back, *not* jettison it completely, so pull this *other* thingamajig, and *don't* punch the canopy off, lock it open by pulling *this* door handle just *part* way back, *not* all the way." She doesn't have to finish the rest of the story. I know the rest. *Don't* jump out of the plane just yet, wait until it comes to a stop and then jump out and run like hell before it blows up.

Other than that, have a nice flight!

Well, there are a few more things to discuss, like how I have to move my right leg out of the way when she switches the fuel selector handle from main to wing tanks after takeoff, then back to main tanks before landing. And here's the flaps control, the flaps are either up or down, nothing in between. And here's the landing gear control lever and indicators, seat adjustment lever, throttle, propeller pitch control, rpm, altimeter, airspeed, forget about the artificial horizon because it is completely dumped, here's the boost gauge for the supercharger, the turn coordinator, rudder trim, elevator trim, fuel pump warning light, oil pressure, coolant temperature, brake differential pressure, etc, etc, etc.

I'm trying to get this all in because I might just have to deal with it all, in the unlikely event that Carolyn becomes incapacitated ("Amazing but True: Spitfire pilot, bitten by tea weevil, goes unconscious. Biplane pilot brings craft to safe landing! Pilot Carolyn, recovering in hospital says: "Mikie is my hero!".... Pilot Mikie says "Aw, shucks, it was nuthin.' I just seen my dooty and I done it.")

What captivates my attention is a big old gnarly rocker switch on the control stick. Carolyn says it's for the guns. Yeah!

Back to reality, Carolyn jumps into the front cockpit and goes through her checklist audibly, then fires up the big V-12 Merlin engine. One thousand five hundred and sixty five horses spring to life! Oh, boy! She signals for removal of the chocks, and we taxi to holding point 24 Bravo.

As we are taxiing, I am noticing an unexpected noise, like short bursts of air being released. Carolyn explains it's the brakes, which operate on compressed air (just like the flaps). Steering on the ground is accomplished by differential braking.

The run-up magneto check is okay; we are ready to go. Carolyn gets clearance from the tower, pushes the throttle gently forward a little at a time, and soon we are rolling down the grass at Duxford, in a Spitfire, and I'm in it! Yes, there is a god!

The speed builds, and the lift lightens the airplane to the point where we are an inch or less off the ground, then we touch down again into a rise in the uneven runway, and then we are fully up in the air again, this time for sure. The wheels come up, but the airplane stays down low, building up speed until we are past the other end of the runway, then we pull up into a gentle climbing left turn into the downwind leg of the pattern. We level out at about 1,500 feet and Carolyn guides this sweetly singing bird out over the farmland beyond Duxford. "There's Cambridge, there's Duxford, and over there is...."

Yeah, right, Carolyn, but I'm not up here for sight-seeing, show me what this baby will DO! I don't say this of course, I'm much too polite, but I sure do think it.

The sky is alive with clouds at every level. Just above us at about 1,800 feet there is a scattered layer of light cumulus. Above that is another broken layer at around 2,500 feet, billowing to around 4,500 feet. Lots more scattered and broken layers are visible through the holes all the way to 15,000 feet and beyond. In several places, all around us, there are dark cells of rain showers. Carolyn finds a likely place to play, but keeps it below the lowest broken layer.

She does a few easy turns to loosen up; then a couple of steep turns, pulling a couple of G's in the process. The Spitfire is wheeling around in a tight circle, one wing pointed straight down at the ground. It's beautiful beyond words to see that perfectly shaped wing, so strong and true, but there is an even more beautiful sight, the other wing, pointing straight up to heaven with a background of God's finest clouds.

Straight and level, boost up, then diving slightly to build up speed to 240 mph. Stick back into 30-degree climb, then stick full left for an aileron roll. Oh yes, we are rolling in a Spitfire, and it is doing it like it's a natural bodily function, no problem at all. Again, into a dive to regain our speed and another roll, another dive and this time it's not a roll, but straight up, up, up, and up-side down, we are doing the loop thing! I tilt my head up and see the horizon, blue side down! Coming out of the loop on the down side, we roll out for a Half-Cuban-Eight. And then another. Then a full loop, pulling about 3.5 G's coming out the bottom.

"You have the airplane!" says Carolyn. This is the moment of truth. I take the stick; the airplane is under my control. "I have the airplane," I confirm. Now what am I going to do?

The control stick is very different than anything I have used before. While the stick is mounted to the floor of the aircraft, and hinged at the bottom to control pitch, the entire stick does not move side to side, just the top third! This is done as a compromise due to the cramped cockpit. There isn't enough room to move the entire stick. So there are two different pivot points to deal with in a climbing or diving turn. In addition, there is no classical pistol grip at the top of the stick; it is a loop-shaped grip, which could actually be gripped with both hands, if you needed to. I find the entire arrangement very awkward, but obviously it's just a matter of what you get used to. Spitfires with this stick sure outclassed a lot of enemy aircraft during the war.

The pitch (up/down) control is very sensitive, a lot more sensitive than the aileron control. As far as rudder controls go, I had a bit of a challenge figuring out the right touch, probably because the prop spins the wrong way (the reverse of US aircraft) therefore reversing the torque characteristics from what I am used to. I could eventually make a decent turn without slipping or skidding too much. I did a few easy turns and then some tight turns, and tried my best to keep from climbing into the clouds, but the pitch is very, very sensitive. It took a few minutes for me to get the hang of it.

We were cruising around the neighborhood at about 2,000 feet, and I mentioned to Carolyn that I wanted to find a little more altitude for some aerobatics. I'm used to having about 3,500 feet under me when I go looping and rolling around the sky. It's comfortable insurance to have some extra time to recover if things get weird, like a wing coming off, or whatever. Carolyn's reply was that it was not going to happen today. The loops and rolls, that is. She no longer lets passengers do that stuff, ever since the ride with the guy who froze at the controls when the engine quit while upside down. (That's a particular personality quirk of this airplane during any maneuvers less than 1G.)

"However, if you want, you can come back in two weeks and Peter (the guy who taught her to fly the Spitfire) will take you up and you can do anything you want! Shall I book you with him?"

Yes! Now we are talking! So it looks like this is just my introductory flight. A chance for Carolyn to get to know if I'm capable and trustworthy behind the stick, and if I pass, then I get invited back to play for real. This is so very cool. I'll be back!

We play a little bit more, then Carolyn takes us back to the airfield and we are blasting down the runway for a low pass, about 20 feet off the deck, and I am looking at Duxford airfield in a whole new way... hey, there's my biplane on the grass parking area... nice plane... and up, up, up we go again for a victory roll. Oh, yes, this is just so much fun I don't want to stop, but I know this is the end of it because we are headed downwind, the boost comes back, the airplane slows, the wheels come down, we turn base, then final, and we are set up real nice for a landing.

I can't see much forward because the back of Carolyn's headrest blocks my field of vision. However, the canopy is bulged out on the sides so I can press my head up tight against the Plexiglas and get just the slightest bit of forward visibility. It would be a real mess to try to land this airplane from the rear seat. Probably have to sideslip it down, then straighten it out at the last second.

I'm surprised that the airplane lands so slowly. Carolyn holds it to 90 knots on final. It stalls at less than 50 knots (my Waco stalls at 59 mph!). However, the true Achilles heel of this airplane is the ground handling. The main gear is surprisingly close together, and there is a lot of weight in the wings, so ground loop accidents were not uncommon. By comparison, the Mustang main gear is probably twice as wide as the Spitfire.

Carolyn is very well set up for landing, and I'm expecting it to be perfect. She probably was too. But the unexpected happens and it bounces. Not real bad, but not the flawless work that has become her standard. I can certainly empathize. Some of my landings have been hilarious to onlookers (but not to me at the moment!). I would term the landing "effective, but inelegant." So what, let's focus on what really matters: We were flying a Spitfire! And now what really matters is where's the loo? I really gotta pee!

Day 83: Nice People, Nice Day

Duxford, England

How does one face the day *after* an astoundingly excellent day? It seems impossible that today could be any better than yesterday, and maybe that means that today will be less than yesterday, and that seems like a negative thought to start the day, so I throw that thought out and think about some good stuff. In fact, today turned out to be a great day.

First of all, my Waco got washed! Notice how I didn't say that I washed it. That was one of the finer things about today. And one of the other really nice things about today was directly related to the washing of the Waco.

It started yesterday afternoon with the Spitfire ride. One of the guys on the ground crew for Carolyn's Spitfire is Graham Marks. He helps get the aircraft in and out of the hangar, oversees refueling, starting, etc. Without him, or someone to do these things, it just couldn't happen. You can't just jump in your Spitfire and go flying. You need help. That's Graham's job. I met Graham before my flight when I asked him to use my camera to take a few photos. He took those shots of Carolyn and me by the Spitfire.

We got to talking a little after the ride, and I helped push the Spitfire back in the hangar. Thunderstorms were due in the evening, and I asked Carolyn if there was any more hangar space for the Waco. "Sure!" Graham helped me push the Waco about a quarter mile from the parking area to the hangar, right in front of the Spitfire. While we are huffing and puffing and pushing my biplane uphill to the hangar, I asked Graham if there was any way I could get my biplane washed. He said I was really at the ragged edge of my luck with a question like that, but he would make a phone call and see what he could do.

He calls his friend Marian, a nurse who works with terminally sick patients. She is temporarily between patients right now (for the most obvious of reasons) and could use the money. She says yes, and they agree to wash the airplane the following morning. That was yesterday.

This morning, I awoke to a sound I hadn't heard in the last several weeks. It was the soft sound of a gentle rain. Looking out the window it was clear that it had been raining most of the night, and the sky promised to continue with more of the same for at least several more hours. It was the kind of morning that is just perfect for staying in bed.

I figured that the rain would be a logical excuse to *not* wash an airplane, if Graham and Marian were looking for one. By mid-day the rain stopped and the sun actually appeared briefly between the broken clouds. I took a taxi over to the airfield to see if the Waco was any cleaner, but I was prepared for a no-show.

It was beautiful! Graham and Marian had worked non-stop since before I even rolled out of bed, and it was way past lunchtime. The biplane never looked better!

This isn't just a story about a clean biplane. It's really a story about some awesome people. Graham doesn't work full time for The Fighter Collection or Carolyn Grace. He is a volunteer! He gets zero pay. In real life, he is paid to be an engineer, making prototypes of whatever. I didn't get all the details of what he does, but it's obvious he doesn't wash airplanes, or refuel them, or push them around for a living. He does it for fun. He isn't washing my biplane for the money, because all the money is going to his friend, Marian! So what Graham is doing is taking his day off from his paid work, and a day off from his volunteer work, to help his friend Marian earn some money, and at the same time helping *me*. Staggering!

And when you consider the kind of work Marian does for her real work, well she has got to be one of those truly saintly people. She has never washed an airplane before, and I'm sure she didn't jump for joy at the idea when Graham first mentioned it yesterday, but here she is helping her friend Graham while helping me!

So how did it ever come to pass that I get to have two of the world's nicest people wash my biplane? I have no idea, but it was a real pleasure to meet these great human beings, and I wanted to share them with you!

Later in the day, I returned to the Duxford Lodge. When I checked in there almost two weeks ago, I thought I would stay only a couple of days. I guess you could say I like the place. The room is comfortable, the food is good (French trained chefs) and the staff are excellent!

Speaking of staff, this afternoon is their "Christmas Party," and they are having a great time. For the first time since I have been here, I get a chance to relax and talk with two of the best of the staff at the hotel, Jannick and Geraldine. I have been smitten with Jannick since she first smiled my way, and uttered a sweet French-accented greeting. Jannick, only 21, enjoys skydiving, except for that one time she got caught in some telephone wires and had to be rescued. She got all excited when she thought she might go for a ride in the Waco, but unfortunately our schedules, and the weather, conspired to keep it from happening. Meet Jannick:

For dinner, I was invited to join Bob and Victoria George and their daughter Marina, who are moving here from Seattle. They are staying at the Lodge until they find a new home in the area. Victoria will be doing her thesis at Cambridge University, and Bob is starting his aviation consulting business in London. Real nice people; real nice day!

Day 84: Floats For My Biplane?

<u>Cambridge, England</u>

I had to move out of the Duxford Lodge today — no room at the inn. It was time for me to see some different sights anyway, so I chose to go to Cambridge. Maybe some of the university life will make me smarter. I could also use a new menu. I have had every breakfast and dinner at the Lodge for the last 12 days: Great food, but I need a change. And while the Lodge is real homey, it is isolated from everything except the airfield, so it will be good to get into a town environment for a while, until the weather front moves past.

The Georges, who I had dinner with last night, drove me over to the airfield in the morning to see my biplane. Bob has some time in a Stearman, and is looking forward to getting back into the air again here in England. He is just totally stoked with the Waco, and as I say goodbye to them and wish them luck with their new life in England, I can see the gears in Bob's head turning, figuring how he can get one of these awesome airplanes.

I spent some time with my navigation charts, planning my next flight. I want to get over to Ireland. That means an over-water flight, across the Irish Sea, a little bit longer than the flight crossing the English Channel, if I cross at the narrowest point. I'd also like to stop at Newcastle-Upon-Tyne on the east coast, by the England/Scotland border, about two hours north of here. It could be a great flight all along the east coast of England.

The weather this morning is unexpectedly excellent. I get the urge to fly north right away and beat the weather system which is headed this way and is sure to keep me from flying for another day or so. It is real tempting to go for it, but since I wasn't expecting this opportunity I haven't prepared properly for the flight. I haven't reviewed the airspace I'd be going through, or checked out the airports I would be using, or alternates. Maybe I could accomplish all this in the next few hours, and still make it to Newcastle today, but I know I wouldn't feel comfortable rushing through it. So even though the day is looking so fine for flying, I let it go. There is always another day.

Some details need attention. My special European flying insurance is going to expire August 31. I need to renew it real soon, or I can't fly. The broker is in Switzerland, but he is out of the country on vacation until after the policy expires. I need to work on a solution.

Another detail is the air show on September 7 at Duxford: They want me to fly in it, and I need to get more info about the specifics. I want to be real clear about it so I don't do something stupid in front of a hundred thousand people.

One more thing: The Waco factory wants to use my biplane to demo it to some prospective buyers in Europe, people they met at the Paris Air Show in June. We need to coordinate our schedules on when that will be. That means that I must give some thought to when I will be going home. It's not a thought that I want to dwell on. I'm having too much fun.

In my conversation with the Waco factory, I learn some startling news. They are building *floats* for the biplane! They will be ready for testing in October. This is just wonderful news to me because I have always pictured my biplane on floats and wanted to splash it in the water. I earned my seaplane license a couple of years ago (in a Super Cub on floats) and it was more fun than I have ever had in an airplane.   To have floats on my biplane would just be spectacular! I can't wait to try it out...

The Mustangs were playing over the airfield again today.

Day 85: Ghosts of Greatness

Cambridge, England

Before the rains came, I had a chance to take a walking tour of Cambridge, and wandered into a little alleyway off a side street, and discovered "The Haunted Bookshop." It's a tiny shop with old books piled all over the floors and desktop and up the walls to the low ceiling. Sarah Key, the owner, sat solidly behind her desk, sorting and pricing volumes, while an assistant handed recently acquired books to her for review. When I asked if she had any books on the subject of aviation, the answer was an immediate "No."

And then a man standing nearby produced "Aerial Wonders of Our Time." Eight hundred and four big pages of text and hundreds of rare photos covering the great advances in aviation up through the mid-30's, the time of its publication in England. What a treasure!

It was the perfect companion for the rest of the day, as it rained persistently throughout the afternoon. Although I was not flying my beloved biplane, I was with Bleriot when he became the first man to fly across the English Channel in 1909, and I could relate with his discomfort and disorientation when out of sight of land and in heavy haze. I also joined Francesco Agello at Lake Garda in 1933 when he flew the 24 cylinder 3,000 horsepower Macchi-Castoldi seaplane to a new word record, a phenomenal 440.6 mph. I looked into the eyes of Lt. Col. Bishop who had 72 victories in air battles in WWI to his credit.

These heroes, these ghosts of greatness and more, kept me company today. And it didn't matter about the rain. We had a fine time.

Day 86: Cloud-Slop

Last night, the TV weather forecast for today showed clouds and lightning bolts and rain all over Ireland and England, except for a thin band of lovely clear green over the east coast of England and Scotland, which is exactly where I wanted to go. Now, you know you can't believe everything you see on TV, especially when it comes to weather forecasts, and even more especially when they use those magnetic stick-on cartoon clouds, lightning bolts, and raindrops. How accurate could it possibly be?

I know this; you know this. But I was ready to get out of the Duxford/Cambridge area, so I just ignored the stupidity of it all and focused on that little green band of clear area that they probably missed with their magnetic nasties.

In the morning, I woke with full resolve to fly to Newcastle-Upon-Tyne, on the Scotland/England border, on the east coast, about 200 miles north of Duxford. I kept ignoring the very gray skies; the low ceilings and the cold, wet air that made me wonder where the summer had gone.

I checked out of the hotel, but told them I might be back in a couple of hours. It all depended on the weather. The streets in front of the hotel were still wet from the rain. By the time I arrived in Duxford, it was looking better, maybe even flyable.

I went right to the tower, and requested a forecast for Newcastle, and points along the way. It sure didn't look like the TV forecast from last night, indicating chances of rain showers all the way. It was obvious that it was going to be one of those flights where it is a waste of time to draw a course line on the charts, as I would be ducking and dodging the weather the whole way, and hoping that it didn't close in behind me and cut off the possibility of retreat.

The only good thing was that the visibility was excellent. I would be able to see rain showers from a long way off. On the horizon to the west, I noticed a slice of sky that was clear and blue headed my way, and thought how nice it would be if I could fly north in that opening. I decided to go. By the time I was rolling down the runway for takeoff, that clear blue sky had disappeared; covered over by a congealed mass of low and fast moving rain clouds.

For the next two hours I was flying in a sky that looked as if it had been the result of an explosion in a cloud factory. It was the worst mess of a sky I have seen, with dark pewter gray clouds at every level, broken and scattered patches of cumulus mixed with active towering mountains of bright white cumulo-nimbus. It seemed as if the hand of God had reached into a cosmic bowl of cloud-slop and flung it far and wide and up and down. There was haze, ground fog, mist and virga and even areas of bilious yellowish-green pollution layers overlying some industrialized areas. Yuk!

I was constantly changing my altitude to stay above or below these random layers, always trying to second-guess what I would encounter next. And at the same time, I was being vectored around by traffic controllers to avoid traffic, or some restricted area.

The flight did have some redeeming qualities. There was a tailwind of about 15 to 20 knots, and since there was a high overcast, the air was very smooth for the entire trip. In summary, although it was busy, it was an easy flight. By the time I landed in Newcastle I was ready to fly some more. It was exciting. I was energized!

I wanted to come to Newcastle to visit the headquarters of The Sage Group PLC, the software company that bought my software company in October of 1992. I had been growing my TeleMagic software package and its dealer network for over seven years, and it was time for me to convert my paper equity into something more real, and to relax for a while. The pain in my side had been growing worse for more than two years, and selling was the only option. The pain disappeared completely two days after the sale. Stress can be a killer.

So my plan was to stop in and say hello to the nice people at Sage and to thank them once more for their confidence in the future of my company, and especially for making it possible for me to retire. About six months ago, I let them know that I might be stopping in on my tour of Europe, but I couldn't tell them exactly when. They didn't know I was coming today, so I wasn't disappointed when I called from the airport and found that the people I knew at Sage were either out of town or on vacation.

The Sage Group is a real success story. Prior to 1981, Paul Goldman had a small printing company and decided he needed a more efficient way to calculate price estimates. He contracted with Graham Wylie to write a computer program to automate the process for his own needs but quickly discovered that they could sell the software to other printers. Next, they worked together to write software to automate the accounting for small businesses and formed Sage.

They have been very successful. For the last full year of operations, they sold more than $200 million of software and services with a 15% bottom line profit, a 30 percent increase from the year before. In the five years since they bought my company, the value of their shares (London Exchange) has increased more than eight-fold.

It's a first class operation in every respect, and it was a good visit. I met with Aidan Hughes, the Finance Director, and we toured their customer service operations and had a polite cup of coffee in the boardroom. Then he drove me back to my hotel. I have always had the highest respect for the people at Sage.

It's a shame that the people I know here were on vacation, I would have liked to take them for a ride in my biplane.

Hmm.... do you think they knew that?

Day 87: Discoveries, Old and New

The weather forecast indicated it would be a typical British day with lots of low clouds, rain, cold and wind. Not the kind of day for flying an open-cockpit biplane. I decided to explore the Newcastle area.

The porter at the hotel arranged for a taxi driver friend of his, Steve, to take me out to Hadrian's Wall, a major archaeological site, a 40-minute drive to the west of Newcastle. It was a very pleasant and relaxing tour, as Steve was in no hurry at all. We motored along high-crowned country roads that were barely wide enough for two cars to pass each other, and in some cases only one car wide, with occasional small roadside spots to pull over and let oncoming traffic pass by. The properties were mostly small plots separated by ancient walls of stone dug out of the farmland. The stones were cut on all sides to fit perfectly with their neighbors on the wall, and no mortar was used. Simplicity and elegance; effectiveness and efficiency.

We finally arrived at Hadrian's Wall; a defensive bastion built by Roman armies around 125 AD, to ward off the attacks from northern tribes, who were in a habit of sacking British towns and taking away silver, gold and pretty girls. Hadrian, the Roman Emperor, must have heard about the Great Wall of China, and figured that an economy version would work here. Unfortunately, as we know so well, walls don't work; especially in this case, because Hadrian's Wall was only about 80 miles wide, and Britain is about 200 miles wide. He probably never even thought of the possibility of the Norsemen sailing their ships around the wall. But an Emperor needs to come up with solutions, and this was the best he could do.

Today, Hadrian's Wall is a sad pile of rocks, rebuilt in some sections by archaeologists, and torn away in other sections by locals in search of free building materials for their homes. If you stand at the top of the hill, and look down the long narrow wall into the distance, you can imagine the hard life endured by Roman soldiers who were stationed here, and the long hours on guard duty, patrolling the walls in driving rain, fierce cold, snow, and the constant fear of being attacked by savages intent on taking off with your girlfriend at the local pub. The pleasures of Rome must have seemed a long way away.

My tour of Hadrian's Wall was interrupted several times with cold rain showers driven by high winds. Soon enough, I decided I had seen enough and opted for the comfort of the car, where Steve had cleverly decided to stay warm and dry while I explored.

We motored back into Newcastle-Upon-Tyne, and Steve pointed out the local attractions, including the remains of the ancient wall which surrounded the heart of the city of Newcastle. He left me to go on foot for a few hours, and agreed to meet me later at the base of the great statue of Earl Gray (after whom the tea was named) that dominates the central section of the city.

By this time, the day had cleared up considerably, and the sun was shining brightly, although intermittently, through fast moving cumulus clouds. The streets were crowded with people and cars. It was payday, the end of the month, the end of summer, and the beginning of the school term (the university has over 20,000 students). For an hour or so I wandered aimlessly, window shopping and snacking on local foods, and eventually found myself drawn into a Dillon's Bookstore.

The place sells no old books at all, so I can't imagine why I went there in the first place. I'm only interested in the old stuff. But I suppose a new bookstore is better than no bookstore at all. The place is large with three floors of books on every conceivable subject.

There were plenty of textbooks for the university students as well as lots of fiction, and I passed by all of the shelves on the first floor without so much as touching a single volume.

The second floor was much the same and when I passed by the section of Biographies, I stopped to scan the personalities featured there, but was not interested in anything I saw. And then for some totally unknown reason, my hand reached out to pull back a small volume for closer inspection. It was completely undistinguished in its color, jacket design, and general nature, and I still have no idea what made me sit down and start to read. The title "The Diving Bell and the Butterfly" was boring and vague, and the author, Jean-Dominique Bauby, was unknown to me. Why am I reading this?

If you read only one book this year, I suggest that you invest the time to read this scant 139-page miracle of literature. It is the too-short story of Mr. Bauby's (previously the editor-in-chief of ELLE magazine) brief struggle with survival after a stroke in December 1995, which left him totally paralyzed with the sole exception of the ability to blink his left eyelid. And yet, with that singular ability to communicate, he found the way to dictate this book, letter by individual letter, painstakingly, over a period of months in the summer of 1996. The book was just published in March 1997 after his death. It is a fantastic story, beautifully written, and stands out as a monument to man's ability to overcome seemingly insurmountable obstacles, as long as there is the will to do it.

I have no idea why my hand chose that book. It may be more properly stated that the book chose my hand. Hopefully, it is because, now that you know of it, your hand will choose it for yourself, and you will be as moved by it as I was.

Day 88: Roots

County Donegal, Ireland

For three months, I have been looking forward to landing my biplane at in Ireland, and especially in County Donegal. I thought that if I were able to get there, then the whole tour would be worthwhile.

Situated on a narrow spit of land just a stone's throw from the North Atlantic Ocean, this little airport is a bright sparkle on the Emerald Isle, in the midst of some of the prettiest landscape in the world.

County Donegal, Ireland is the birthplace of my great grandfather. For me, it is like coming home.

Early this morning, in Newcastle-Upon-Tyne, the weather looked marginal. It was only my optimism that made it seem flyable. There was a low solid overcast, and the air was very cold, but the visibility was good. I resolved to check out of the hotel, go to the airport and wait until conditions improved enough to fly. I would wait all day if I had to, and then check back in to the hotel if I couldn't fly. My caution was unwarranted, as the sky soon brightened, the clouds separated and there appeared great patches of blue. By the time I got to the airport, it was a spectacular day to fly!

My plan was to fly directly to the west coast of England, the small military airport of West Freugh, refuel and check the weather before crossing the Irish Sea, bypass Belfast and fly straight for Londonderry in Northern Ireland, where I would stay overnight, then fly to Donegal in the morning. It went better than I expected, in some respects.

Preflight preparation was interrupted several times with many people coming around to check out the biplane, take pictures, ask questions, tell stories, etc. This is the first time a Waco like mine has ever been in England, so there are plenty of people who want to get a look.

I wish I had taken more time to talk with one person in particular. It seemed as if we had much in common. His name is Gary Foster, and he works at Samson Aviation, the FBO where I hangared my plane. He will be going on vacation to the US next week and the first stop is Philadelphia, my home town, to go to the Eagles/Packers game, then on to San Diego, my new home, for a couple of weeks. He wanted to rent a plane in San Diego, so I suggested that he call John Hughes, a fellow Brit, at Oceanside airport. It was amazing to find someone in such a remote corner of the world as Newcastle, and within just a few moments of small talk, find so many common threads.

Taking off on runway 07 into the calm air of Newcastle, I turned left to 270 degrees, staying below the cloud bases at 2,400 feet. Soon I was flying over Hadrian's Wall, reflecting again on the folly of it all. As I progressed farther west into a mild 10-knot headwind, the clouds thickened and forced me lower and lower until I was cruising at only 1,200 feet. And then the clouds separated again, and the high ground fell away, and I was flying over wide beaches and rugged cliffs enjoying the scenery.

Then the cloud layer reappeared. This time I had to climb above the layer that was facing me, and eventually I was forced to more than 5,500 feet, and getting very cold. There was no relief in sight as I neared the west coast of England. West Freugh was closed for the weekend, so I would have to continue across the Irish Sea above the clouds, without refueling, and with no land, and very little sea, in sight. It wasn't anywhere as nerve wracking as my crossing of the English Channel, but I would have to admit to being a little on edge about it. All I could see in all directions were clouds, all the way to the horizon. It was only by looking straight down that I could catch a brief glimpse of the Irish Sea.

I was in touch with Belfast Approach Control the whole time, and they told me the weather at Londonderry was good, with 2,500-foot ceilings and 30-kilometer visibility. The only problem was how I was going to get down under the clouds so I could find Londonderry, and I wanted to get lower to get warmer.

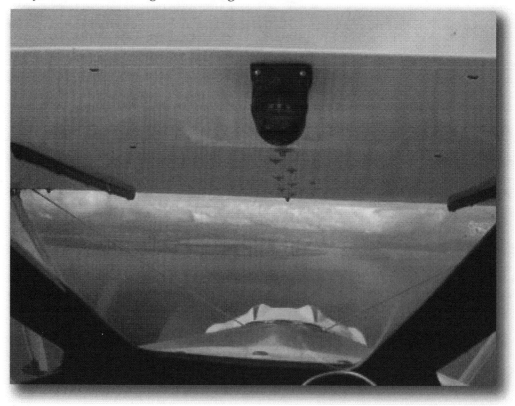

Just in time, a hole in the clouds appeared, and through the hole I could see the east coast of Ireland! The hole was just barely big enough for me to dive through, but I figured I wasn't going to get a better chance, so I went for it. It was so good to see Ireland from the air, even if it was Northern Ireland. Actually, it was great to see Any Land after being stuck on top of the clouds over open water.

By the time I was over land again, I found myself back in the old game of Squeeze Play again. The clouds lowered and the ground rose up, leaving me less and less room to maneuver. The visibility dropped dramatically as rain showers developed and faded as if in a vague dream. I was able to continue to Londonderry only by weaving through valleys that seemed to always be in the right places to avoid the heaviest of the rains.

I couldn't avoid all the obstacles, however. I was just too busy dealing with the rain and terrain, as well as looking for traffic, and I didn't look at my charts for a few minutes, so I missed the military parachute jump zone and flew right through it. Fortunately, it was not raining jumpers at the time, but the air traffic controller mentioned that we would have a discussion about it when I landed. He had noticed that my ground track was taking me into the zone, and tried to radio me, but my radios were acting up again and I couldn't understand him, even after asking him to repeat several times. I really must get those radios checked out.

The people at Londonderry were very pleasant and helpful. They told me that all of the restrictions and regulations regarding Customs clearance, "Special Branch" notification and airport prior notice had been eliminated, and that I could fly on to Donegal without anything more than a flight plan required because it was considered an International flight from Northern Ireland to the Republic of Ireland. Maybe someday it will be all one Ireland again.

I had planned to stay over in Londonderry, but Donegal was only 42 miles away. I could almost see it from the control tower at Londonderry. The visibility was still good, and even though I would possibly have to skirt a rain shower or two on the way, I decided to go for it. It was just too tempting. I had a quick lunch, refueled and I was back in the air within 90 minutes.

This was probably the easiest flight I have ever had, in spite of the unfamiliar terrain, the low clouds, and the rain. I felt a great ease come over me as I flew for the first time in the Republic of Ireland, watching the small green pastures and farmlands slip slowly under my wings. This is the land of my ancestors. The McCafferty clan has been here for hundreds of years, and although I wasn't born here I am probably the first in our family to fly over this countryside. I feel very much at home.

The landscape of County Donegal is quite varied: vast stretches of patchwork farms, lots of hills, rivers, valleys, lakes, peninsulas, islands, villages and one little airport sitting all by itself next to the ocean. I went the long way, taking some extra time to enjoy the scenery, and then at long last, after three months of anticipation, I finally touched down at Donegal. It was so very sweet.

The photo above shows our roving biplane pilot, just landed at the County Donegal airport. The monument stone is cut in Gaelic, the local language. English is taught as a second language.

Day 89: Mourning the Princess

County Donegal, Ireland

As my biplane rested quietly in the hangar at Donegal airport, the day wore on in a relentless drizzle from a gray and gloomy sky. The rain-dappled window of my room looked out onto a landscape made barren and featureless by a veil of fog and cloud. Cold it was, a cold that seeks your bones.

It was a day fitting for the mourning of Princess Diana. When I reflect on her premature and wasted passing, I am given to thinking of the greatness in each of us, the gifts we all have to share with each other, the gifts of friendship, compassion, warmth and love. In her, these traits were so highly visible, and they are also quietly at the core of these people in Donegal, and in all of us, if we choose to set them free.

This morning I started to notice the first signs of a scratchy throat, probably a souvenir of yesterday's damp and chilly flights. It would have been perfect if this hotel had a fireplace to keep warm, but it doesn't, so I had to seek the medicinal internal warming of Paddy's Irish whiskey, civilized with a cup of tea. I used this same remedy in Paris with great success. The symptoms persisted, but the concern evaporated.

Donegal is a land situated on the northwest coast of Ireland, bravely facing the harsh cold storms that attack from the North Atlantic. The people who have survived in this climate have had to learn to deal with Nature on its own terms. Their lives are simple, and move with a pace that is in keeping with the environment. Their homes are simple, many still with thatched roofs. The stores sell only basics, as the people have neither the desire nor the wealth to seek the frills of more complex civilizations.

There is, however, a song that can be heard on the lips of every person you meet, and that is their language. It is a lilting, singsong lullaby, a playful, teasing, fun-loving spirit that comes from their soul. They may have the most minimal personal possessions, and almost no hope of ever achieving more in this remote place, but their voices are priceless living works of musical art, free for the asking and many times even if you don't. They are a friendly people, uninhibited and yet shy, blushing easily and brightly through pale white-skinned faces. These are the Irish, my people, and my heritage.

Those Irish who are still here on this island are descended through centuries of grinding hardship and persecution, a legacy which most of them bear with stoicism. It is only a minority who has taken to extreme political measures to force their voices to be heard. The great majority is peaceful, loving, family oriented and religious, enduring the hardships of the present and praying for peace in the future.

The photo below shows the view at low tide on a cold and rainy day, from the Ostan Gweedore Hotel and Leisure Complex in Bunbeg, County Donegal, Republic of Ireland.

Day 90: Miracles and Monarchs

Doon Well, Ireland

There is an ancient holy place in County Donegal called Doon Well, the site of a natural spring, the waters of which are said to have special healing powers.

Beside the well grows a bush upon which are tied countless pieces of fabric from the bandages of the pilgrims who have come here for healing. Among the branches and stuck in the ground around the bush are crutches and walking sticks, some of which must have been here for a long, long time.

It is Donegal's most celebrated Holy Well, and has been a place of pilgrimage for hundreds of thousands of people in the past century alone. But its origin and the traditions associated with it go back much further.

There are many other holy wells scattered throughout Donegal, some of much greater antiquity than at historic Doon. But none is held in greater veneration or visited by such vast numbers. Year by year, especially from the beginning of May until late September, never a day and hardly an hour passes without its quota of pilgrims. They come in silence and barefoot, reverently reciting the traditional prayers and partaking of the water and bearing away with them the bottles of holy water for use by the sick and infirm at home or to send to relatives and friends in distant lands. It is said that hardly a single Catholic home in all Donegal is ever without Doon Well water.

But the visitors to the well are not from Donegal alone. They journey from many other countries across the seas, because the fame and efficacy of its never-failing springs have been wafted to all parts of the world, wherever Donegal people are to be found.

The history of the well is none too factual, but it is established that it goes back for hundreds of years. Doon Well is credited with having been blessed by the saintly Lector O'Friel. Nothing can be said with certainty as to when he lived, but it is a historical fact that one of that name worked in this lonely part of Donegal during the fifteenth century. Lector O'Friel was a man whose sanctity of life was matched only by his wonderful power as a healer. Sufferers from all sorts of painful and apparently incurable maladies came or were brought to him in quest of cures. Many and extraordinary were the stories told of the efficacy of his prayers for those with bodily afflictions.

Tradition tells us that in his old age, when his vigor was waning and the shadow of death was hanging over him, people became disturbed at the thought of losing such a holy and charitable man in whom God had implanted such power for miraculous healing.

"When I die, my powers will live on after me," he told them. He blessed the well and told them that those who drank or applied its water would have the benefit of his prayers of intercession.

Down the years, countless stories have been told of cures to all sorts of ailments at the spot and of how disabled or crippled pilgrims were able to leave behind their sticks, crutches and bandages after one or more visits.

One cannot go to Doon Well and fail to note the lofty "Carraig a Duin" (Doon Rock) standing sentinel-like nearby. Most visitors make a point of climbing to its uneven summit, from which there is a breathtaking view of the lovely countryside for many miles in all directions.

It was while standing atop this great rock eight years ago, that I first got the idea that I would like to fly low over this magnificent countryside. It was the genesis of this great adventure.

Here in truth one rubs shoulders with history, making physical contact with the era of the celebrated Clan O'Donnell. It was on this spot that those great chieftains of the O'Donnell tribe were inaugurated. The last O'Donnell to be crowned at Doon Rock was Niall Garbh, a cousin of Red Hugh in 1603. Here also it was that Sir Cahir O'Doherty, just out of his teens and the last Chieftain of Inishowen, was slain in battle in 1608.

Just two hundred yards from Doon Well, and in the shadow of Doon Rock, my great grandfather Hugh McCafferty had a farm and married the girl next door, Mary McGinty. The Great Famine and the financial ruin that resulted forced them to emigrate, first to Scotland where they had several children, and then on to Philadelphia, where they had several more, establishing the McCafferty clan in the New World where it subsequently flourished.

About eight years ago, I visited Doon Well, and talked with Charles Gallagher who lives in the house directly next to the well, and he showed me the place where my great grandfather's cottage once stood, and the rubble of the foundation that was all that was left of it. I took away with me a rock from that foundation as a piece of the past, with the intention that one day I would have it split up into pieces, each mounted and framed, and given to my parents, siblings and children.

Yesterday, I saw Charles Gallagher again. He seemed not to have aged at all in that time, and remembered me easily. We talked of the past, and of Hugh McCafferty's farm and cottage, and Mary McGinty, and he told me of the young lad who was building a new home right on top of the site where my great grandfather's home once stood.

I walked the short way from the Well, and up the un-named and unpaved lane to the site of the old McCafferty home, and winced when I saw the bare new cinder block shell and the construction debris desecrating this good place. I walked fully around it looking for any signs of the old cottage foundation, and I was saddened to find that it was gone without a trace.

I inspected this new home more closely and saw that it was situated with a great central room facing to the northeast, looking out over the small farm once owned by Hugh McCafferty, and beyond it the view of dozens of farms in the valley and up the gentle hills into the distance. It was a fine picture of Ireland, and I thought how Hugh and Mary must have loved this view, which has probably not changed much in the hundred plus years since they were forced to leave.

So, the next time you ask me "How are you?" and I say "Doon Well," you will know that I am in fact "doing well," and that I am also remembering and saluting a place of great personal and family significance.

Day 91: Incommunicado

The largest town in County Donegal is Letterkenny. Unfortunately, the airport there is quite small. The short narrow grass runway was very soggy, and there is a slight dogleg in it with a fence at one end and a hill at the other. Ultralight airplanes use it, but this is no place for my biplane, so I left the Waco at Donegal airport.

I wanted to visit Letterkenny, because it is the nearest town to Doon Well, and I thought I would like the town environment instead of the isolated place I've been staying for the last two days.

What I found was that my computer's modem wouldn't connect with the phone system at my new hotel, and I spent the day dealing with computer and phone stores to fix the problem, but we never did get it figured out. It seems as if the modem has been fried. The thing that compounds the problem is that I didn't bring the separate floppy disk drive with me, and there is no way to install a new modem without loading the new drivers from a floppy disk. So I have to turn over my computer for the evening to a local computer store so they can try to install a generic external modem that won't need drivers. It's all techie mumbo-jumbo, but the bottom line is that I will be spending the night without my computer for the first time in months. It's very difficult for me to let go.

I have been incommunicado for two days now, and am having e-mail withdrawal symptoms.

I also spent some time on the phone, dealing with some of the details that have been piling up. The Waco factory says that they have demo flights scheduled in Paris from September 25-27, so my tour will end the 27th at the latest. It will be my job to get the biplane back to France by then, if possible, and if not possible due to the weather, then the factory pilot Carl Dye will fly it IFR from wherever it gets stuck.

The end of this tour is not something I want to dwell on at this time, but I suppose I have to face it sooner or later. Another reality is the special European flying insurance. I have already had it renewed for one additional month, and it expires on the end of September. And last, but certainly not least, is the weather, which has taken a dramatic turn from summer to winter. If for no other reason, this adventure will soon be over; simply because it will no longer be fun to fly in this weather.

Here is Mount Errigal, the highest elevation in County Donegal at 2,400 feet. Healthy people like to climb it. I figured I would stay healthier if I didn't.

Day 92: Typically Irish Weather

<u>Letterkenny, Ireland</u>

Here was the weather forecast for today: "Widespread heavy rain at first with a risk of flooding, very windy with southerly gales and severe gusts of 50-60 mph. Brighter showery weather on the west coast will spread eastwards to all areas by mid-afternoon. Some heavy showers likely later. As the rain clears to showers, very strong southerly winds will veer westerly and moderate. Further heavy showers tonight."

Yikes! I'm glad my biplane is in the hangar. Sixty mph winds could blow my biplane away, *far* away!

My computer came back today with a newly installed external modem. It was a relief to get e-mail again. I took the computer back to my room and plugged it in to recharge the batteries, telling myself to be careful about the cord that had to be run from the desk on one wall to the electrical socket on the other wall. Can you believe only one socket in the room, and on the opposite wall from the desk? Who designs these rooms anyway?

I tripped over the cord almost immediately! It brought the computer crashing down to the floor and I had that sick feeling I get every time I do something completely stupid. I figured the hard disk could never survive, but amazingly, it was fine. No data lost, everything checked out just fine, except the electrical cord. When I plugged it back in, I got no juice. The end that goes into the computer was bent, and the guts of the power supply socket were screwed up as well. It is only by playing the most ridiculous game of finding and then holding the cord in the right position will the computer accept electricity so that the battery can be charged. It reminds me of the antics you have to go through to get a "rabbit ears" antenna to work on a TV. Every time I turn my back, the thing resets and turns off.

I tried to track down some of my surviving relatives in the area without much luck. I have a few leads that might come to fruition tomorrow.

Day 93: Meeting the Relatives

Termon, Ireland

The little village of Termon isn't even on my map of Ireland, but it's about 10 miles outside of Letterkenny. I took a taxi to "The Lagoon," the pub in Termon owned by John McCafferty (not a relative). I met him the last time I was here in Ireland and he was very helpful in locating the few remaining relatives I have left here.

Although the local phone book lists 110 people named McCafferty with a phone, there are probably many more without one. I called the phone number I had for a Margaret Toland, but it was no longer in service. John told me that her home is now vacant and that she has moved to Creeslough, farther north.

The only relative left in Ireland with the name McCafferty is Paddy McCafferty, who lives alone on a desolate hillside, well off the paved country road. Even John, who knows these parts like the back of his hand, had trouble finding the overgrown grass and mud path that leads to Paddy's house. Paddy has lived in this same home since he was nine years old. He is now 74. He doesn't drink, doesn't smoke, and has never married.

He gets by on a small pension, and he tends a few cattle in the nearby pasture. Friends in the area look in on him from time to time. He has no car, but gets to the store by walking the short way across the fields to Termon. He has no phone, and can't see why he needs one. His conversation is liberally sprinkled with phrases like "Can't complain" and "That's the way it goes" and "What can you do about it." He seems resigned to his solitude and poverty, and not necessarily unhappy about it.

Not too far away lives Jimmy McDaid, whose aunt was my great grandmother, Mary McGinty. We visited for a while and he showed me photos he has collected of his family, and gave me a small picture of himself and a few of his family standing in front of the remains of my great grandmother's cottage at Doon Well. He also showed me a collection of letters he has, dated as early as 1850, written between various members of his family. From him, I learned that my great-great grandfather Patrick McCafferty was a shoemaker and that the original farm where he raised his children was five acres in Doon Well. These are little facts, but they help put together some of the missing pieces of family history.

Jimmy McDaid is still living in the house where he was born almost 80 years ago. A very old photograph of his mother hangs framed on the wall. A religious man, he has been away from home on a few occasions, primarily to make pilgrimages to shrines of Our Lady (Lourdes, etc). Jimmy has a keen interest in genealogy and can trace his family through seven generations, all the way back to the mid 1700's. Like Paddy, Jimmy doesn't smoke, and rarely drinks. He seems quite content and says there is nothing he needs. He is in excellent health with a firm handshake earned from many years of working in the construction trades.

It was the highlight of my visit to Donegal to be able to meet and spend a little time with a couple of my relatives in Ireland, and to learn a little more about my ancestors and how they lived.

The weather continues to be unflyable with high winds and rain all day.

Day 94: Flight of Fancy

County Donegal, Ireland

Most of the day was wasted waiting for my computer to be delivered. Repair was not possible, so I have to be very careful with it to keep from inflicting more, possibly fatal damage to the power supply. After checking out of the hotel in Letterkenny, I took a taxi to the Donegal Airport. I sat in the back seat and feigned sleep so as to avoid conversation with the driver, but I was in fact looking out the side window, watching the extraordinary landscape slip by through half-closed eyes.

The weather today was the same as it has been since I arrived in Ireland, rain showers, low ceilings, windy and cold. Inside my taxi, I was warm and dry, and it was easy to imagine that I was flying low over the beautiful countryside, as I have imagined it so many times before. From the comfort of my taxi, I was indeed flying over the green heather-covered hills and rocky glens, the streams and lakes. From the safety of my taxi I didn't need to be concerned with the low ceilings obscuring the mountains, for in my mind I could fly in ways that could never be done in reality.

As each turn of the road presented some new breathtaking vista, I was there in my biplane, creating an even more beautiful scene to the few farmers and sheep that might have chanced to look up at the moment. It was a most memorable flight of fancy, one that I will recall for many years after my flying days are done.

I have been longing to fly this wonderful land, to completely circumnavigate the coastline of Ireland, and to investigate its airports and villages, but it seems as if I have come here a little too late in the season. When I arrived at the Donegal airport, the cold wind was still gusting strong and straight across the runway, the low clouds spewing intermittent showers. Only three airplanes used the Donegal airport today. Mine was not one of them.

Day 95: "The Craic Was Mighty"

The weather persists in thwarting my hopes for flying. Today's weather was the worst so far: virtually continuous rain, very low ceilings, fog, and *cold*. I never even attempted to go outside the hotel.

It was a great day to stay warm inside, and even if it was a perfectly flyable day, I would probably have done the same thing as a couple of billion people around the world and watch the live TV broadcast of Princess Diana's funeral. I thought I would have been stronger, and for most of it, I retained my composure, but at the sight of so many other people so obviously moved, I found myself fighting to hold back that first tear, ultimately without success.

In the midst of all of the depressing news, including the passing of Mother Theresa, I heard the one truly beautiful thought that made me smile and see that there is, if we only look for it, a positive way to see everything. Of the many hundreds of thousands of people who sent messages to the press and to the family, one that was reportedly sent in from a little girl expressed the thought that God must be happy and excited to be receiving into heaven both Diana and Mother Theresa in the same week.

In the evening I was pleased to be the guest of Adrian Towey, the Donegal airport commercial manager, and his wife Anne, for dinner at their home. We had a fine dinner and I enjoyed meeting their four young children and Anne's brother in law, Jim. After dinner, we sat around the kitchen table for hours and engaged in the Donegal tradition of lively conversation ("craic" in Gaelic) on a wide range of topics. While the rest of them enjoyed their spirits, I held myself to one glass of beer, planning on flying tomorrow, an optimist to the end. It was a great compliment Anne paid me when we hugged and parted, saying she enjoyed the evening, and that "The craic was mighty." Aye, it was. I love the way these people talk!

Day 96: The End

County Donegal, Ireland

Today is my birthday. I was really looking forward to flying today. The weather forecaster I talked with yesterday sounded hopeful, and the TV weather program showed a big high pressure zone headed this way. I was determined that I would fly in sunny skies at last.

It didn't happen. The airport doesn't open until 11:30 am on weekends, and even by that time the day showed no signs whatsoever of getting better. The ground was dry all day, and that certainly was a positive, but it was very cold and made worse by the high humidity and gusting high winds. If I had pressed the limits of my flying ability, I could have gone flying, and I was tempted to, but in the final analysis, it would just not have been any fun to be flying around in such miserable conditions.

Of course, it wasn't much fun to be walking around in these conditions either, but I took a brief walk on the beach anyway. There is an absolutely beautiful beach just a couple of hundred yards to the west of the runway, hidden from view of the terminal building by the sand dunes covered with grasses.

While walking alone on the beach, I was filled with the sense that this adventure has already come to an end. The time has come to stop waiting for the weather to break in my favor. It is time to come home.

Back at the hotel, I called the Waco factory and gave them the word. Carl Dye, the world's greatest Waco pilot, will come from Lansing, Michigan to Donegal Ireland, fly my biplane to Paris, disassemble it and ship it back to the factory where it will be reassembled and then fly it back home to me in California.

It is impossible for me to express my emotions at this time. I have had an extraordinary adventure these past three months. It has been the experience of a lifetime. It will take years for it to sink in. I am extremely fortunate to have been able to do this.

Thank you all for coming along.

Epilogue: The Duck

(Three Years Later)

It was a perfect spring day in <u>Del Mar, California</u>. The onshore wind was light, the sky clear, and although it was almost sunset, the air was still warm. I was standing on my west facing, second-floor balcony, 50 feet from the edge of the cliff with a view for miles along the Pacific coast.

On this stage stretched out before me, life was being lived in all its glory: dolphins playing in the waves, surfers lazily waiting for the next set, pelicans gliding effortlessly on almost nonexistent puffs of air pushed up by the slightest swells.

Passing before me was an endless parade of flying things: the fighters from Top Gun school at nearby Miramar, helicopters, commercial jets, assorted general aviation aircraft, and in addition to the pelicans, there were gulls in abundance, egrets, herons, sandpipers, ravens, terns and hawks. However, today it was a solitary duck that introduced himself to me in a most extraordinary way...

As I breathed in this magnificent scene, it was only natural to think of Flying, and my open-cockpit biplane, "The Spirit of Adventure," which at that moment was enduring the indignity of being stripped, poked and prodded by mechanics giving it a thorough annual inspection. I knew it would pass as easily as I passed my pilot medical checkup last week. All systems were "Go" for my seventh summer in the air.

And yet, a dark and melancholy thought had been nagging at me lately: "When does one stop flying?" This question was so foreign to me because flying was an obsession, an addiction. I needed flying like my lungs need air.

I won't bore you, dear reader, with stories of my exploits, which have been well below the level of legends like Lindbergh, Saint-Exupery or Mermoz. I was so careful that I never even scratched any of the great airplanes I flew. I was never betrayed by an airplane, never had to deal with an engine out or fire in flight. My logbook totals a measly one thousand hours in only six years.

But my time aloft was far from boring, at least to me! I was unbelievably lucky to learn flying, and get my license in the most excellent open-cockpit biplane of all time, a work of vintage art that I owned and could fly at my whim. Together, we toured all over the USA and Europe, from border to border, coast to coast and all in between, on months-long barnstorming adventures-of-a-lifetime.

Each flight was a miracle. Together, we struggled for air, cresting the Rockies and the Alps, and crossed the Irish Sea, the Baltic and the Channel. We boiled over deserts, froze in the mountains and survived weather that seemed bent on extracting the ultimate price. Like aliens, we dropped from the sky and landed in hundreds of exotic places big and small. There were close formations, dogfights in play, and lots of aerobatics, even near misses and other heart-stopping frights.

We hot-dogged and scud run, flying low as a matter of choice, the lower the better, and played in ways that were so unwise yet seemed so necessary. For extra fun, I bought or begged time as pilot in command of the P-51 Mustang, Spitfire, B-17, floatplanes, gliders, Stearmans, a Pitts and even a few ordinary spam cans. I mention these things not at all to boast, but to illustrate how difficult it was for me to answer the question that had been tugging at my mind these past few months...

"When does one *stop* flying?"

An answer came into my head: "If you are thinking about not flying, then you shouldn't be flying." It seemed true, because it is the corollary to the proposition which states that while one is engaged in the art of flying, one must be thinking *only* of flying."

It was a quick and simple answer, but I didn't like it, and rejected it immediately.

At this precise moment the duck appeared, entering the left corner of my left eye, flying fast and low (we have a lot in common!), following the path at the edge of the cliff. He was all business, flying straight as an arrow, not a moment to lose — probably late for dinner with the wife and kids, and wanted to get home before dark. That was the entirety of my thinking about this duck, lasting for all of a second or two at the most. An insignificant thing.

The thought drifted back into my mind: "If you are thinking about not flying, then you shouldn't be flying." It seemed too easy. I was looking for a better answer.

The duck then made an instantaneous course change (about 45 degrees) and headed directly my way! What made it even more curious was that he never wavered, never skipped a wing beat, and never slowed. For the first quarter-second of this new behavior, I was merely interested. What could he be going after in my general direction? In the next quarter-second, I realized that he was doing something very strange. There was nothing of interest to a duck in my general direction. What was even more unusual was that not only did he change heading he changed altitude. My balcony is a full 15 feet above his previous cruising altitude. It dawned on me that he was not making a course correction to avoid something in his path, and he was not going after something I hadn't yet discovered, rather he was heading with laser accuracy at a point between my eyes! Did I miss something in my education? Do ducks attack humans?

Within that moment of awareness, this duck showed up, full speed, two feet from my face. I just started to take evasive action (yes, I know, I could have said "duck") when he did the most spectacular thing I have ever seen done by any flying creature. He stopped in mid air with a tremendous flapping of his wings, acting as an air brake, almost hovering for an instant, showing perfect control. He then executed a sensational wingover and spiraled down to land on the grass, and without so much as the slightest extra movement of a feather, he stood there like a statue and looked up, unblinkingly, into my eyes.

It occurred to me that in some cultures, this would be considered an omen. But what could it mean? For the answer, I tried to remember what I was thinking when this creature (this Messenger?) showed up. Of course: "If you are thinking about not flying, then you shouldn't be flying."

A few moments passed while I tried to figure out what was going on, and all the while the duck remained absolutely motionless, staring up at me with rock solid eyes. I couldn't allow myself to believe all of this. But there he was!

I regained my composure, took a deep breath, and formed that fearful, fateful thought as a question for my visitor: "Is that why you are here, to confirm my intuition that if I am thinking about not flying then I should not be flying?"

The very moment I finished asking the duck this question (telepathically, of course, because I am not given to talking aloud to poultry), he immediately lifted up, returned to his original course and altitude and was gone as if nothing at all out of the ordinary had happened.

For quite a while after that event, I considered other possibilities for the meaning of it all. At one point, I even wondered if I might have had a run-in with this duck on one of my low flying capers. Did I scare him with a near miss, and this was his way of getting back at me? No way, he would never be able to recognize me without my helmet and goggles. So why did this happen?

To me, there was only one explanation: the duck was a Messenger, pure and simple. The message was clear, not a shadow of doubt.

I haven't flown my biplane since that day, and I have never regretted the message that was delivered to me. The time had come. I felt it coming for some time. I knew the moment of decision was near, and somehow, at just the right time, this clairvoyant duck came along with the answer to the ultimate question of "When?"

One of the reasons I had been delaying answering this big question was that I didn't have my next move figured out. If I wasn't going to be flying, what could possibly take its place? Without that question answered, I was stuck. Then the duck confirmed that the need for a safety net is all in the mind.

I saw that it was just one more flight into the unknown. In this light, I eagerly looked forward to the new adventures that would soon be revealed. When one door closes, another opens. Yin and yang. All things are perfect.

Nowadays, I do a different kind of flying. Whether I am sitting in rush hour traffic, or walking on the beach, all I need to do is look up and my thoughts and feelings fly me in a sky of low scattered puffball clouds, a throbbing radial engine pulling me along on fabric covered wings, the wind in my hair, the tug of the stick on my right arm. Sometimes, the air is crisp and wet from early morning ground fog, sometimes salty from the surf spray, and sometimes heavy with the scent of young jasmine flowers, lining a wandering valley stream.

My flying machine is always full of gas and oil, freshly washed and polished. The weather is always just right, and yet, always different. Control towers and radios have yet to be invented, so there are no rules or government officials to enforce them. My aerobatics are flawless, and every landing pure joy! I fly alone or with good friends, always at the perfect time, always without rush or compromise.

Just before falling asleep each evening, I cut the engine, rudder into a radical sideslip, wing wires whistling, and drop low over the trees for a three-point dead-stick landing on a manicured field of soft smooth grass, at the edge of the sea. Lindbergh looks on, smiling.

I sleep snug beneath the wing, dry against the dew, the full moon rising, and I dream of the day just done, and the day to come. And it is all very, very good. But sometimes, when I again stand on that same spot, I do secretly wish the duck would come back.

Appendix A: Acknowledgements

Mom and Dad - for your eternal patience with me
Michael James McCafferty - my son, my hero
Kendra McCafferty - my sweet and lovely daughter
Carol Soria - for running things flawlessly at home, while I go fly
Carl Dye - the world's greatest Waco pilot
Don Kettles - the world's best Waco salesman
Waco Classic Aviation - the company of artists who built my biplanes
Lowell Williams - flight instructor, friend, P-51 Mustang ace
Art Annecharico - friend and wingman on many flights
Vince Moore - flight instructor
Larry Grismer and Donnya - for kindness and favors too numerous to list
Annie Le Bris - friend & spotter pilot for forest firefighters
Shari Breton - pilot, friend and good company on the first leg to Paris
Addison Pemberton - we went flying at just the right time
Bill Allen - biplane pilot, aviation historian, friend
Dan Murray - builder, restorer, biplane pilot
Bernard Chabbert - the French connection
René Brillant - for saving my life that day in Nangis
Helene Brillant - wife of René, for her hospitality
Matthias & Nici Zuellig - flying on my wing for much of Euro '97
Barry Tempest - top man in the U.K. air show scene
Bill O'Dwyer - for teaching me about the "first to fly"
Antoine Saint-Exupery & Charles Lindbergh - for writing what I feel about flying
Sean Curtis - friend from home, and in Paris, Sardinia & Corsica
Ann von Gal - cover design and layout assistance
Mary E. Gonzalez - copy editing and proofreading, via elance.com
Barry Dunleavy - for the sense of urgency to finish this book (see Preface)

Appendix B: About the Biplane

The Spirit of Adventure I

The photo above was taken on the day my biplane was rolled out of the factory, the first day it saw sky, the first time its tires touched grass, the first time the engine breathed air and spit fire, sometime in the early summer of 1993.

It was love at first sight.

My first flight with it was July 18, 1993. We flew it to Oshkosh, WI, the biggest air show in the USA, where it was on display for the week, and then we flew it home to San Diego. I flew it exclusively during training and earned my Private Pilot license in it November 18, 1993.

The Spirit of Adventure I   February 24, 1994   I didn't do it!

One of my instructors decided to do a check flight after some routine maintenance, but he came in for a landing with the parking break on. Boy, was he surprised when it flipped over instantly upon touchdown! He was unhurt (except for his pride), but the biplane was a total loss. I traded the broken bits, and the insurance, for a new biplane.

"The Spirit of Adventure II"

Above photo is biplane number two, delivered in May 1994, the one I flew in the USA and European adventures. It was manufactured from scratch (not restored), according to the specifications of a 1935 Waco YMF-5.

The engine is the same as used in 1935. The cockpit was state-of-the-art.

Here's a partial list of the "bells and whistles":

- Horizontal Situation Indicator (HSI)
- Traffic Collision Avoidance Detection (TCAD)
- Global Positioning System (GPS), Arnav Star 5000
- Moving Map Display, Eventide Argus 7000
- Nav/Comm: two KLX155's
- Stormscope BFG
- G-meter
- Vertical Speed Indicator (VSI)
- VOR/Glideslope
- Vacuum-operated Artificial Horizon
- Magnetic Compass
- Turn Coordinator
- Altitude
- Engine Speed, rpm
- Manifold Pressure
- Exhaust Gas Temp
- Cylinder Head Temp
- Oil Temp
- Oil Pressure
- Airspeed
- Alternator Output, Volts, amps
- Battery Indicator, volts
- Individual fuses for each item
- Video recording devices and controls

Certified for flying instruments-only (IFR), and for night flying. Time between overhauls on the engine is 1,200 hours. It has never been in an accident or incident, not a scratch.

The biplane is also outfitted with a video camera in the right lower wing, wired to a VCR and monitor in the cockpit. With this setup I can make videos (or watch them!) as I fly.

Other special features: Auxiliary fuel tanks. Total fuel 72 gal. Total endurance is about four hours. Range approximately 400 miles, depending on winds, at a cruising airspeed of 100 mph. Baggage capacity: 75 lbs. in rear baggage compartment, 25 lbs. in the front baggage compartment.

My Waco is now in California, flying rides out of Attitude Aviation, Livermore, CA.

For more information and photos of this unique aircraft, click on the link below and visit the website of the Waco manufacturer:

Classic Aircraft Company, Battle Creek, Michigan

Appendix C: Emergency Supplies

Kit 1.

    First aid kit
    Hunting knife with sharpening stone
    Magnesium fire starting tool
    Flashlight
    Compass
    Matches, waterproof, (2) boxes
    (8) AA Duracell batteries
    Potable germicidal water tablets
    Sewing kit with safety pins
    Thermal blanket
    Mirror signaling device
    Sunscreen SPF 30
    (2) razor blades
    Fisher Space-Tec pen
    Metal coiled cable wire
    Toilet paper roll
    (2) large black plastic garbage bags

Kit 2.

    Sunscreen, SPF 30, mosquito, flea & deer tick repellent
    Insect repellent, Deet, for black flies & ticks
    (2) disposable warm packs
    Emergency survival handbook
    Rope, 50 feet, 3 mm 100% nylon
    Signal Flares, Package of (3)
    Splints, kit
    Signal whistle
    Matches, (2) boxes, windproof and waterproof
    Batteries, (4) AA Duracell, with battery tester

Appendix D: Checklists

Preflight Inspection

Fuel quantity	Check/fill
Oil quantity	Check/fill
Fuel quality test	Check
Walk around inspection	Check
Passengers	Briefed
Ignition key	In place
Baggage compartment	Locked
Tie downs	Remove
Wheel chocks	Remove

Before Engine Start

Toe brakes	Set
Parking brake	INOP
Tail wheel steering	Engaged
Trim	4 turns up
ELT	Armed (left)
Seat	Adjust/Locked
Seatbelt and harness	Fasten
Left circuit breakers	In
Right circuit breakers	In
Electrical switches	Off
Compass slave	Set
Fuel selectors	Push In
Fuel quantity	Compute
Manifold pressure	Field Pressure
Flight controls	Check

Engine Start
- Mixture — Rich
- Carburetor heat — Cold
- Throttle — Cracked
- Primer — Cold=10, Hot=5
- Primer — Locked
- Magneto key — Battery
- Battery master switch — On
- Navigation lights — On
- Voltage — 23-25 Volts
- Control stick — Aft
- Rear visual check — Clear
- Prop area visual check — "Clear!"
- Starter — Engage
- Magneto key (after start) — Both
- Oil pressure — Check green
- Alternator switch — On
- Avionics master switch — On
- Intercom — Check
- Warm up — 600 rpm for 30 sec.
  1,000 rpm until temp needle moves

Before Taxi
- Clock — Reset to zero
- Transponder — Standby – 1200
- ATIS — Write it down
- Altimeter — Set pressure
- TCAD — Set pressure
- Ground control — Contact
- Brakes — Release

Taxi
- Brakes — Check Left and Right
- Turn coordinator — Check
- Attitude indicator — Check
- HSI — Check
- Clearing turns — Execute

Run-up

Oil pressure	Green
Oil temp	Needle moved
Toe brakes	Set (no parking brake)
Power up	1,500 rpm
Oil pressure	Green
Key to left magneto	90 rpm max drop
Key to ignition	90 rpm max drop
Key to both	Check
Carb heat on	RPM drop
Carb heat off	1,500 rpm
Alternator amps.	Set, 9-15 amps
Pitot heat	On, +1 amp.
Pitot heat	Off
Left circuit breakers	Check all in
Right circuit breakers	Check all in
Power	Idle
Flight controls	Check
Tower	Contact

Taking the Runway

Passengers	Check seatbelt
Transponder	Set to Altitude
Lights	On
Compass	Check Runway heading

Take Off

Clock	Run
Throttle	Take Off power
Engine instruments	Scan
65 mph	Lift off

Climb

Mixture	Rich
Power	Full throttle
Airspeed	Vy=76 mph Vx=72 mph

Cruise

Power	2,000 rpm
Mixture	Lean as required

Descent
    Power   Below 2,000 rpm
    Carburetor heat   As needed
    Mixture   Rich
    ATIS   Obtain info
    Tower   Contact

Before Landing
    Landing light   On
    Fuel selectors   Both On
    Seatbelt and harness   Fasten/tighten
    Mixture   Rich
    Carb heat   As needed

After Landing
    Landing light   Off
    Transponder   Standby
    Carburetor heat   Cold
    Pitot Heat   Off
    Ground control   Contact

Shutdown
    Brakes   Parking brake is INOP!
    Tail wheel   Unlock
    Power   Idle 2 minutes
    Mixture   Full Lean to shutdown
    Electrical switches   Off
    Magnetos   Off
    Fuel selectors   Off (push in)
    Ignition key   Remove
    Avionics master   Off
    Alternator field   Off
    Battery master   Off
    Flight plan   Close
    Logbook   Entry
    Fuel   Top off
    Learn   Make notes
    Squawks   Log

Appendix E: Emergency Procedures

Engine Fire at Start
      Starter   Keep cranking!

Engine Fire at Start	
Starter	Keep cranking!
Mixture	Idle cut-off
Throttle	Open
Fuel selectors	Off
If fire continues	Abandon ship!
Fire extinguisher	Use
Electrical Fire in Flight	
Battery master	Off
Alternator field	Off
If fire persists	Use fire extinguisher
All electrical switches	Off
Circuit breakers	Check (do not reset)
Land	ASAP
Engine Fire In Flight	
Fuel selectors	Pull
Throttle	Closed
Mixture	Idle cut off
Power off landing	Execute
Electrical Failure in Flight	
Ammeter	Check
	If zero, check for faulty alternator
Alternator switch	Off
Avionics master	Off
Alternator circuit breaker	Check/reset
Alternator switch	On
Avionics master	On
If power is not restored:	
Alternator switch	Off
Reduce electrical load	Turn off stuff
Land	ASAP

Loss of Oil Pressure
    Prepare for power off landing!
    Land   ASAP

High Oil Pressure
    Prepare for power off landing!
    Mixture   Rich
    Power   Reduce
    Land   ASAP

High Cylinder Head Temperature
    Mixture   Rich
    Power   Reduce
    Land   ASAP

Power Loss at Take Off
    If sufficient runway remains,   Land straight ahead
    Fuel selectors   Push Forward (off)
    Mixture   Rich
    If power not regained,   Power Off landing!

Power Loss in Flight
    Airspeed   75 mph
    Carburetor heat   On
    Mixture   Rich
    Fuel selectors   Push forward (on)
    Magnetos   Check
    Wings   Rock
    If power not regained   Power Off landing!

Power Off Landing
    Landing field   Locate

Landing field	Locate
Wind direction	Determine
Radio	Last ATC or 121.5
Call	"Mayday, Mayday, Mayday"
Transponder	7700
Descend	to 1,000' above touchdown pt. on downwind leg
Trim	75 mph
Magnetos	Off
Passengers	Seatbelt and Harness tight
Battery master	Off
Fuel selectors	Off
Mixture	Idle cut off
Seatbelt and harness	Tight

Spin Recovery

Throttle	Reduce power
Stick	Neutralize
Rudder	Opposite rotation
Rudder	Neutral as rotation stops
Stick	Back for dive recovery

Caution: A one turn spin and recovery requires approximately 1,500'.
Each additional turn requires approximately 800'.

Limitations

Maximum engine speed	2,200 rpm
VNE – never exceed speed	214 mph
Power off stall	59 mph
Maximum gross weight	2,950 lbs
Maximum aerobatic weight	2,650 lbs
Maximum "G" at max weight	+5.2 -2.1

Made in the USA
Charleston, SC
21 December 2010